THE WISDOM OF STUPIDITY

BY ROY DEVON

(with Julian Butler and Bob Priestley)

HEADPRESS

A HEADPRESS BOOK
First published by Headpress in 2019
headoffice@headpress.com

THE WISDOM OF STUPIDITY
The true story of Smile Orange Films and how you can
become semisuccessful for a short time like they did.

A CIP catalogue record for this book is
available from the British Library

ISBN   978-1-909394-38-4 (paperback)
ISBN   978-1-909394-39-1 (ebook)
NO-ISBN (hardback)

HEADPRESS. POP AND UNPOP CULTURE.

Exclusive NO-ISBN special edition hardbacks and other
items of interest are available at HEADPRESS.COM

ABOUT THE AUTHOR

> " To those that have given up on life, I dedicate this tome. "
> Please accept (and pay for) this, my lifeboat to you.

Roy Devon is an author who has just completed writing this book. Since leaving school in 1960 Devon has existed on the breadline spending his life begging publishers for his next meagre commission. It was an editor's vague promise of an advance for a book on low-budget filmmaking that brought Devon to this exciting subject. So, with his 2% royalties safely secured, Devon dove headlong into the project. By looking up what a low-budget film was.

During further research Devon interviewed low-budget filmmakers Smile Orange Films, the only team with enough spare time to give him their views. Devon's 96 hour interview session with the team led him to base the whole book on their memoirs alone and he planned to have the book finished by the weekend. Three years later Devon finally emerged with a manuscript called *The Whining Odd Sodomy*. Devon's publisher then got him an updated computer with a new spell checker and, a further two years later, he finally delivered *The Wisdom of Stupidity*.

Roy Devon lives at the Davidwellsley Car Park Safariland with five wives and one cat.

ALSO BY ROY DEVON

FICTION
Shopping in my Stockings

NON-FICTION
The Alternative Music Scene of Bradford:
How New Model Army Played Some Music

Burying Dirt: Forensic Science and Unearthing the Soul of Lies

Birdshit on Flowers: Why Art is so Fucking Abysmal

STAGE PLAY
Man Finishes Cigarette before Entering Shop

CONTENTS

INTRODUCTION BY THE CO-AUTHORS

Please rest assured that every tale in this book is completely true. Although we did have to leave out some of the best stories. So you won't get to hear those. But you can rest assured they're good ones. Like that crack dealer hanging out of the car door, being told to 'fuck off you white bastards', or that time we stole a train. We've said too much already, those stories are just a little bit of personal. Soz.

So, yes, a lot of the stories, peoples and films in here are true, living and real. We have created a couple of fake characters but mostly these people have been kept away from the real shit. It may be hard for you, the reader, to distinguish between them and/or it may not. Maybe it doesn't matter either way. As there is wisdom in our stupidity, there is also truth in our lies and bathos in our pathos. The fake characters are a dressing, a façade, a motherfucking illusion and from our darkest shadows comes the brightest illumination.

Hope you enjoy it anyway, not that we care because we are both dead. Or, if not, at least pretty fucking poorly.

JULIAN BUTLER & BOB PRIESTLEY
(SMILE ORANGE FILMS)

FOREWORD

A foreword is a piece of writing sometimes placed at the beginning of a book or other piece of literature which covers the story of how the book came into being. The term comes from the sport of rugby league where the foreword is the person who takes the ball on the burst, driving forward into the pack. Whilst avoiding a scrum hard on. This is the forward to *The Wisdom of Stupidity*.

The Wisdom of Stupidity is a guide to filmmaking but it is also the story of Smile Orange Films. What can you say about Smile Orange Films? They made films for people who like confusion. Fans of *Hellzapoppin* (dir: Michael Winner, 1943), for example. Smile Orange Films are also the team who accidentally made Britain's most financially successful feature film and the hit TV series *Focus North*. For a while they seemed to be on the cusp of greatness. Then they disappeared. Then they reappeared. Then I interviewed them for this book. Then they regurgitated many of their most treasured brain fruits. Then I wrote them down and published a book. Then you bought and read the book.

So who is *The Wisdom of Stupidity* designed to be read by? *The Wisdom of Stupidity* is exclusively made to be bought by absolutely everyone. From successful media fat cats to the professional industry money-makers. From keen pro-sumers to clueless amateurs like yourself. But the book's appeal doesn't stop there; it's also aimed at people with no interest whatsoever in anything to do with filmmaking (people like Decky from Shipley, or Captain Mark Phillips). Finally, *The Wisdom of Stupidity* aims to tap into the huge international market of people with no interest whatsoever in anything at all.

I hope you find the book successful and that, whilst reading this foreword, you did not get a scrum hard on.

The Kingdom of Video awaits.

ROY DEVON
DAVIDWELLSLEY CAR PARK SAFARILAND

THE WISDOM OF STUPIDITY

THE TRUE STORY OF SMILE ORANGE FILMS AND HOW YOU CAN BECOME SEMI-SUCCESSFUL FOR A SHORT TIME LIKE THEY DID.

PART ONE

PRE-PRODUCTION

StorytellingGBCreative

135C THE STABLES, LEEDS, WEST YORKSHIRE, LS3 5GH

Smile Orange Films
34 Park Street
Bingley
BD16 5TYU

3rd March 1992

Project Name: *I'llkillya!*
Funding Request NO: 920860294LE

Dear Judd, Gustine and Rod,

Thank you for submitting your request for information about film funding. Our remit is to support and invest in your regional film, TV show, videogame or pub quiz machine. We're talking films mostly though. Possibly high end TV, but I have no real interest in television to be honest. No interest in games either. Or playing pub quiz machines. Awful things. My daughter, Gilly, she's always on them. She spends too much time on them when she should be on her horse.

I'm not that interested in this job to be honest. My main worries are private schools for Gilly, holiday homes and horses. Barns don't convert themselves you know! Anyway, it's our remit to keep the wrong types out of the film industry, so it's a 'no' this time I'm afraid. I'm sorry, it's just our policy.

I look forward to discouraging you further, so please have an appointment made in the near future. Sorry, not next week, bit busy. Maybe the month after that. Oh hang on am in Turin that month... oh then its school hols, maybe after that.

Ciao

Amanda Fees-Rodeane
Head of Funding
StorytellingGBCreative

CHAPTER ONE
IDEAS

WHAT ARE IDEAS?

Ideas are information that one mind or many minds possess. No one knows if ideas are stored in the Hippocampus or the Medulla Oblongata or even in the pebbles in one's pocket. It is important to remember that there isn't a single story that exists that does not contain at least one idea. That is apart from *Transformers 3: The Rise of the Decepticons* (Dir: Michael Winner, 2010) which was an experiment in ridding a project of all ideas. Two hours of flashing and banging and rumbling sub-bass and screaming generals and girls in vests and children saving the world. These may sound like ideas but they aren't. They are happenstance.

WHERE DO IDEAS COME FROM?

Ideas often come from working collaboratively and working collaboratively can start at a very young age. In 1979 a group of children from Gilstead Middle School in Yorkshire, England, had their first collaborative idea: They decided to bury decomposing animals in an area of the school playing fields they called the Roxy Tox Box. These children would go on to become Smile Orange: A group of filmmakers, musicians, actors, scientists, thinkers, pet owners and dads that would make Britain's most successful feature film and eventually become the subject of this book.

But for now, the only idea that mattered to the nine year old members of Smile Orange was to improve their Roxy Tox Box by adding their own faeces to the rotting stew as an offering to their imaginary god, Salamanca the Slow Worm. The full and true reasons for this have been lost in time, but it is also not relevant to this book. So don't concern yourself with this detail, put it out of your mind, and read on immediately.

HOW IS THE SUCCESS OF AN IDEA MEASURED?

The success of an idea can be measured in many ways. Filmmakers often use box office receipts and online views as a gauge to indicate accomplishment; bakers go by their leftovers at the end of the day and publicans in the North of England judge it by the number of broken teeth and

This is an old, non-bayonet, inefficient tungsten clear-glassed light bulb. The light from bulbs like this often hurt the eyes of stoners.

blood stains at the end of a Friday night. However, the young members of Smile Orange considered their idea a success when a terrified Dominic Murgatroyd was successfully chased around the playground with a stick covered in fetid goo from their Roxy Tox Box. But please do not think that they were bullies. No, it is too early in the book for you to make that judgement. For now let's just assume that the young Smile Orange team were ABSOLUTELY AND IRREFUTABLY CORRECT IN DOING THIS!!!

Two members of the fledging group were Julian Butler and Augustin Bousfield

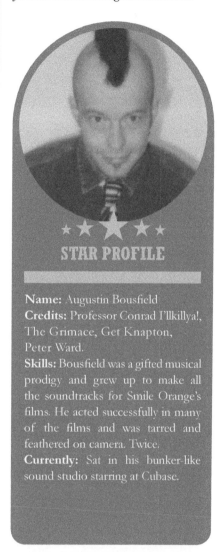

★ ★ ★ ★ ★
STAR PROFILE

Name: Augustin Bousfield
Credits: Professor Conrad I'llkillya!, The Grimace, Get Knapton, Peter Ward.
Skills: Bousfield was a gifted musical prodigy and grew up to make all the soundtracks for Smile Orange's films. He acted successfully in many of the films and was tarred and feathered on camera. Twice.
Currently: Sat in his bunker-like sound studio starring at Cubase.

★ ★ ★ ★ ★
STAR PROFILE

Name: Julian Butler
Credits: Angry Man Fong, Dougie Rivers, Teddy the Chauffeur, Alan Pigshafter Graves.
Skills: Butler was nine years old when he became friends with Gus Bousfield when the couple bonded over their love of *Doctor Who* monsters. Butler went on to act in many Smile Orange film productions and was great at playing politicians, bouncers, debt collectors and war criminals. His co-stars say that Butler was fun to work with despite the fact that he always wanted a piss.
Currently: Producing Antipodean sporting television.

Bousfield tarred and feathered for the second time.

WHY SHOULD I TURN MY IDEAS INTO FILMS?

There are many reasons why you should turn your ideas into films, the most valid of these being that making films will get you out of playing rugby at school. In 1986 the future members of Smile Orange Films were sixteen and attending

I used to play rugby with Butler; he was a good, clean player and we won the Bradford Schools competition. But we wanted out. The idea of doing the school magazine on video was ridiculous though — as if we were some guerrilla reporters on a TV show like *Network Seven* or something. But I was just glad to get out of games because it meant I didn't have to jump on peoples' heads in the mud.

GUS BOUSFIELD
(SMILE ORANGE FILMS)

Bingley Grammar School where they were press-ganged into the school rugby team. Luckily Butler and Bousfield heard that sports lessons could be avoided if they volunteered to write for the school magazine. What's more, they'd discovered the school's Ferguson Videostar VHS camera which they wanted to play with. Putting two and two together, Butler and Bousfield convinced the school that, instead of playing sport, they would write the school magazine and, what's more, for the first time, it would be in an exciting new 'video magazine'.

WHO SHOULD I CAST IN MY FILMS?

The best way to cast a film is to do what Butler and Bousfield did: They gathered a group of children consisting of everyone too ill or odd to play rugby and started filming anything they did that made them laugh. They soon forgot that they were meant to be making a video magazine (this ability to ignore briefs would become a future Smile Orange house-style) but some of the films the team made became classics of their time.

This is the game of rugby. Like all sport, it is meaningless. With the exception of the Isle of Man TT Races.

A Camcorder with a big push button on it for you to record with. This is not the type of camcorder that Smile Orange Films used but this is an easily available and free image for me to bang in here.

SMILE ORANGE FILMOGRAPHY

WEBBOX BOOM BOOM (1986)
Experimental / 124 minutes / VHS / Colour
Fireworks placed in Webbox dog meat sausages explode sending pet food flying through the air to a soundtrack of whoops and screams. Part documentary, part stunt action, part two hours of black screen when the camera was left on by mistake.

Webbox dog food exploding. Actually, no, this isn't Webbox dog food exploding. This is really an industrial sized can of beans exploding.

HOW ELSE SHOULD I RECRUIT ACTORS FOR MY FILMS?
Filmmakers recruit actors for their films in various ways; some are paid huge amounts of money and some, like Smile Orange Films' Bob Priestley, will do it for Seabrook crisps. Sa' vin'. Whilst Smile Orange Films were making their first productions, Priestley was doing his English resits in the classroom directly above. The laughter, screams and explosions he could hear made him want to join in. Finally, after resitting his exams, Priestley's dream came true and Butler and Bousfield gave him his dream acting job: Starring in a film of some bangers going off in some dog food.

Want to make compelling cinema? Blow up some dog food with fireworks and film the results. Yorkshire's own Webbox Chub Rolls are highly recommended, they also make great missiles that explode disgustingly when thrown. But always be sure to have your camera with you or you aren't actually making films.

JULIAN BUTLER

(SMILE ORANGE FILMS)

The Webbox idea developed and soon we were building huge bonfires, putting industrial sized tins of peas and aerosols in them and then leaping over the fire in the hope that they would explode just as someone was leaping over it. We got some great footage of kids getting caked in mushy peas.

GUS BOUSFIELD

(SMILE ORANGE FILMS)

Soon we were filming all the time. Capturing anything that made us laugh: Friends bombing into canals fully clothed, interviews with alcoholic men in shopping centres and spoofs of TV shows like Doctor Who and Rentaghost.

JULIAN BUTLER

(SMILE ORANGE FILMS)

WHAT WILL MY IDEAS LOOK LIKE WHEN I'VE FILMED THEM?

Your ideas, when filmed, will look like shit. Whereas Smile Orange's ideas, when filmed, were video gold. One Smile Orange idea was, during an art exam, to film cast member 'Jenks' jumping off a cupboard in a plastic bin. He broke his arm, went to hospital and was unable to finish his exam. The Smile Orange team found this hilarious and tried to capitalise by sending the clip to ITV's *You've Been Framed*.

SMILE ORANGE FILMOGRAPHY

JENKS AND BIN (1986)
Short / 32 Secs / VHS / Colour
'Jenks' violently breaks his arm after falling to the ground in a bin. A modern take on the Icarus myth. With Icarus in a bin.

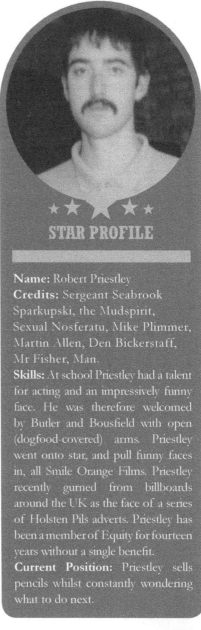

★ ★ ★ ★ ★ STAR PROFILE

Name: Robert Priestley
Credits: Sergeant Seabrook Sparkupski, the Mudspirit, Sexual Nosferatu, Mike Plimmer, Martin Allen, Den Bickerstaff, Mr Fisher, Man.
Skills: At school Priestley had a talent for acting and an impressively funny face. He was therefore welcomed by Butler and Bousfield with open (dogfood-covered) arms. Priestley went onto star, and pull funny faces in, all Smile Orange Films. Priestley recently gurned from billboards around the UK as the face of a series of Holsten Pils adverts. Priestley has been a member of Equity for fourteen years without a single benefit.
Current Position: Priestley sells pencils whilst constantly wondering what to do next.

Priestley starring in a Holsten Pils advert (right). He was paid a thousand sheets, claimed it was the best work he has ever had and said 'I wouldn't mind a few more weeks of that.'

Jeremy Beadle:
Anti-Smile
Orange?

> The video was rejected by You've Been Framed as being too gruesome, too snuff. I felt that the show's presenter, Jeremy Beadle, was being hypocritical — he rejected the film of Jenks' knackering his arm and yet Beadle had a knackered arm himself. What sort of morally bankrupt logic was that? If anyone should have accepted Jenks' knackered arm it should have been Beadle. Beadle and Jenks should have been brothers in (knackered) arms.

BOB PRIESTLEY

(SMILE ORANGE FILMS)

WHAT IS DEVELOPMENT?

Development is the exciting process of expanding an idea and imagining what it would be like as a moving image product such as a film, television show or flick book. This means that development often has nothing to do with reality; famous actors can be cast without ever contacting them, scenes can be imagined without ever having to film them and locations can be used that have never been found. Therefore It is not unusual to end up with an idea for a film starring Sir John Gielgud showing his tits to Audrey Hepburn whilst Ray Winstone smokes cheese with Fidel Castro on an aircraft carrier under the Atlantic Ocean within a fishbowl-like force-field across a manifold of quantum realities. This will, for numerous reasons,

never be made. Therefore when you work in development, chances are, you'll put a lot of effort into something that won't get any further than the piece of fucking paper it's written on.

> Development. de-vel-op-ment [dih-vel-uhp-muhnt] noun
>
> 1. NOT, as many in the Church would have it, in any relation to the Devil and his gait and mince. Instead, the true reasons behind the origins of this word are shrouded in mystery but can be divided into various parts: 'de' — from divide, 'vel' — from later Illium dialect for 'various', opme — Sanskrit for 'parts' with the vulgar honorific plural form 'nt' added to show who knows what in this context.

ETHAN MACPEDANT

(INTUITIVE ETYMOLOGIST)

WHAT ARE DEVELOPMENT MEETINGS?

Development meetings are meetings of Development, Developmenting and ultimately Developmenterising. In these meetings your favourite ideas can expand into something more substantial. In 1986, at the age of sixteen, Butler, Bousfield and Priestley had already made short films and so it seemed a natural progression for them to develop some into longer 'non-short' films.

The team's development process involved them sitting watching VHS films rented from the local video shop on a Saturday night in one of their bedrooms. It was during one such session that the

We'd purposefully choose the worst films we could find. The covers were always a giveaway — there were some very funny bad video covers in those days.

JULIAN BUTLER

(SMILE ORANGE FILMS)

HIS HANDS TEAR THROUGH FLESH AND BONE!

NIGHT BEAST

Picture of a typical meeting.

friends stumbled across a film called *Nightbeast* (Dir: Don Dohler, 1982). *Nightbeast* was a horror film about an alien crash-landing on Earth and going on a killing spree for no reason. The film was the second most hilarious thing the team had ever seen.

It was after watching *Nightbeast* that the group realised they didn't have to develop a new film at all. They just had to take the piss out of this one. The team voted to remake *Nightbeast* and, in doing so, were years ahead of studios like Universal and Paramount in remaking a 1980's horror

Smile Orange, impersonating Funkadelic, on the way to the video shop [Image removed for legal reasons].

Video cover for Smile Orange Film's Nightbeast. The claims of this cover are correct. Fifty men were actually killed in the making of the film.

PRO TIP

The most important question when developing ideas is 'what time is bedtime?'. I want the ideas to stop running around in my mind so I can trot up the wooden hill to Bedfordshire. I lie down all quiet and still until morning time when I'm up and run around large as life again, ready to have more ideas.

NICKY HINCHCLIFFE

(TOP HOLLYWOOD DIRECTOR)

film. They were especially ahead of the game because they were still living in the 1980s when they did it.

WHAT IS THE FUTURE FOR IDEAS?

An old friend of mine, Malcolm from Cottingley, told me that ideas move so fast that it is almost impossible to predict what they will be in the future. In the time it's taken you to read that line, Frank Ribblesdale, the BBC's Head of Grandad Factual, has come up with the ideas for three new television shows: *Let's Go Forgetting*, *Death Live* and *Adrian Edmondson's Stick Time*. And it's all gold, baby!!!

But Smile Orange Films move even faster. Developing the idea for *Nightbeast* had taught them that development is basically talking nonsense and typing up that nonsense and then acting on that nonsense to make celluloid nonsense. And so, despite having their short films rejected by ethically warped TV shows, the incubating Smile Orange team took their first childlike footsteps towards fulfilling their ultimate destiny to make Britain's most profitable film.

Smile Orange, impersonating Soft Cell, on the way to the video shop [Image removed for legal reasons].

Early Smile Orange costume fittings often took place in front of a closed blue garage door and in the rain (L-R: Bousfield, Duckworth, Tennyson, Butler).

"

It must eternally be remembered that one must be prepared to suffer for one's art, either in the accomplishment of it, or the failure of it. The trying is the main thing, and although this is distinctly un-Jedi-like, it is a far more useful maxim for life than that utterly vacuous pseudo philosophy of there only being 'do or not do'. Trying begets doing and non-doing, it precedes and causes it.

Leonardo Da Vinci didn't just do the Sistine Chapel's roof, he tried it and succeeded. Heracles didn't just do his twenty labours, he tried them first and then got the job done. Or didn't. It's exactly this sort of mainstream catchphrase logo that is dragging us back into the Dark Ages and leading the kids astray culturally in ALL areas AND I WON'T HAVE IT ANYMORE, you hear me!?!?!!

Overall, the suffering as well as the success must be part of the ethic of development. It is the process, the starts, false starts, the progress, the set-backs, and the numerous give-uppings, as well as the unlikely successes, which are vital in the artistic life.

ETHAN MACPEDANT

(INTUITIVE ETYMOLOGIST)

CHAPTER TWO
THE PRODUCER

WHAT IS A PRODUCER?

According to all the producers I have interviewed the most important person on a movie set is the producer. Look on this chapter like a strong, friendly handshake from a producer with handruff (see Glossary).

A typical film producer.

FILM FACT

Nosferatu producer Albie Grau's body weight was equivalent to thirty-two eyes.

Radio Rentals. Maybe they put the full stop at the end of their logo after it closed down?

WHAT'S DOES A PRODUCER DO?

A producer needs to have a good overview of all the other crew members on a movie set. For an inexperienced twit like you it's hard to grasp what everyone on a set actually does so here is as easy-to-follow guide:

THE PRODUCER: Responsible for everything that happens behind the camera.
THE DIRECTOR: Responsible for everything that happens in front of the camera.
THE CAMERAMAN: Responsible for everything that happens inside the camera.
LOTS OF CHEAP CHILD LABOUR IN CHINA: Responsible for making everything twelve thousand kilometres below the camera and then shipping it to the set.

WHY DO I NEED A PRODUCER?

To make a good film you don't need a producer. When Smile Orange Films (including Julian Butler, Gus Bousfield and Bob Priestley) made *Nightbeast* the cast and crew instinctively knew to rent a VHS video camera from Radio Rentals

and make the film in one night at their mum and dad's house whilst they were away. It was so obvious to them to make their film this way that no one actually needed to say it.

HOW DOES A PRODUCER MANAGE A BUDGET?

It is the producer's job to keep a production 'on-budget' so that nobody gets attacked by debt collectors. A budget can be generated in various ways, one of them is by applying for funding. For Smile Orange Films, funding for their film Nightbeat was sadly not forthcoming due it not being applied for. A solution was found when *Nightbeast*'s budget of twenty pounds was collectively financed from the team's pocket money.

After the collection of the monies from themselves the Smile Orange team then released the funds to themselves and went on a prop and wardrobe buying session at Manchester's Affleck's Palace. This session ended with the team being dropped off back at their mums' houses joyously clutching their purchases: A silver tracksuit, a skull mask, a toy spaceship and some toy slime called Gak.

Still from Smile Orange Films' *Nightbeast*. Al Birdsell (left) and ColinTennyson (right).

SMILE ORANGE FILMOGRAPHY

NIGHTBEAST (1988)
Horror / 42 mins / VHS / Colour
Nightbeast starts when the eponymous alien crash-lands it's spaceship on Earth and proceeds to rampage through the Texan/Yorkshire countryside pulling out its victim's guts, ripping off their limbs and microwaving their heads. I am not describing every shot here. But I could, and I want to, and each shot is worth it. But I am not. Basically scene after scene depicts a small community massacred by *Nightbeast* for genuinely no reason. It is *Nightbeast*'s inexplicability that makes it so terrifying. It does occasionally eat its victim's flesh but this is not to quench any actual hunger but just to amuse itself. Eventually *Nightbeast* is killed when a mattress is dropped on its head.

Gak. A slimy modelling compound. Variations included Gak-in-the-Dark, Magnetic Gak, Mood Gak, Gakoids and Smell-my-Gak.

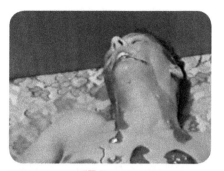

Gak used in *Nightbeast*. Pure cinema.

WHAT IS THE PRODUCER'S JOB ON SET?

It is the producer's job on set to insist that all departments are working towards delivering the scriptwriter's vision. Smile Orange's *Nightbeast* never had a script, the producers didn't even know what one was. This made the producer's job very easy. Whilst shooting *Nightbeast* the cast and crew basically turned up, dressed up, rolled the camera and waited for funny things to be said and happen.

AS A PRODUCER HOW DO I MANAGE POST-PRODUCTION?

The producer's role often continues

Because *Nightbeast*'s costume was basically a mask and a silver tracksuit we all had a go at playing the character at one time or another during filming. In a single scene *Nightbeast* would be beanpole thin, then suddenly short, then finally fat.

GUS BOUSFIELD

(SMILE ORANGE FILMS)

If you weren't acting as a victim, holding the camera, or squirting blood into shot from a Fairy liquid bottle then you were going to play *Nightbeast*. But when Tom Ashcroft played *Nightbeast* — that was always the funniest.

JULIAN BUTLER

(SMILE ORANGE FILMS)

★ ★ ★ ★ ★
STAR PROFILE

Name: Tom Ashcroft
Credits: Nightbeast
Skills: Cottingley bedroom interior socialite, Xbox hero and Aagrah curry house enthusiast Ashcroft was The Beast. He owned the role. Ashcroft was a performer so accomplished that he often managed to play *Nightbeast* and one of it's victims in the same shot.

into the post-production stage of the filmmaking process. The post-production suite is where the rushes are edited and a narrative begins to emerge. The process can take many long hours, weeks and sometimes months before a watchable first cut of your product is ready to be viewed by a test audience. *Nightbeast*, evaded the post-production process as it was edited 'in-camera' then watched in hysterics half an hour after filming.

HOW DOES THE PRODUCER SOURCE A SOUNDTRACK?

One of the hardest jobs for a producer can be sourcing a suitable soundtrack. If you are producing a science fiction film about a killer alien called *Nightbeast* then every one of the gore-soaked deaths needs a terrifying piece of composed horror music. The theme tune from the Sinclair ZX Spectrum computer game *Geoff Capes Strongman* is perfect for this. Smile Orange Films recorded this tune onto a cassette player then played it on set, providing a live soundtrack for whatever scene was being filmed. At

Mr Ashcroft being spectacular as *Nightbeast*.

Cover for the 48K Spectrum game *Geoff Capes Strong Man*.

one point in *Nightbeast* the tape can be heard rewinding and 'oh shit… hang on' whispered before the track is finally cued up and then played.

WHAT IS THE FUTURE OF PRODUCING?

Finally *Nightbeast* was complete and pretty much instantly forgotten by the filmmakers. The group finished school and split up for a while, going off to various educational establishments or jobs. Gus Bousfield worked at Bingley Hospital and Julian Butler and Bob Priestley went down to art schools in London. In the capital they hoped that

Stills from Smile Orange Films' *Nightbeast* (1988)

Still from Smile Orange Films' *Nightbeast* [Image obsured for legal reasons].

they would meet interesting people, people who were sane and wise, people who would show them the way forward, people who would help them forget their naïve bumpkin films and show them the way to enlightenment. They were in for a rude awakening.

Nightbeast's title sequence: Perfectly shit.

We did the *Nightbeast* opening titles and credits by writing them on a bit of paper and the camera had a basic Chroma key facility and then we would use this to project these titles over a TV image, all in real time. It was shit, but somehow perfect.

GUS BOUSFIELD
(SMILE ORANGE FILMS)

We edited as we went. We would film a shot and then pause the camera, then set up the next shot, then unpause the camera and film that. Until the film was done. Every shot was filmed in one take. In fact most scenes were filmed in one take. We didn't watch anything back whilst we were filming. Then, at the end of the night, we just watched the finished film from start to finish. I remember laughing constantly for forty minutes. Tom Ashcroft was laughing so much that he was screaming for it to be turned off mid-way through. It was that funny. Then we just added titles and credits and it was done.

JULIAN BUTLER
(SMILE ORANGE FILMS)

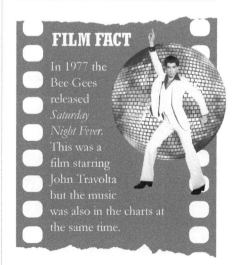

FILM FACT

In 1977 the Bee Gees released *Saturday Night Fever*. This was a film starring John Travolta but the music was also in the charts at the same time.

CHAPTER THREE
THE PRODUCTION COMPANY

WHAT IS A PRODUCTION COMPANY?

A production company is an association or collection of individual people who get together on dark corners or front rooms or dark front rooms or front corners to mock other people's television and film shows. Eventually these groups spout their opinions to such a degree that they call their own bluff and decide to make their own television and films. Soon it becomes evident to them that making films and television is not as easy as it looks — they realise that Noel Edmonds does have some skills and running a production company is like passing a large stool — It might be shit but it's still very hard to do.

WHEN SHOULD I SET UP MY PRODUCTION COMPANY?

A production company should only ever be started when there's absolutely nothing

One interesting thing that happened in London was that I showed *Nightbeast* to a philosophy student called Brian Turner. Brian got so obsessed with our film that he immediately made two feature length *Nightbeast* sequels (See Appendices for more on the making of these).

JULIAN BUTLER
(SMILE ORANGE FILMS)

else to do. In 1992 Julian Butler and Bob Priestley finished their degrees in the country's capital and, with nothing better to do, decided to re-join Gus Bousfield in the North of England.

At first Butler, Bousfield and Priestley found plenty of things to entertain themselves; such as sitting in the public viewing gallery of Bradford Magistrates Courts watching

Bradford's Magistrates' and Coroner's Court, the location for many brilliantly entertaining indecent exposure cases.

Restricting our urges to laugh became impossible and I just laughed out loud. The next thing I knew a court official, red with anger, threatened us with contempt of court saying that if we didn't stop we would be in the dock ourselves. Sitting there after that, not even allowed to smirk, whilst a flasher humbly apologised for his actions to a group of stern-faced magistrates, that was one of the hardest things I've ever done.

BOB PRIESTLEY
(SMILE ORANGE FILMS)

The poster for the film that inspired a wedding video company.

criminals being sentenced for minor misdemeanours. On one such court trip Butler and Priestley witnessed the trial of an eighty year old man who'd been caught indecently exposing himself. It was hard for the duo to hold their laughter in, especially when a police officer stood up in the dock and started describing the crime in detail:

"…t'ccused revealed his penis and asked some lasses he'd 'appened across int' playground 'do you 'appen to know what 'appens when you do this?' T'ccused then proceeded t'masturbate…"

Another one of Butler and Bousfield's methods for passing the time was to go and see strange films and theatre. One such cinematic screening was of a 1970s Jamaican comedy called *Smile Orange* (Dir:

PRO TIP
Your local Magistrates' courts can be visited for free any day of the week. Proceedings are enjoyed much more from the viewers' gallery instead of the dock.

trevor rhone's
smile
orange

starring
CARL BRADSHAW   GLEN MORRISON
VAUGHN CROSSKILL   STANLEY IRONS
ROBIN SWEENEY   CHARLIE BABCOCK

Production Manager: Yvonne Jones-Brewster   Editor: MIKE GILLIGAN
Photography: DAVID McDONALD   Executive Producer: MILTON L. VERLEY
Producer: EDWARD G. KNIGHT   Director: TREVOR D. RHONE

Michael Winner, 1976) at the Bradford Playhouse. The film is *Confessions of a Window Cleaner* set in Jamaica. For Butler and Bousfield Smile Orange's heavy West Indian patois rendered the entire film unintelligible, but despite, or maybe because of, this the duo loved it.

To continue attending screenings of funny films Butler and Bousfield needed money, so the duo were forced to take desperate measures: They set up a company making wedding videos. Butler and Bousfield advertised in the local paper's classified section and a couple came over to enquire about having their wedding filmed. Having never actually filmed a wedding the duo panicked and

> We had a meeting with a prospective bride and bridegroom and showed them our edit. I remember the girl going awwww when she saw the bird. It was an embarrassment.

GUS BOUSFIELD (SMILE ORANGE FILMS)

SMILE ORANGE VIDEO PRODUCTIONS
****

"Memories preserved for years to come."

Using "state of the art" video and sound technology, we aim to provide a friendly and efficient service, enabling you to take advantage of the ability to watch, listen, watch again and relive your happiest memories.
Weddings have always been our speciality but of course we will video birthdays, twenty-firsts, engagements, galas and sports events or just any occasion you or your friends wish to remember. Our service is always discreet (You'll hardly know we're there.) We tailor ourselves to your most specific needs.

We are both trained in film, video and media skills and have worked in this field for a number of years.

PRICES

   Weddings> £130 All inclusive (times)
   Or Separate> £85 Church Service only
                £45 Reception

   Extras are negotiable in price as is filming other events or occasions.

Equipment and options available.

   Titling
   Stereo sound (Hi-Fi quality) recording.
   Super VHS editing and recording
   Optional music or personalised soundtrack (Including your favourite music if requested)
   Transfer to VHS or Beta formats.
   2 Copies of the final version free subsequent £10 each.

   Demonstration cassette available on request.

Is this a flyer? Or just a memo? Or a price list? I dunno but, whatever it is, Smile Orange Wedding Videos used it to grab the attention of those eager to marry (or those whose bedroom circumstances had forced them to get married). Although of course, in the end neither of these parties got a video made. They pretty much told Smile Orange to fuck off.

borrowed some footage from a friend that he had filmed of his sister's wedding. They cut in some shots of birds they'd filmed and added silly music over the top.

During the meeting the bride asked what the production company was called. Bousfield, thinking on his feet and to make Butler laugh, said 'Smile Orange Films'. The company name stuck, although the bride and bridegroom never got back in touch.

So it came to pass that Smile Orange Films were born. Unfortunately the wedding video market hadn't turned out to be as lucrative as they had hoped and so the team immediately began thinking

A typical wedding videographer.

Name: Brian Turner
Credits: Van Helsing, JC Gustav McMann, Pierre, Banzai Brian, The Bus Stop Philosopher, The Ronin, Night-Beast.
History: Butler and Priestley met Brian Turner when he was a philosophy student in London. Inspired by Smile Orange Films Turner immediately brought together his own ensemble of long haired yahoos, called them Ontolocide Uberbilde Films and made two sequels to the Smile Orange's *Nightbeast*. Turner went on to act in many of Smile Orange's films and then moved to Japan. Smile Orange's Julian Butler showed his respect for Turner's work by travelling all the way to Japan and shitting on his tatami mats.
Skills: Thinking
Current Position: Training others to think.

I think, as a name, Smile Orange Films is as good as any other. Some of the names of other production companies sound awful, I can't think of an example but generally they are quite tedious.

GUS BOUSFIELD
(SMILE ORANGE FILMS)

film. How they were going to do it would be another matter.

WHAT IS THE FUTURE FOR PRODUCTION COMPANIES?

Malcolm in Cottingley says the future for production companies is bright: Open-plan offices will be replaced by walk-desks. A walk-desk is a small table attached to the user with shoulder straps. It allows the wearer to work at a desk whilst walking around. Stem cell research will also develop Post-it-Skin: Your DNA will be mixed with sunflower DNA, leaving you with yellow skin that falls off in massive square flakes. You will then be able to write messages on these flakes and shed them near the person who the message is for.

about writing their next feature film and the very first thing they learned about scriptwriting was not to bother doing it. This revolutionary technique would lead them to make Britain's most profitable

CHAPTER FOUR
THE SCRIPT

PRO TIP

A scriptwriter is a genius! You get dazzling results from putting this one in front of a buttons board. Top thinkers these mums and dads. Magic thoughts onto a blank piece of paper, up in shining light all through a computer screen. They transplant a heart from thin air straight into actors' mouths. Where do they get it from? No one knows! Glad they do it though. Beautiful, beautiful always using beautiful.

NICKY HINCHCLIFFE
(TOP HOLLYWOOD DIRECTOR)

WHAT IS A SCRIPT?

Scripts are made of paper and covered in words. Within the realm of the

A typical script

filmmaking arts there is no more important component than the script — It is the skeleton and central nerve system and titanium plates used to keep folk upright who have been hit by cars in gruesome accidents on the M62 (Or were just too obese to get out of the way) of film.

WHAT ARE THE ORIGINS OF SCRIPTWRITING?

Greek philosopher Platypus was the first person to write scripts. He lived in a time before the concept of pretending to be other people on stage was invented. Before Platypus all theatrical plays were documentaries; you came up on stage, said your name, you sang a song about your brutal life and were off. Throughout the Mediterranean, the matter of how good your story was would mean the difference between being beaten to death or beaten to death and your guts hung

Greek playwright and philosopher Platypus who, whilst performing a sword fight live on stage, had his nose stabbed to bits

Not be outdone by Platypus, another Greek philosopher, Koalas, stabbed his own face off, night after night, for no real reason whatsoever..

had (and had had) the more fists, bile and scorn could come their way if their story did not match expectation. As theatres grew and stages became further away however, a popular alternative to the throwing of clenched fists was the casting of stones, and the practice of stoning eventually became the recourse of public justice against untruthful individuals. These original practices are also still in use in the darkest and most remote corners of Yorkshire. Platypus was finally arrested, sentenced to death and made to drink hemlock. He was then reprieved, revived and encouraged to say it again by his biographer Hippostance who then put him to death again.

on ropes and your 'pottery' being kicked down a volcano.

This was known to be extra tough with the more popular bards and (sooth) sayers, as the larger the audience a player

FILM FACT

What's is the secret to successful scriptwriting? It's simple: You need to write. Any good scriptwriter will fill notebooks, pen drives, floppy-discs, zip-dongles, jazz-buckets, pixelsacks and USB-fingers full of their nonsense before they get anything made. An experienced scriptwriter will have unfilmed treatments, discarded feature films, forgotten comedy series, song lyrics, raps, half-finished short films, scraps, lists, character profiles, half ideas and entire musicals coming out of their arse.

SHOULD I USE SCRIPT-FORMATTING SOFTWARE?

There are many excellent free script-formatting software programmes available that help the scriptwriter to make their work legible and understandable. By no means use them. They are called things like Superscript, Lazywriter and CottingleyInternationalWordCraft. Whatever you do, stay away from them.

HOW DO I WRITE A FEATURE FILM SCRIPT?

Writing a feature film script is one of the exciting phases of the filmmaking process. To do this you will need a story. Finding a story is easy: Imagine you are telling a friend something funny that happened to you or something you imagine happening. That is a story. Smile Orange Films were lazy and so they decided to base their first feature film script on the stories in their favourite movies. So they scribbled down a two page synopsis featuring robots, super heroes, kung fu fighters and cops and their script was done. As you can see

their writing technique was, more or less, less is more. They called the film *I'llkilhya!*.

Lanky lads in balaclavas clutching weapons [Image obscured for legal reasons].

SMILE ORANGE FILMOGRAPHY

I'llkilhya! **(1992)**
Martial Arts / 120 mins / SVHSC / Colour
Three aliens that look like naked men, arrive on Earth and start killing people. Unfortunately they mess with the wrong person — kung fu hero Ken Fury who sets off on a one man mission to avenge his family's death at the hands of these monsters. Meanwhile the local cops blame Fury himself for the murders and set off to beat the living shit out of him. The ensuing film features kung fu schools, evil demons and huge-penised superheroes. Most of *I'llkilhya!*'s actors aren't over the age of twenty and this gives the film the look of an ISIS recruitment video; lots of lanky lads in balaclavas clutching weapons that they have no idea how to use. *I'llkilhya!* ends with a huge battle where Ken Fury destroys the mutating population of an entire alien planet. The nudity is filmed in tasteful long shots.

This nudity has been handled tastefully (T-B: Bousfield, Butler, Priestley).

An actor with
an enormous
penis.

HOW DO I SAVE MY SCRIPTS?

Saving your writing in the correct way and in the right format is a very important aspect of a scriptwriter's professional practice. You do this by pressing 'Control' and 'S' frequently. Or hit 'file' and then hit 'save'. I think. If you're on a Mac then I haven't got a clue. This book doesn't have all the solutions. Soz

WHAT IS THE FUTURE FOR SCRIPTWRITERS?

The digital age has changed the world for scriptwriters. Voice recognition and mind-output recorders are here and implanted in my mate Malcolm from Cottingley's head. Or so he tells me. For Smile Orange Films, back in 1992, this utopian dream was far in the future. Instead they had to sit around practically naked, tapping out things on a keyboard made sticky with spilt juice.

After scripting *I'llkillya!* The Smile Orange crew discovered that writing is easy but making sense is harder. Luckily they also believed that sense is overrated and so they limped proudly into action and began pre-production on their sci-fi kung fu buddy cop epic. Find out in the next enthralling chapter if it will be

Various kung
fu moves in
I'llkillya!

Various mutants in *I'llkillya!*

PRO RANT

Don't spend all day writing something while saving it successfully, and then edit this and that bit out by deleting it and then accidentally deleting the whole thing at midnight when you mean to save it — oh, poor you — thus necessitating an all-nighter to try and get back what you had down before. It will never be as good, you dumb-arse! No, double dumb-arse on YOU, before you can say it to me.

BRIAN TURNER

(ONTOLOCIDE UBERBILDE FILMS)

FILM FACT

There are no interesting anecdotes about the scriptwriting process.

a decision that will leave them writhing in torment for the rest of eternity. Or will they be alright with it?

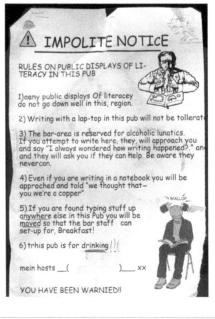

⚠ IMPOLITE NOTICE

RULES ON PUBLIC DISPLAYS OF LI-
TERACY IN THIS PUB

1) aeny public displays Of literacey do not go down well in this, region.

2) Writing with a lap-top in this pub will not be tollerat

3) The bar-area is reserved for alcoholic lunatics. If you attempt to write here, they will approach you and say "I always wondered how writing happened?." an and they will ask you if they can Help. Be aware they nevercan.

4) Even if you are writing in a notebook you will be approched and told "we thought that— you we're a copper"

5) If you are found typing stuff up anywhere else in this Pub you will be moved so that the bar staff can set-up for, Breakfast!

6) trhis pub is for drinking!!!

mein hosts __(   )__ xx

YOU HAVE BEEN WARNIED!!

Publicans! Are you annoyed by scriptwriters frequenting your establishment and not purchasing enough drink? This poster is the solution to all your problems [See page 263 for full-size publican print version].

CHAPTER FIVE
FILM FUNDING

Some money.

"

Yes! The gravy train at last!

DANNY BOYLE

(DIRECTOR)

WHAT IS FILM FUNDING?

Film funding involves the gaining of monies required for the creation of a proposed film, it is one of the hardest areas of film production due to the fact that it's impossible. But try not to let this fact overwhelm and scare you, there will be lots of time for other, more violent things, to do that.

WHAT IS THE HISTORY OF FILM FUNDING?

DHSS Film Funding offices. All creative talent reaches its zenith here.

The Greek philosopher Platypus wrote at great length about his problems getting film funding. His main problem was that he was living three thousand years before film existed. Platypus was painfully aware of this problem and therefore became the world's first person to complain about not getting any film funding.

WHAT IS THE DHSS FILM FUND AND HOW DO I GET AT IT?

The DHSS Film Fund is a highly generous film funding body with an office in most cities and towns throughout the UK. The heads of funding there are some of the friendliest people you will meet and have done more for the British film

Some more money.

industry than any other organisation. For many years the DHSS Film Fund has kept creative people like you in the enviable position of being able to moan at length about not getting work whilst not actually needing to get it. Smile Orange Films decided to fund their next feature film, *I'llkilhya!*, entirely through the DHSS Film Fund.

HOW DO I GET MONEY FROM OTHER GOVERNMENT FUNDING BODIES?

For some reason some filmmakers aren't content with the piles of free money that the DHSS Film Fund provides them to make their shit projects. This type of greedy filmmaker believes they need even more money. For them, funding is the glue that sticks their dreams to reality, the adhesive that holds their ideas to the delicate face of the Multiverse, the great steely-pointed barbed hook securing their gossamer-like creation to the fabric of the cosmos.

These fools then go cap-in-hand and handicapped (mentally) to the masters of the gluepot, the stickiest of all: The government film funding bodies. There is

nothing more pathetic than a filmmaker trying to do this. Forget it. Crowd funding is also a waste of time. You don't need it. If you have access to a phone with a camera you can blissfully make films from now to eternity. Begging for funding is the most disgusting area of the filmmaking process and YOU DON'T NEED IT!!!!

WHAT IS THE FUTURE OF FILM FUNDING?

According to Malcolm in Cottingley, a day of reckoning will soon come for the people who work for film funding bodies when they themselves have to beg for their money in front of a court of yawning bores. A similar theory was espoused in an illustration he once saw on a Merzbow CD, depicting a man in an abattoir being slaughtered by a cow. It will be just basic karmic reversal. But still fun.

With their DHSS film funding safely procured and karma on their side (at least for now) the members of Smile Orange Films were excited to move onto the next thrilling stage: Filming what was to become Britain's most profitable film.

It was to be a decision that would change/fuck up their lives for ever.

CHAPTER SIX
THE SHOOT

This is a big red button similar to those found on a camera. It's not the big red button you will find on your camera, you will have to do some research for yourself to see that one. This is just a generic big red button. Maybe the 'stop button' for Chernobyl? It doesn't look used so it probably was. No joke. Truth. Chernobyl was no joke. Wolves with four spines have taken over there.

> The Smile Orange way of filming was amazingly productive. We worked together like a happy blob. Or a Roman orgy. But why can't professional shoots be more like that? Fuck me! The professional world is completely unprofessional. The things I've witnessed whilst working professionally — I might write about it all in the sequel to this book. But for now be content to know that there are multimillion pound operations nowhere near as slick as a bunch of untrained stoners with their dad's camera.

JULIAN BUTLER
(SMILE ORANGE FILMS)

WHAT IS THE SHOOT?

The shoot is when cameras are switched on, pointed at stuff and you press record.

Pressing record is the crucial element here. Mistakes can happen if filmmakers don't take time to familiarise themselves with pressing record, so, please, please, please learn where the record button is and use it. Or, like Brian Turner from Ontolocide Uberbilde Films, you will live to regret it. On that day, Turner got out of his car, carrying his camera, to film a crucial scene for his film *Nightbeast II*. He pressed record and filmed the whole scene. He then got back in his car and pressed the record button to stop recording. When Brian got home and watched the footage he discovered he had filmed himself travelling to the location as well as getting out of the car. He had then recorded himself getting back in the car and driving all the way home.

Do you get it? Do you know what he did? If you don't you've been wasting your time reading this. I feel for you. You're a fuckwit. No, I won't be stopped,

Paul Merton would be pissing himself at this it's so fucking funny. Look at that! It's funny isn't it? Top sticks!

you're a fuckwit. If you can't work it out then you're a human turd, go back to your mother's tit.

Sorry, was I travelling rapidly outwards there? I'll get back on track.

WHAT IS THE HISTORY OF THE SHOOT?

The earliest films were of trains and ladies and gentlemen and horses running about everywhere. It's fascinating to see the world as it was in those days. These films are a piece of history captured and rendered pretty much unwatchable by bad camerawork filmed by grotty little men in moustaches and starring human beings with exaggerated facial expressions that people insist are still funny. Are they really funny though? Who laughs at such shit? Paul Merton that's who. And who looks to him, hmmm? Who? Really? Do you? No. Not really. At least the little potato man is tangible and actually knows something about the newspapers.

WHEN DOES A SHOOT HAPPEN?

A shoot can happen between morning and evening and actually sometimes at night too, yes?

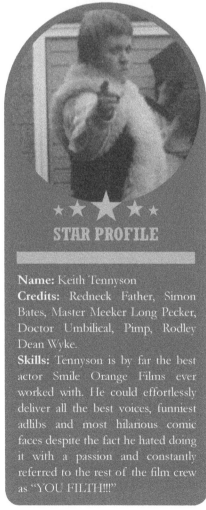

★ ★ ★ ★ ★
STAR PROFILE

Name: Keith Tennyson
Credits: Redneck Father, Simon Bates, Master Meeker Long Pecker, Doctor Umbilical, Pimp, Rodley Dean Wyke.
Skills: Tennyson is by far the best actor Smile Orange Films ever worked with. He could effortlessly deliver all the best voices, funniest adlibs and most hilarious comic faces despite the fact he hated doing it with a passion and constantly referred to the rest of the film crew as "YOU FILTH!!!"

HOW DO I CAST MY SHOOT?

Some of the most common stuff that gets shot at shoots are actors. Actors are twelve-dimensional beings. We three-dimensional humans only get to see their crudely projected three-dimensional image. Therefore we must never hope to tell actors what they should do or say or wear or who they should slap in the face.

The whole cast and crew of Smile Orange Film's *I'llkillya!* consisted of just seven friends and consequently there was no need for small talk. A scene started when the camera rolled and finished when the camera stopped, during which the actor was trusted instinctively to know what to do. They could ad-lib lines, use any objects within reach as props or slap another actor clean in the face (see Glossary: Cause). Every scene was filmed in just one take, in one shot, in real time. Some of the best actors in *I'llkillya!* were Graham Duckworth and Keith Tennyson.

HOW ELSE DO I CAST MY SHOOT?

Another casting method used by Hollywood films is to use anybody who happens to be on set. This is how Smile Orange met their greatest fan, Johnny Pigram. Pigram just happened to be visiting Smile Orange's set but as soon as Smile Orange caught sight of him they knew he was cinematic gold and he turned out to be a talented actor. Pigram is Smile Orange's one true fan, he is the only person who still watches the films and he is probably the only person who

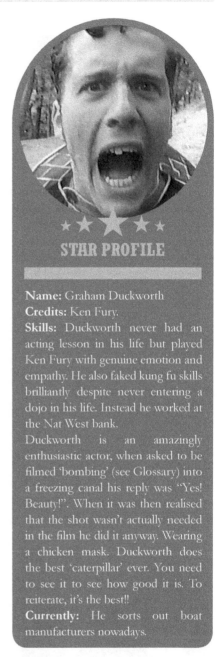

★ ★ ★ ★ ★
STAR PROFILE

Name: Graham Duckworth
Credits: Ken Fury.
Skills: Duckworth never had an acting lesson in his life but played Ken Fury with genuine emotion and empathy. He also faked kung fu skills brilliantly despite never entering a dojo in his life. Instead he worked at the Nat West bank.
Duckworth is an amazingly enthusiastic actor, when asked to be filmed 'bombing' (see Glossary) into a freezing canal his reply was "Yes! Beauty!". When it was then realised that the shot wasn't actually needed in the film he did it anyway. Wearing a chicken mask, Duckworth does the best 'caterpillar' ever. You need to see it to see how good it is. To reiterate, it's the best!!
Currently: He sorts out boat manufacturers nowadays.

will read every word of this book. Hello Johnny Pigram!

WHAT CAMERAS SHOULD I SHOOT WITH?

To shoot a film you must use a camera. *I'llkillya!* was shot on Julian Butler's dad's VHSC camcorder, a camera that was

Hi Johnny Pigram.

made by a company whose name nobody can now remember. Like Smile Orange you shouldn't give a shit about the manufacturer of the camcorder as long as it's your dad's. The camera was operated by talented cameraboy Andrew Boldy.

WHAT IS A TYPICAL SHOOT?

On a typical Hollywood shoot someone like Robert Redford and some mates will arrive in the park, they will put on masks and start acting, often before the camera arrives. Further actors will get the bus there, follow the shouts, find everyone else and then sneak up and jump in front of the camera as it's filming. Then someone like Dustin Hoffman will fling themselves out of a tree onto a bracken bank. Scene one in the can. Break for crisps. Oh, hang on, that was an *I'llkillya!* shoot wasn't it?

SHOULD I GAIN PERMISSION BEFORE SHOOTING IN A LOCATION?

There is no need to gain permission to shoot in a location. Especially if you

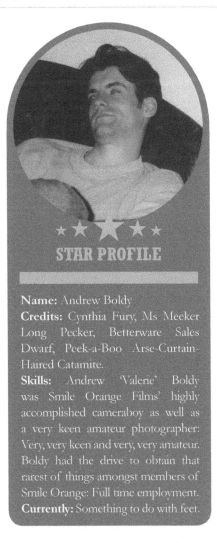

The Panasonic MC-10, a very good camcorder.

★ ★ ★ ★ ★
STAR PROFILE

Name: Andrew Boldy
Credits: Cynthia Fury, Ms Meeker Long Pecker, Betterware Sales Dwarf, Peek-a-Boo Arse-Curtain-Haired Catamite.
Skills: Andrew 'Valerie' Boldy was Smile Orange Films' highly accomplished cameraboy as well as a very keen amateur photographer: Very, very keen and very, very amateur. Boldy had the drive to obtain that rarest of things amongst members of Smile Orange: Full time employment.
Currently: Something to do with feet.

are filming a kung fu fight on a Chinese bridge within the grounds of some posh residential apartments. Even If your actors bomb into the ornamental pond there is still no need to gain permission. Even if

Robert redford laughs at a baddie.

Filming *I'llkillya!* was always very warm and nice and summery. I guess there were a lot of funny and talented people doing it as far a low-budget filmmaking goes. The nice thing was that the improv would make you laugh as people did it, a funny punch and a funny mask and funny dive, in those days it would be very entertaining. Most shoots now are very dry and boring.

GUS BOUSFIELD

(SMILE ORANGE FILMS)

you encounter an angry security guard there is still no need to gain permission. Even if, as you leave, the security guard asks 'hang on! Have you been in that bloody pond?' all you need to do is just

Before making films, Butler (left), Boldy (right) and Priestley used to draw on the ground to make money. This portrait of Leonard Nimoy actually looks like the new guy who plays Spock. Could it be that JJ Abrams based his whole *Star Trek* rebrand on this image? No.

PRO TIP

When Ken Fury flees from the police in Illkillya! the drama of the scene is heightened because it is shot from an elevated point of view. Amazingly, this incredible shot was achieved by the cameraman climbing up a tree. Use trees in your shoot, they are often free. For now.

run away. Again, gaining permission to use a location is never required.

WHERE DO I OBTAIN PROPS FOR MY SHOOT?

There are numerous ways a professional art director obtains props for a shoot.

FILM FACT

Almost every single prop in your film can be constructed from papier mâché (French for mashed potato). Props in *I'llkillya!* made this way include an orange mask, a yellow mask and a pink cock.

This is that bridge I were on about in that paragraph about that bridge. Does look a bit Eastern doesn't it? Maybe it's the squares and the colour red maybe?

During production of *I'llkillya!*, the Smile Orange team would often improvise with things they found on location. A great example of this is when, walking down the street one day, eagle-eyed Julian Butler spotted the biggest pile of dog shit he'd ever seen. Butler rang Bob Priestley and cameraboy Andrew Boldy immediately and insisted they shoot a scene where the cops step in the dog-mess and proclaim "someone's had the shit kicked out of them". If you too want to capture such moments of pure cinema then similarly you must be willing to use whatever crap is lying around. Good joke.

Another recommended way for a Hollywood art director to obtain their props is to steal them. One day Smile Orange Films' Priestley and

PRO TIP

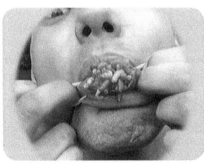

Maggots in mouth.

When filming maggots coming out of your mouth please put them in a condom first. Also, be ready with an explanation when your grandad turns up and is slightly bewildered by what he sees.

Massive dog shit.

Butler decided they would visit a BBC drama location in the Yorkshire Dales. They wanted to learn how to produce

the world's finest television, see the glamour of the industry, witness some professionals in action and then steal from them. It was the camouflage netting the BBC used to hide the crew portaloos that went walkies. One of the mutant aliens in *I'llkillya!* is made of this netting. An added bonus came when Priestley and Butler watched the BBC show later and spotted the glimmering roofs of the exposed toilets in the background of a wide shot.

Duckworth as Ken Fury. The only ever documented example of a young twenty-year-old Yorkshire lad showing emotion.

Smile Orange's Meccano-camera-cradle. A model superhero is suspended in front of the camera. The camera is put into the cradle and then travels down some fishing wire strung between two trees, giving the illusion of flight.

WHAT IS THE FUTURE FOR PLANNING SHOOTS?

Malcolm in Cottingley says 'Who knows what the future for planning shoots will be, no one can plan for it'.

This still from *I'llkillya!* shows the camouflage netting that some people might have said was stolen from the BBC. Others say it never happened and it would never stand up in court anyway. Because it never happened. But nonetheless, here is a picture of a great big camo net and it did stink of piss. But even DNA samples taken from the net and matched with the DNA of the stars of the BBC drama (Riddle of the Stones, or whatever it were called) would not even stand up in court after this many years. Because some say those same said stars were pissing everywhere at the time and might have pissed near Smile Orange when they were filming *I'llkillya!*

PRO TIP

In the middle of a scene in *I'llkillya!* one of the actors makes an excuse to leave the set and walks out of shot. After a pause the camera, on its tripod, begins a long pan to the left. Finally the camera stops panning and the same actor then calmly re-enters the shot and continues acting. Note: If your actors can also operate cameras you should employ them.

CHAPTER SEVEN
THE FIGHT SCENE

WHAT IS A FIGHT SCENE?

Fight scenes are the times in films when fists fly, hair is pulled, windows smash,

FILM TIP

To achieve realistic punch effects in a fight scene fill fairy liquid bottles full of neat washing-up liquid mixed with red food colouring and squirt them in the eyes of your actors whilst they are being punched in the face. This is also a great way to gain realistic screams from your talent. The screams of Smile Orange's Bob Priestley in *I'llkillya!* were obtained in this way.

Butler stabbing Priestley in the eye with a sword in an attempt to recreate a kung fu fighter being stabbed in the eye with a sword.

tables are thrown, kicks are kicked, bites are bitten, wives scream, Christmas trees topple and the pigs turn up to arrest someone who has nothing to do with it.

ARE THERE ANY GOOD MANUALS WRITTEN ABOUT FILMING FIGHT SCENES?

There are many informative manuals available to instruct you how to film fight scenes. One of these isn't the BBC manual *After Lunch We'll do the Fight*. If you want to know how to film a Shakespeare-esque fight from a BBC drama, set in the olden days, over a dinner table with chicken legs then don't buy the book because it won't even tell you that. All it does tell you is how to pack your armouries van correctly and how to drive it safely back to the BBC's Shepperton Studios. Wherever that is. Even though we pay for it. That's a licence fee reference by the way.

Priestley screams after having neat fairy liquid mixed with food colouring poured into his eyes.

Keith Tennyson (in long wig and beard), Graham Duckworth (in novelty hat) and some local talent shooting an *I'llkillya!* fight scene.

CAN FILMING A FIGHT SCENE BE DANGEROUS?

No, filming fight scenes is never dangerous and there is no need to meticulously choreograph them with highly experienced stuntman and women. All Smile Orange Films did was watch a lot of popular videos and re-enact the fight scenes from these films in front of the camera. These fight scenes were from well-respected classics such as *Two Crippled Heroes, Five Superfighters, Shogun Assassin, The World Famous Temple of Shaolin, The Fatal Flying Guillotine, Mafia vs Ninja, Black Belt Jones, Revenge of the New One Armed Swordsmen, Seven Golden Vampires, Iron Armor, Shaolin Death Squad, 72 Desperate Rebels, The Butcher, Zu Warriors from the Magic Mountain, Five Fingers of Steel* and *Thundering Mantis.*

Bob Priesley playing the Mudspirit covered in reservoir oomska

ANALYSIS OF THREE PIVOTAL FIGHT SCENES FROM THE FILM *I'LLKILLYA!*

Below is an analysis of three classic fight scenes from Smile Orange's *I'llkillya!*. Just what it is that makes each scene so successful?

FIGHT 1: KEN FURY VS THE MUDSPIRIT.

Movie fight scenes are often filmed in extreme conditions and Ken Fury's fight with the Mudspirit was no exception. It

Butler and the crew joyfully squirt fairy liquid into Priestley's eyes.

PRO TIP

Effects of bodies being punctured can be created by filling little water bombs full of fake blood. The actor then smashes this against their body so it explodes at the moment when they are hit by a sword / arrow / nunchaku / scythe / tong-fi stick / throwing-star / hammer / axe / knuckleduster / chain / club / chainsaw / mallet / flick-knife / mace / machete / bottle of acid / branch / fist / foot / knee / palm / forehead.

was the middle of winter and the Mud Spirit is played by hypothermic actor Bob Priestley. Priestley's skinny nude body was covered in freezing mud and dung, with only his own dreadlocks keeping him warm. Extreme conditions like this heighten drama and can give rise to great performances. Unfortunately that didn't happen this time.

FIGHT 2: THE COPS VS PEDESTRIAN

The West Yorkshire Armed Response Unit that turned up during this scene had been phoned by Bingley's Neighbourhood Watch Association. The police stopped the filming immediately and interviewed various members of the Smile Orange crew who told them that a scene was being filmed where a dummy is run over by a car driven by fake policemen brandishing cheap plastic toy guns. Before leaving, the police then reassured the Neighbourhood Watch Association that they were now safe from a bunch of children brandishing toy guns driving over a Penny for the Guy.

The scene in *I'llkillya!* that was so realistic that the police were dispatched to save a terrified community from balaclavaed dummies with broken hands.

Kneecapping is an easy special effect to create: Tape a banger to a balloon to your knee. Light banger. Stand well back. Unless banger is strapped to your knee. Then stand still and TAKE THE PAIN!!!

I'llkillya!'s kneecapping sequence. Pure cinema.

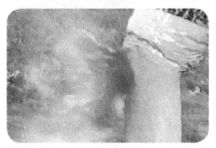

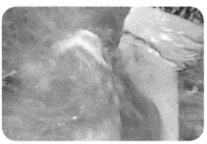

FIGHT 3: THE ORIGINAL DIEHARDS VS THE SEVEN JOINTS SPIRITUAL WHIP SCHOOL

Acquiring lots of actors to star in large fight scenes is essential. The process is easy: Go round every pub in your area on Friday night and hand out flyers asking anyone who wants to be involved in a huge fight to meet at your local park the next day. Come Saturday afternoon and the park will be populated with a large collection of hung-over gentlemen gagging to beat each other up. One of the gentlemen who responded to the Smile Orange flyers was called Danny Price. Price was an excellent martial artist and owned his own taekwondo school and so, for Smile Orange Films, the price was right. Excellent pun. That day's filming went well. At the end of this process Smile Orange Films had captured some of Britain's greatest fight scenes. They had them on tape, now they just needed to polish that turd and edit that bastard all up.

Pre-social media crowdsourcing at it's best.

The magic of creation (L-R: Butler, Bousfield, Duckworth).

WHAT IS THE FUTURE OF THE FIGHT SCENE IN THE FUTURE?

Malcolm in Cottingley says: Society is becoming more violent and soon we'll all get cameras fitted in our eyes. Then all our lives will become action films and I'll be scared to go out in case I get chopped up by ninjas. Due to global warming the abominable snowman will come down from the Antarctic, wander loose in the cities and fight tramps for scraps of food. The live streaming of these fights via tramps' eye-cams will become the most popular type of action film on (and off) the planet. Yes.

MY MORNING

I'm usually bang wide awake at the crack of dawn. Due to the pain. When this happens I just lie back all cosy in me doona and check for leakage from a busted open stitch. Usually by this time I'll be shaking all over due to the lack of painkillers (as nine times out of ten the drip has popped out while I've been writhing in my sleep and wetting me Manchester). Then my sheila, Tamsyn, brings me heaps of morning pills — ooohhh yeeeaaah — best part of the day! Tamsyn wraps me in cling film so I don't get me stitches wet when I'm in the shower, then I bang her like a dunny door in the wind. Then she's off to work a very satisfied woman. I love her guts.

Anyway, throw on the Crocs, wife-beater and budgie-smugglers then jump in the Ute and hoon me way over to the shoot. When I get there I check for seepage, have a paracetamol and chuck a Berserker energy drink down me neck. After that kicks in I have a shout at the director

A Stunt.

and do a stunt — maybe hooning up and down in a muscle car and then crashing it. Hard yakka. I'm injured! The director bites me arse out. Shit as. The faaking sook! So I hoon over to the on set triage nurse Millicent Bax. Then the paramedics air-lift me to hozzy. I'm besties with all of the staff here on the Gold Coast. Then it's scans, plaster casts and stitches.

In the arvo Tamsyn will swing by while she's getting a tetanus boost and pick me up in the Ute. Then it's daks down, strides off and I'm in there like a roo-rat up a gum tree. Pav for afters, fair dinkum. Sometimes my bestie Shauny Lee will hoon over on his jetski. Shauny's a barista in Bali. He only ever wears bathers and thongs. Shauny's such a great mate, he says there's not much difference if I'm in a coma or not! If, like now, all my fingers are ripped off then he'll even swipe Blendr for me.

As you can see most shooting days are pretty chilled and go to plan but some days I don't get hurt first time and then I don't know what's happening. But, no dramas, I load up on painkillers, although I'm not even crook, chuck a cleanskin down me gullet and I just keep stunting until I get hurt and then I know where I am and heading to hozzy. You ripper!!! Too easy.

BOB VON DAMAGE

(STUNTMAN, GOLD COAST INFIRMARY)
(TRANSCRIBED BY SHAUNY LEE)

CHAPTER EIGHT
LINEAR EDITING

WHAT IS EDITING?

Editing is what you do when you want to rearrange pictures of people and stuff that your video camera was pointing at after you pressed the record button.

WHAT IS LINEAR EDITING?

Linear editing is non-computer based editing. It means each shot has to precede the last one and you cannot go back and move shots around once they are laid down. This means that when you make mistakes you can't change it so you will then decide you like it that way. Smile Orange Films' *I'llkillya!* was edited using a linear edit suite.

FILM FACT

The weight of the mass of an average man's imaginary bag of groceries is equal to the minutes of every film. In grams only.

Non-linear editing is computer based editing. It means that shots can be moved around on the timeline endlessly until the pompous producer and pontificating director are happy with the order they come in and the highly important video of the boss's children's Christmas pantomime is finally fucking finished.

FILM FACT

In optimum lighting conditions It takes seven editors seven minutes to beat up seven producers. However, because editors work in darkened rooms, when light levels fall below 10% one editor can beat up seven producers. The only way one editor can beat up seven producers in natural light is if the editor resorts to a warp spasm.

This is a non-linear editing suite. You can fit all of this shit into your phone now.

If you are ever in Nottingham and looking for a good papier mâché penis-maker you can't do better than Big Pat (far left).

I was involved in aiding and abetting the creation of large papier mâché masks and an unfeasibly large acid-ejaculating penis round a three bar gas fire in a rented house in Mapperley St., Nottingham

BIG PAT

(HOUSEMATE)

WHEN DOES EDITING START?

When the filming stops, the editing starts. Waiting for filming to stop can take a long time. *I'llkillya!* took two years to make. This is mostly because it could only be filmed on the Saturdays when lead actor Graham Duckworth wasn't watching Leeds United play at Elland Road. It was then time to start editing.

Oh, I forgot, I also accompanied the guys to a windswept quarry where I took part in the filming of a fight scene. It was a fun packed day! I was given a role as a waist-coated, Elvis-headed fish-filleter being dispatched and urinated on by an alien.

BIG PAT

(HOUSEMATE)

WHERE SHOULD I EDIT?

One place to edit your film is in suites situated within state-of-the art post-production houses where highly trained professionals facilitate filmmakers by feeding their raw footage through complex and incredibly expensive image manipulation equipment. Another place

to edit your film is in a University where you gain access to free editing equipment by pretending to be a student.

In 1993 Smile Orange Films' Gus Bousfield was completing his degree at Nottingham Trent University when he noticed there were several empty edit suites there. Bousfield alerted Julian Butler who immediately hitched down to Nottingham and moved in for free with Bousfield and his fellow housemates. Big Pat was one such housemate.

On the first Monday morning after moving to Nottingham, Butler picked up his bag of video tapes and music cassettes and walked straight past the Head of Media Services at Nottingham Trent

Apparenly this picture has something to do with Nottigham Trent University.

I would get through about a scene of *I'llkillya!* and a 'teenth a day. I was learning how to use the edit suite at the same time and each night I would learn what worked when I'd show what I'd edited to Big Pat and Gus. Another housemate worked at HMV and he had a huge collection of stolen VHS tapes. We would watch lots of these and any tricks that we liked would usually turn up in the next day's edit. 'Shrooms strictly at the weekends only.

JULIAN BUTLER

(SMILE ORANGE FILMS)

University and into one of the edit suites. He locked the door and started editing.

WHEN SHOULD I USE MUSIC IN MY EDIT?

Music enhances the emotional content of a shot and can be used at any point in the editing process. Inspired by Wagnerian

Napalm Death's Shane Embury is the go-to grindcore guy. Nice illiteration.

Opera each character in *I'llkillya!* is introduced with their own theme music. Police Officer Sparkupski arrives to Eric Weissberg's Banjo plucking, Ken Fury arrives to Isaac Hayes and *Nightbeast* arrives to Napalm Death.

HOW DO I MIX SOUND ON AN EDIT SUITE?

An edit suite can be used to mix your film's sound. During post-production on *I'llkillya!* Butler, Bousfield and Priestley would get together with the rest of the crew and re-record adlibbed dialogue over the top of edited scenes. The great Italian filmmaker Frederick Fellini often used a similar technique. Smile Orange Films, being a set of pigs, were ignorant of this heritage, they just found it funny.

WHAT IS VIDEO GRAFFITI?

Once Butler and Priestley had learned to dub over their own films they enthusiastically started re-dubbing other people's — by renting tapes from the video store and re-dubbing them with chunks of their own dialogue. These tapes would then be returned to the video shop for the next unsuspecting renter to borrow.

Composer Richard Wagner. The go-to guy for classical music. He composed music which had a theme tune for each character. Smile Orange Films stole this idea and did it better.

Bingley Town Centre. It was near here that video graffiti was invented.

I'Ilkillya's talking Buddha. A great example of the technical abilities of Nottingham's go-to tech guy, Misery Guts.

Butler and Priestley christened this process 'Video Graffiti' and the video shops of Bingley were awash with these doctored tapes. Butler and Priestley also discovered that the more subtle the dubbing the more chance the tape had of being kept in circulation by the video shop. The duo would often re-dub only a single line in a whole film.

> ## FILM FACT
> At a free buffet, editors will take a beef sanger from the bottom of the pile instead of the top. This is because all editors are bottom feeders who think backwards.

Butler and Priestley provided this wonderful service at no extra cost to the video watchers of Bingley. Eventually Video Graffiti became so popular in the town that people would rent certain films out just because they wanted to see the Smile Orange version.

HOW DO I KEEP POST-PRODUCTION STAFF HAPPY?

Impossible. One day, after months of happily editing for free at Nottingham Trent University, Butler was confronted by the Head of Media Services (or Misery Guts as he'd been nicknamed by Butler and Bousfield). Misery Guts gruffly pointed

out that he'd discovered Butler was not a student at the University. This was surely the end for the editing of I'llkillya!

But, in film, appearances can be deceptive. Instead of throwing Butler off the course he wasn't even on, Misery Guts cracked his first smile in twenty years and allowed Butler to carry on. He even went on to help with various effects, including a talking Buddha.

HOW DO I MAKE THE CREDITS FOR MY FILM?

Credits are created by using machines specially designed to impose words over video. The final stage in the completion of I'llkillya! was applying the credits. These were created by Butler and Priestley back in Yorkshire, in the damp offices of Bradford's Oaktree Community Video.

It's easy to understand why Oaktree Community Video Ltd were wary of Smile Orange and their film that depicted, glorified and laughed at violence. Oaktree Video are the sort of people who say 'I want to bring art to the masses' but as soon as some shell-suited fuck called Decky turns up wanting to edit his rabbiting with ferrets videos then they say 'oh, not THOSE masses, we meant the nice masses'. These places were originally set up on a wave of 1960s optimism but by the early 1990s most of these them were suicidally disillusioned having seen their world stamped on like a boot stamping on a human face. Ironically this was also a scene depicted in I'llkillya!

Oaktree Community Video owned a community editing suite and titling machine so we turned up out of the blue expecting to use it. A more paranoid bunch of people would be hard to find. They would stare at us suspiciously as we tapped in the list of stupid made-up names that constituted our film's credits. We were baffled as to why these hippies were reacting to us in such a negative fashion.

BOB PRIESTLEY
(SMILE ORANGE FILMS)

HOW DO I MAKE A TRAILER?

With credits now added, Yorkshire's finest kung fu film was finished. It just needed a trailer. To make this, Butler and Bousfield went to see Dave Spane. Spane ran a film course at Bradford and Ilkley Community College where, to ensure that numbers stayed up and he kept his job, anyone could enrol. One of the fellow students enrolled on the course, possibly just to keep out of the cold, was a seven foot high, backcombed beanpole, stuttering, ecstasy dealing genius called Shaun Shallots. Also on the course was a short stocky man who

FILM FACT

An editor's average life span is less than that of a paediatrician.

I'llkilllya's title sequence utilised glass, acrylic paint, car paint, hammer and fire.

was Compo's stunt-double in Last of the Summer Wine. No one here knows this man's name. Tim Peck might know. I had it then, no it's gone. It was here, amongst these luminaries, that the trailer to *I'llkillya!* was edited.

HOW DO I AVOID EDITING?

Editing can be a fulfilling and creatively rewarding process. But usually it's not. It's a fucking bore. One way to avoid

The Arse-wipe.

> Maybe the folks at Oaktree Video were just sacred of us? Bob Priestley has always thought that Smile Orange were actually quite scary. But, as I pointed out to him — a lot of people weren't_scared by us. Quite the contrary — they would come up to us and start laughing and join in the ranting. AND they always seemed to be the best people. So actually scaring people off was a good way of whittling the wheat from the chaff, rendering the fat from the bone, thrashing the pigs in the slaughterhouse.

JULIAN BUTLER

(SMILE ORANGE FILMS)

FILM FACT

A 'wipe' is the name given to a video editing technique where one shot moves to cover the previous one. Illkillya!'s Mudspirit scene ends with a circular wipe to black, the final shot we see before the wipe is the Mudspirit's bum. The technical term for this is an Arse Wipe. Excellent joke.

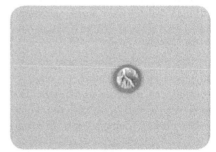

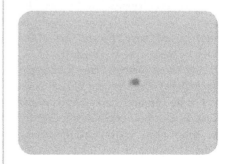

SMILE ORANGE FILMOGRAPHY

THE TASCHE AMSTERDAM SHOW (1994)
Studio chat show / 3 Episodes.
Various durations / Betacam / Colour
Bradford based studio chat show filmed as-live but never broadcast.

doing any editing is to mix your film live. This involves setting up numerous cameras in a studio and using a vision mixer to change camera angles whilst the action is happening. A lot of television is made this way and, to try it out, Smile Orange used the studios on Dave Spane's course to make The Tasche Amsterdam Show, a studio based chat show starring Gus Bousfield as the eponymous host.

This was a chat show where the host interviewed anyone and if no one was available, he interviewed himself. The show was crewed by anyone who could hold a camera. Multiple layers of jarring music and sound effects were also mixed in by whoever happened to be using the sound desk. The Tasche Amsterdam Show ran for three episodes until it was axed. By the people who made it.

Still, Smile Orange Films were going places: They had a feature film, a trailer and were making important contacts such as Compo's body double. What's his name now? It's on the tip of my tongue. Anyway, It was finally time for

PRO TIP

If you are sat in an edit suite watching someone else editing, all you hear is '... repeated statement, repeated statement, repeated statement, re-peat-ed sta-te-men-t, re-peat-ed sta-te-men-t, repeated statement, repeated statement, repeated statement, repeated statement, repeated statement...' for twenty hours fucking straight.

BOB PRIESTLEY (SMILE ORANGE FILMS)

the Multiverse to witness Smile Orange's mighty power. But how? Please read on…

CHAPTER NINE

MARKETING

WHAT IS MARKETING?

Marketing is making people aware that you wish to sell something. When you look at the word 'marketing' you will notice that it includes the word 'market' i.e. you're taking your 'something' to a market to sell. The word marketing also includes the word 'ing', this is a small village in Yorkshire.

WHAT IS THE HISTORY OF MARKETING?

Marketing started a long time ago. No one remembers how it happened. Because there was no marketing at the time.

WHAT IS THE DIFFERENCE BETWEEN PUBLICITY AND MARKETING?

Publicity and marketing are two different things. A public information film saying 'don't eat fireworks' is publicising something but not marketing it. This may or may not be true. To be honest I'm just thinking aloud. I'm a fucking philosopher now! Fuck off Žižek, you thick cunt!

★ ★ ★ ★ ★
STAR PROFILE

Name: Big Al Birdsell
Credits: Craig Knapton, Al Brewsty.
Dialects: Joe Pesci, Tony Bennett, Hughey from The Fun Lovin' Criminals.
Skills: Birdsell is physically ungainly yet strangely beautiful. He is also a crooner and, due to his loud voice, one of the country's leading hecklers. Once, at a stand-up show, he mercilessly taunted two famous comedians. He then got on stage, grabbed the mic off them and used it to promote his new bar. True story, I say, true story.
Currently: Manchester landlord.

Most of you don't even fucking know Žižek from a fucking hamster and you won't grasp what I'm saying. Imagine what I could achieve if I did actually apply my mind to something. But I'm not gonna. So fucking snooze on.

WHAT IS MARKETING WITHIN THE FILM INDUSTRY?

Film marketing includes posters and flyers and adverts and web campaigns and stickers and promotional objects and keyrings and baseball caps and T-shirts and bedspreads and wallpaper and action figures and food tie-ins and children's food tie-ins. You might even be able to get cakes with a lead character from a film on them. I swear I've seen Teenage Mutant Ninja Turtle cakes in Greggs.

WHAT IS WORD-OF-MOUTH MARKETING?

An example of word-of-mouth marketing is a bouncer telling another bouncer that 'that Children of the Corn is good innit?' It is this grass-roots level of brand loyalty that film marketeers aspire to. Word-of-mouth marketing, when harnessed successfully, will have many bouncers all over the North of England praising your film to each other in this way.

WHAT IS A FILM PREMIERE?

Perhaps the most important part of marketing any film the premiere. It is here where a massive audience of paying customers will eagerly consume your film product. After your premiere you will meet distribution companies that want to give you money, your film will get written about in trade papers and bloggers will praise it endlessly to the online community. It is an irrefutable universal truth that these things will happen and this book is no way selling you a false dream.

In January 1994 Smile Orange Film's *I'llkillya!* premiered to a full house at Bingley Little Theatre. Smile Orange actor Big Al Birdsell did a beautiful turn, singing 'The Girl from Ipanema'

Flyers like this are a fantastic way to market your violent film [Image removed for legal reasons].

The debut premiere of your film should be advertised with a flyer exactly like this one [Image removed for legal reasons].

> The film premieres were part of the gag. It was like we were trying to be comparable with Hollywood, pretending to be lavish and holding premieres as extravagant as those in Cannes.

GUS BOUSFIELD (SMILE ORANGE FILMS)

with Gus Bousfield accompanying him on a sit-down electronic keyboard. The premiere also featured Butler and Priestley performing as 'blue' Northern comedy duo Rivers and Rhodes and trying to induce epileptic fits by flashing a strobe light directly into the audience's

eyes (more about Rivers and Rhodes later). Ontolocide Uberbilde Films' Brian Turner also appeared in his performance artist persona, Drunken Dad, dressed as a Musketeer, clutching a rubber hand, and falling off the stage.

HOW DO I DISTRIBUTE MY FILM?

Once you've premiered your film you need to distribute it. A deal with a major Hollywood distribution company is one way to do this. But the Smile Orange Films way was to get a hundred VHS copies made by a local duplication house, market them with photocopied flyers and sell them via mail order. Cameraboy Andrew Boldy and graphic designer Juliet Uren designed the cover artwork and flyers for the film. The flyers were given out at film festivals, media events and bus stations. A cut out coupon on the back featured a chainsaw logo along a dotted line instead of the usual scissors. Sadly, no one actually used a chainsaw to cut it out. This marketing strategy led, surprisingly, to all the VHS tapes quickly selling out.

The debut premiere of your film should be advertised with a flyer exactly like this one [Image removed for legal reasons].

[Violent kung fu image removed for legal reasons.]

HOW DO I GET MY FILM REVIEWED IN THE PRESS?

Getting your film reviewed by the press is an important part of the filmmaking process. Marketing departments of film production companies constantly send promotional copies of their film (or 'screeners') in packages to press departments of magazines and trade papers. These packages might include

Do not overlook small budget fanzines when marketing your films. Why? Because the sooner you stop caring and lower yourself to this level, the better.

A Bag of Sand

The Fanzine/Contact Journal for Low Budget and Amateur Genre Film-Makers

Last is an extended trailer for a film called ILLKILLYA, which apparently is two hours long (the full version). This is kind of indescribable, a bit like a martial arts version of BAD KARMA, but not as good. It's basically a big spoof on 1970's kung fu films, and features lots of incredibly silly effects. There is no attempt at seriousness here, and whilst it looks quite amusing, at two hours I'm not sure I could sit through the whole thing! Copies of the film can be ordered from J. Butler (address printed on the video sleeve) for £15. I'm not printing the address here because I wrote to Mr. Butler weeks ago at the address given and have received no hint of a reply... (Stop press: At last! A reply! See news section and the full review of ILLKILLYA elsewhere in this issue!)

"ILLKILLYA" 2 hours
Directed by "Run Run Sore"

This video supposedly carries an "18" rating, but whether or not it's real (or if the makers have just hi-jacked the BBFC symbol) I wouldn't like to say. I certainly wouldn't put it beyond them! Yet again I'm stumped for words, as this really is alarmingly strange. Perhaps I should give up reviewing amateur films and start up a 'Forrest Gump' fanzine instead.

Nope, I'm sorry, but I really don't know what to make of this. It's so indescribably terrible, and yet rather enjoyable, that it could almost be some kind of pastiche of a home movie, something put together by jaded TV directors, fed up with the limitations of working for the BBC and desirous of letting their imaginations have free reign, whilst summarily taking the mickey out of amateur movie makers like you and me.

Or it could just be a load of crap made by a bunch of northern loonies. Basically, if you loved Take-over TV, and deeply wished that every episode would run on and on for hours, you'll adore ILLKILLYA. If not, you'll probably still find something to enjoy in this film, even if by the end watching it becomes more of a chore than a pleasure, because the genres it chooses to lampoon are many and varied!

Most obviously, it's a spoof kung fu movie: Not a Jackie Chan-type thing, but those awful 70's efforts with the expected awful dubbing, exotic weaponry, and "I must avenge the death of my father!" storyline, all of which have been reproduced and spoofed almost to perfection. Some of the voices used are excellent impersonations of those annoying dubbing artists we kung fu fans have to listen to time after time in virtually every Chinese actioner! It doesn't stop there, though, as ILLKILLYA also takes off 1970's cop shows, kids superhero shows and quite a lot of other things I can't even remember.

The plot (I use the word in the loosest possible way) has a scientist named "Illkilya" transported to alien planet during World War 2. Years later, a gang of aliens appear on Earth (their appearance is a superb joke on the Terminator films – I think – as they appear naked, and then the first thing they encounter, in the middle of nowhere, is a rotary clothes drier covered in various handy items of clothing!) and begin searching for a young guy called Ken Fury, slaughtering everyone else they meet in their path. Ken Fury seems to live inside a bad kung fu film, whilst the police who are after the aliens are Starsky and Hutch / The Sweeny rejects in 1970's clothing with 1970's attitudes! Eventually, all of the genres cross over with each other, and the finale resembles a decidedly 'adult' version of the Mighty Morphin' Power Rangers!

There are so many crazy ideas packed into this film I can't begin to list them all, but my favourites were the way in which Ken Fury's second set of arms are made to work in the finale (don't ask!) and the various 'designs' of the bizarre alien lifeforms that the heroes take on in the final scene. There are also plenty of special effects, all of them deliberately terrible, such as the 'flying' superhero which is obviously a model on a bit of string, and the ridiculous fake limbs and heads, most of which look like they came from jumble sales rather than special effects workshops.

Yes, there's plenty to enjoy, but what annoys me about films like this is that, like Take-over TV, they merely perpetuate the myth that anything filmed on video is basically made to be laughed at with complete and utter derision. This is particularly the case here, as ILLKILLYA is now available is a superbly designed box, complete with highly professional advertising leaflets, and yet the film itself is amateurish and puerile beyond belief.

Still, if you want something you won't get anywhere else, I can say with complete conviction that you'll find it here! It's also obvious that a hell of a lot of work has gone into ILLKILLYA, and that it must have taken a long time to complete (cast members hair-styles change frequently throughout the film!) so I guess the makers are justified in selling their product in the hope of making their efforts pay. But still, I can't help wishing that, if only the effort had been made to put something halfway professional together, ILLKILLYA could have been SO good! A kung fu movie made by people who so obviously know and love the genre could have been brilliant, if only the had copied the genre's good points as accurately as they have it's worst features!

Oh, but I must just say, Smile Orange productions (the makers) have taken huge liberties with copyright laws, editing in clips from actual movies throughout!

21

23

I'Ilkillya! in Loaded: A rare example of an article in the publication that didn't feature breasts. Instead it featured a massive dick.

gifts such as baskets of fruit and bottles of wine but never tins of cold carboniferous sardine spines.

Smile Orange Films decided they too wanted to send the I'llkillya! trailer to the press in the hope that the publicity would increase sales. But there was one problem: The DHSS Film Fund wouldn't stretch to buying the blank VHS tapes needed.

Article in Eastern Heroes magazine.

I rang up for a free video from the Army. The tape was supposed to give me more information about joining a regiment called the Green Howards. However, once the Army had my address they kept badgering me to join the Green Howards for at least eighteen months. Like a fucking dog with a bone. I never joined the Army and I got two tapes from them. I think I know who had the victory there. I won the battle… and the war!

BOB PRIESTLEY (SMILE ORANGE FILMS)

Luckily a simple solution presented itself when the British Army launched a new recruitment drive — by giving away promotional VHS tapes. Butler, Priestley and Bousfield rang the Army countless times and, using pseudonyms, ordered numerous free tapes.

FILM FACT

Very occasionally your VHS copy of I'llkillya! will stop working. To mend your tape take it out of the player, look at it and put the tape back in the player. Press play and continue watching. This ALWAYS works.

T&A, Monday, January 3, 1994   **NEWS**
It's martial arts movie madness – with Bingley's own Bruce Lee

MONKEY BUSINESS... They're out of their tree! From left, Bob, Graham, Julian and Andrew Boldy during intro action

Kung Fu carry on!

BY day he's a bank clerk in Bradford – but by night he's the Bruce Lee of Bingley.

by PAUL PARKER

ROLE MODEL: Bruce Lee

MASKED MAYHEM... Filming a sinister movie scene

the film and amongst the thousands and thousands of cassettes, books and zines in their catalogue. *I'llkillya!* was the only self-made feature film they sold.

HOW DO I GET MY FILM SHOWN AT FILM FESTIVALS?

Festivals are the springboard to success for many films and, despite any form of standardisation system, selection panellists are definitely the best qualified people to decide what films get shown. There is absolutely no better way to spend your budget than by lining the pockets of these people. Film festivals are not in any way basically just a fucking money-raking racket.

Smile Orange Films sent the

It is a good idea when being interviewed by your local paper to include utter nonsense in your answers.

Smile Orange Films then took these promotional tapes, recorded their trailer over them and sent them out, as screeners, to promote *I'llkillya!* .

The screeners did their job and soon *I'llkillya!* was featured in numerous magazines. Loaded ran a full page article on Smile Orange Films which led to *I'llkillya!* sales rocketing to almost a hundred. The film was also reviewed in numerous film zines including *Bag of Sand*, *Sad Man Eating Mushrooms* and martial arts movie magazine *Eastern Heroes*. Anarchist publishers AK Press agreed to distribute

SEX, GEWALT & GUTE LAUNE

VOL. 5

66

PRO TIP

The main reason we got shown at so many festivals was because it was a rare thing to have made a feature film back in the early nineties. They were expensive to make, there was no YouTube or Vimeo and films were seen as a sort of form of high-brow art. Now, of course, every cock and ball is at it.

JULIAN BUTLER

(SMILE ORANGE FILMS)

I'llkillya!'s trailer appeared on the German video compilation *Sex, Violence and Good Moods*.

Henry Rollins from the punk group Black Flag signed this certificate and therefore had something to do with *I'llkillya!* Nobody knows how or when but never the less here is the proof and you can't argue with it.

I'llkillya! trailer round numerous film festivals with a note saying 'your fees are more than our film cost to make and we're not going to pay them'. In 1994 it was very rare to have made a low-budget British feature film. It was even rarer to have made one on VHS for a budget of £000 000 000.00. Most festivals waived their fees. The film started to get screened.

I'llkillya! was shown at London's Leicester Square Odeon as part of the

In the mid-90s I attended an Exploding Cinema event somewhere in South London with director Alex Chandon. The best film of the night was the *I'llkillya!* trailer. Recognising fellow film freaks, we exchanged details and subsequently met up again at the Raindance Film Festival in Leicester Square where the full version of *I'llkillya!* was screened.

NEIL KEENAN

(SHIRT-LIFTING FILMS)

Butler and Priestley attending the *I'llkillya!* screening at the British Short Film Festival.

Maybe our whole 'careers' from then on are based on a misreading of the festival screenings? Perhaps the audience were laughing at us and not with us. Maybe we just mistook mocking laughter as a compliment?

JULIAN BUTLER

(SMILE ORANGE FILMS)

Raindance 'We Show Owt' Film Festival as well as the British Short Film Festival in the Haymarket. Wherever that is. At a Bradford International Film Festival screening Smile Orange provided sick bags for the audience and at the Prince Charles Theatre, London, after a Halloween Film Society screening, Bob Priestley overheard two girls say 'oh well, boys will be boys'. At an Exploding Cinema screening, Henry Rollins was lucky enough to enjoy the film as were filmmakers Neil Keenan and Alex Chandon, two filmmakers who went on to do nothing with their lives.

> I could not understand why, when offered a staircase with such short risers and long treads, that other producers weren't utilising such a perfect means of generating publicity.

BOB PRIESTLY
(SMILE ORANGE FILMS)

Smile Orange Films handing out flyers at yet another London *I'llkillya!* premiere (L-R: Butler, Boldy, Bousfield and Priestley).

HOW DO I GAIN PUBLICITY AT A FILM FESTIVAL?

If your film is being shown at the Plaza Cinema on Regent Street, London then stunt-rolls down the grand steps of the cinema is a good way garner publicity. If you make sure you do your stunt-rolls at the packed opening night of the British Short Film Festival then you will gain even more favourable exposure. Or not.

I'M THINKING OF RETHINKING MY FILM MARKETING STRATEGY? HOW DO I DO THIS?

Sometimes your film marketing strategy will need rethinking due to a change in public perception. It was at the initial screenings for *I'llkillya!* , as people guffawed out loud in their hundreds, that it slowly dawned on Butler, Bousfield, Boldy and Priestley that their film was considered to be a comedy.

At first this baffled the team. Admittedly *I'llkillya!* did look ridiculous but there were no attempts at actual jokes, they'd only ever made the film to amuse themselves. Now, unexpectedly, it seemed to be amusing others as well. This was even more baffling because none of the Smile Orange team liked comedy films.

> I still think today that we're not really funny. For us, being considered 'comedy' was an insult. If we were writing and someone said a predictable, Radio 4 style, joke, we would give them a disapproving look and say "hmmmm, comedy" and dismiss the joke. For us there are 'funnies' (things which we find funny) and there's 'comedy' (jokes, comedians and stand-ups which aren't funny). We get bored with 'set up, joke, set up, joke, ad infinitum'. We seem to like 'set up, shot of a weird thing, non-punchline, more weird stuff, fade to black, fade up on a close up of an arse, an explosion in some dog food, cut.

BOB PRIESTLY
(SMILE ORANGE FILMS)

This is a bit of that 'personal' mentioned in that opening bit of this book. Something to tantalise you, but you'll never know what is really going on. Isn't there a lot of Ice Cubes in this picture? Yeah there is! And what does that mean eh? Smile Orange can't remember so you'll never know.

SMILE ORANGE FILMOGRAPHY

MESCALINE (1996)
Music promo for Sultans of Ping / Rhythm King Records / 4 mins / Hi8 / Colour
Promo made as a follow up to the band's shit record 'Where's me Jumper'.

From Monty Python to Eddie Murphy, Smile Orange Films hated it all. Comedy always told you when to laugh and that wasn't funny. Even today, the team avoid any film starring comedians like Will Farrell, Adam Sandler or that small man with the big head (Note to self: Must come back and remember his name later).

Even the idea of being considered filmmakers baffled the filmmakers. Smile Orange thought of themselves as just a way of doing things. A celebration of joyful rubbish. In essence, a 'way'. For them, making films was just another branch in the path of the Smile Orange way. This way could be applied to anything; a fashion show, a radio show or making thrones at the tip.

WHAT CONSTITUTES A SUCCESSFUL MARKETING STRATEGY?
A successful marketing strategy will

We once spent a whole day making huge thrones from rubbish at the tip which we then sat on like kings. Maybe we should have continued doing that instead of making films. The thrones we'd be making by now would be incredible

JULIAN BUTLER
(SMILE ORANGE FILMS)

SMILE ORANGE FILMOGRAPHY

FEARS OF A CLOWN (1993)
Short / 5 mins / SVHSC / Colour
Clown sacrifice film made for ITV's
Hotel Babylon.

You probably can't tell what any of this is can you? Well, it's a clown burning.

usually lead filmmakers to gain more work and, at this point in Butler, Bousfield and Priestley's careers, they started getting little scraps thrown to them from the table. Firstly they got asked to make a pop promo for indie band Sultans of Ping. They got paid 200 sheets and celebrated by spending their first ever proper budget on Pot Noodles.

Next, *I'llkillya!* started getting attention from television channels. Clips from *I'llkillya!* were introduced by dub-businessman Normski on BBC2's Dance Energy and the BBC's The Sunday Show

To all these people who wanted a piece of *I'llkillya!*, I felt like saying 'do you not see? We like you, but you're irrelevant. What you are thinking right now doesn't matter. That prestigious film school you went to doesn't matter. That OBE you have doesn't matter. That severe ginger fringe you have. It doesn't matter.

BOB PRIESTLY
(SMILE ORANGE FILMS)

filmed a segment with the team.

Another television opportunity materialised when ITV's failed youth series *Hotel Babylon* were doing a piece on low-budget filmmakers. They planned to film Smile Orange at work. But Smile Orange were far from 'at work' on anything so they lied and said they were filming a scene in which they would lynch,

Behind the scenes of the *Hotel Babylon* shoot. Some dads can be seen. Battery belt eh?

L-R: Priestley, Arnold (OBE), Butler and Bousfiled.

tar-n-feather, decapitate and burn a clown.

The *Hotel Babylon* producer was Andrea Arnold, the ginger haired crumpet from 1980s children's show No73. It was a freezing boxing day when Arnold travelled up from London to meet Smile Orange Films and she was visibly shivering. On the other hand Bob Priestley, who played the clown, was stripped naked, tarred and then feathered and set alight. AND HE ENJOYED IT! Let's hope Arnold managed to get a proper coat when she directed *Wuthering*

Heights in Yorkshire years later.

Butler, Bousfield and Priestley also decided to pretend that their dads produced the films and had them interviewed on camera. This interview was eventually cut from the show. Interviews with directors Edgar Wright and Alex Chandon did make it into the show. Not because they had anything more interesting to say than the far superior (and much more well hung) Smile Orange. Their interviews were left in the show merely because they did not feature any of their parents.

Years later Andrea Arnold incorporated what she had learned from watching Smile Orange at work into her own films. She went on to win an Oscar. And an OBE.

Local news [removed for legal reasons].

HOW SHOULD I ACT WHEN CELEBRITIES SHOW INTEREST IN MY FILM?

If a film is successfully marketed then everyone will want a piece of your flabby gaping rectum. At one point Butler got a call from the Grammy nominated producer of 'Pump up the Volume', MARRS' Dave Dorrell. Dorrell wanted to show I'llkillya! in a music show pilot he was producing. Butler had loved MARRS and was too star-struck to talk to Dorrell so he asked Bob Priestley to take the call and pretend to be him. Priestley was a fan of country music and didn't really care for Dorrell and his stupid new sampled music, Butler only heard the conversation from his end which went like this:

Priestley: "Give me the fucking phone, yeah what do you want?... (pause)... yes, I'm Butler... (pause)... no... (pause)... yes... (pause)... very good... (pause)... no, I like country music... (pause)... happy... (pause)... if you like (pause)... OK then.. (pause) ..why not? (pause) ... shouldn't be a problem... (pause)... I'll ask him, I mean... er... yes... (pause)... I'll get back to you... (pause)... we come down to London?... (pause... Priestley looks to Butler who shakes his head)... no... (pause)... no... (pause)... no... (pause)... no... (pause)... mmmmmm? No... (pause)... do it here and send it?... (pause)... hello?..." (Puts phone down)

HOW DO I MARKET MY FILM ON TELEVISION?

Films are often marketed on television by an interview with the director or the movie's stars. When a researcher rang Julian Butler and asked if Smile Orange could appear on Channel 4's *The Big Breakfast* he grasped the opportunity. The researcher seemed to be under the impression that Butler, Bousfield and Priestley were able to perform real kung fu but, for the record, Butler never actually said they were trained martial artists. "So you have some costumes and everything?" was all he was asked. "Yes, we definitely have some costumes," he replied. Butler, Bousfield and Smile Orange actress Sue Wright drove overnight to be at the *Big Breakfast* studios by 5am. On the way they picked up Bob Priestley who had, for no apparent reason, moved back to London.

WHAT DO I WEAR WHEN MARKETING MY FILM ON TELEVISION?

It is important to look smart when appearing on television. *The Big Breakfast* researcher's face dropped when Smile Orange Films arrived and she saw what they were wearing. Instead of kung fu fighters she'd got a gang of scary lunatics.

True to Butler's word they wore 'some costumes', but definitely not kung fu costumes: Priestley looked the most

Priestley, in 'costume', just before appearing on Channel 4's *The Big Breakfast*.

ridiculous in blue leggings on which he'd biro-ed the word 'Stüssy', Butler wore a shell-suit and a fisherman's maggot carrier, Sue Wright was dressed in a smart suit and Bousfield just looked naturally ridiculous. The researcher basically ran from the room.

Two minutes later she returned dragging a producer behind her. The producer, probably knowing they had nothing else to fill the gap said 'yeah, that'll have to do'. They were on.

HOW DO I ACT AROUND OTHER CELEBRITIES ON TELEVISION?

Appearing on live television is a great opportunity to make contacts and Smile Orange Films networked effortlessly with the other celebrities in the green room / portacabin. Stunt biker Eddie Kidd was there and became cross when Priestley moved his rubber stunt brick. Burt Kwouk was there too along with presenters Gaby Roslin and Mark Little, some models in bikinis, another bloke in swimming trunks, Lily Savage, Alexei Sayle and a Gladiator (who Butler annoyed when he asked him if he took steroids). Contacts like these are priceless and will definitely lead to collaborations in the future. In this case they didn't.

WHAT SHOULD I DO DURING MY TELEVISION APPEARANCE?

Appearing on television to promote your film is a great opportunity to show viewers how intelligent and eloquent you can be. In *The Big Breakfast* script the Smile Orange team were meant to show off their kung fu skills. But Smile Orange didn't have any kung fu skills, so, instead, viewers saw some tired Yorkshire stoners dressed as broken athletes spinning around on the spot.

Their interview went even better, with Priestley telling Mark Little that the film was an outlet for the team's aggression and without it Yorkshire would have witnessed a 'Kung Fu Hungerford'.

At the start of the next segment Bousfield and Priestley were meant to dive in front of Roslin and Little and fight each other. But Priestley felt that this would be boring and so when Bousfield threw him to the floor he got up on all fours, pushed his rectum directly into the camera and audibly let one go.

For a second the whole 'jokeyness' of the studio froze. The same thought raced through every single mind at exactly the same time: "He just farted!' Then the gates of the collective unconscious closed again, everyone snapped back into action and Roslin carried on. Angrily. Probably because she was having to hold her breath.

Later, safely back in Yorkshire, viewing the taped show, the whole thing seemed worth it for that brief second when Priestley let out an extremely loud fart right into the faces of the great British public.

WHAT IS THE FUTURE OF MARKETING?

I asked Malcolm in Cottingley about the future of marketing and his reply was extremely illuminating: 'In the future, anything told to your face is a lie and all truth will be leaked. You'd better believe this but... hang on. I've painted me sen into a corner here. How do you know that what I'm telling you is the truth then? Mmmmmm. Forget it then. What else have I got for you... er... have I told you about me mate who walks everywhere? He's popping over to visit me from Golcar. He'll be here in three days.'

It was because of it's intensive marketing campaign that *I'llkilhya!* gained its' success, but remarkably Smile Orange Films were aiming for an even greater greatness. Their plan was still to make the most successful British film ever. So the next stage was to capitalise on *I'llkilhya!*'s success and this meant only one thing: Making another film.

PART TWO

PRODUCTION

StorytellingGBCreative

135C THE STABLES, LEEDS, WEST YORKSHIRE, LS3 5GH

Smile Orange Films
2050 Cardigan Road
Headingley
Leeds
LS7 5YUE
5th June 1995

Funding Request NO: 0860294LE
Project Name: The Hunted Yorkshire Grim Ass.

Dear Jillian, Grus and Babbie,

Hi Guys and apologies for the delay in responding, we are against the pump here at StorytellingGBCreative (by the way, a great slate of new projects on their way from us. Gerard Depardieu is attached so get excited!). For this reason I cannot facilitate your request for information. But, as a goodwill gesture, I will give you my quote on producing from my forthcoming presentation at the Media Ethics Conference at the Dogmeat Factory, Sheffield:

'*Producing is as creative as writing. It's like writing with money. Excel sheets are the new jazz. Not that I know anything about jazz. Apart from cool jazz. Light bar jazz, with beats underneath. That's what I like. But I will look at you like a parrot if you mention Sun Ra (is that how they're spelt?)*'

Okay, must run

Kind Regards

Amanda Fees-Rodeane
Head of Funding
StorytellingGBCreative

CHAPTER TEN
CAPITALISING ON SUCCESS

The ladder to success. There's your bottom rung. One step up from the drain.

Lester Pigott (second horse from left).

WHAT IS SUCCESS?

Success is the accomplishment of an aim or a purpose. The level of success depends on how much the aim has been accomplished. For example: Jockey Lester Piggott is highly successful because he has accomplished every single thing he set out to do. Apart from doing stir for tax evasion.

Someone is moderately successful when their aims are only slightly accomplished. For example: Despite having failed to pull at a club, or even on an online dating site, a young man will gain moderate success when he manages to masturbate into a sock with a limp dick at two in the morning.

HOW DO I CAPITALISE ON SUCCESS?

Capitalising on the success of your first feature film is very important if you are going to continue to work in the film industry. Smile Orange Films had tasted the brief smell of success when *I'llkillya!* had been screened at film festivals, shown on TV, featured in numerous magazines and sold on tape in its tens. The next step seemed obvious — to ignore all this and make the most disgusting and offensive

be interested in making the most horrible film ever? It had something to do with the team's attitude to money. Up to this point, to avoid problems, Smile Orange Films had nobly ignored the material distractions of wealth by agreeing that no one in the team be paid a penny. Soon, they found themselves in poverty.

So when Smile Orange Films saw that a film competition called the Dick Awards was offering a large lump sum as prize money, they danced a little happy dance. Dick was the name of an art house film made entirely from close-ups of penises. The film had done bafflingly well financially. This prompted Dick's producers to set up a film competition where a large cash prize could be won for similarly themed filth masquerading as art. They called the competition the Dick Awards. Here was a way for Smile Orange Films to make some money, they just needed a script.

The name Dougie came from the time when, at Blackpool's Pleasure Beach, we saw a man with a megaphone recruiting members of the public to come and have a fight with some wrestlers that were stood menacingly behind him. The public could earn ten quid per round — 'a little bit of extra beer money or sommut like that' as the man said.

BOB PRIESTLEY

(SMILE ORANGE FILMS)

Sequence from Smile Orange's Blackpool wrestling footage. A man (left), wearing the staple 80s look of highlights (or tints) in his permed hair, white socks and shiny shoes, takes a full fist to the face from a wrestler known as The General (right). Note: The man is not Dougie from Manchester. But he might have known him. Or fought him.

film ever made. And so the next Smile Orange film, The Hunt for the Yorkshire Grimace, was an attempt to make not exactly a horror film, just a horrible film.

But why would Smile Orange Films

The Blackpool wrestling was both hilarious and scary at the same time. Somehow we managed to sneak our Radio Rentals full-sized shoulder-mounted VHS camera in to film it. The terrifying thing was that these meat heads were beating each other up in their everyday clothes, wearing shiny slip-on shoes. One even had a huge perm with highlights! It was like a horror film. They fought for real too, no fake moves. Anyway, each bloke was introduced to the crowd in true wrestling fashion before they fought and one was called 'Dougie from Manchester'. For some reason that made us laugh and we quoted it incessantly to each other. Then later we used it in *The Hunt for the Yorkshire Grimace*.

JULIAN BUTLER

(SMILE ORANGE FILMS)

HOW DO I WRITE A SCRIPT THAT CAPITALISES ON MY SUCCESS?

The concept for the script was easy: For years Smile Orange's Julian Butler and Bob Priestley had been making each other laugh with two imaginary characters who were racist, sexist, homophobic, alcoholic, baby-raping murderers. They were also Northern stand-up comedians. This idea made Butler and Priestley laugh a lot and so they decided to make these characters, the two worst people on Earth, the heroes of Smile Orange's next film. The duo's names were Dougie Rivers and Gary Rhodes. For short; Rivers and Rhodes.

SMILE ORANGE FILMOGRAPHY

RIVERS AND RHODES. LIVE AND LEWD FROM GINA AND PAULA'S FRONT ROOM (1987)
Live comedy show / 10 mins / Umatic / Colour
The great Northern double act's first ever stand-up performance in front of an audience of one person.

RIVERS AND RHODES LIVE AND LEWD FROM A COACH COMING BACK FROM BLACKPOOL (1988)
Live comedy show / 10 mins / SVHSC / Colour
Rivers and Rhodes' notorious bus based performance. There was a riot on the coach during the same trip and many members of the audience were taken to court for destroying the interior of the vehicle.

RIVERS AND RHODES LIVE AND LEWD FROM BINGLEY LITTLE THEATRE (1993)
Live comedy show / 210 mins / SVHSC / Colour
Rivers and Rhodes' third performance; live at the *I'llkillya!* premiere. The film ends when the camera battery runs out.

Butler and Priestley knew that they had to flesh out Rivers and Rhodes into, at least, one dimensional characters. So the duo started dressing up in filthy dinner suits and performing live as the duo: At birthday parties, in friend's front rooms and on National Express coaches. Every performance was filmed.

The act was an obvious piss-take of Bernard Manning and involved telling appalling and offensive jokes as badly as they could. But, Butler and Priestley discovered to their bemusement that, no matter how bad the jokes were, members of the audience still laughed. The new Smile Orange film had the characters, they just needed the jokes.

I definitely thought that when we performed as Rivers and Rhodes and people laughed, this could masquerade as success no matter how meaningless and hollow. And if taken to an extreme, this could go as far as notoriety and celebrity.

BOB PRIESTLEY

(SMILE ORANGE FILMS)

There they are. Early R&R. Aye. Correct.

HOW DO I WRITE JOKES FOR MY SCRIPT THAT CAPITALISE ON MY SUCCESS?

Writing and crafting your own jokes is a rewarding and artistic experience and

This is a brilliant shot of George Roper (left).

> I was desperate to see how Roper worked the gig. On entering the club he kept low key, and sidled up to the DJ to get some local Bradford info from him. I was impressed. Roper then stood in one spot for an hour and was funny, a really good performer. Later in his set he then told a joke about a gay club (it wasn't anything offensive, just a bit silly, to be honest. We were disappointed). But what he did was use the name of the most well-known gay club in Bradford, The Sun. This tailored his show to a Bradford audience and made his act more pro. I thought being an old school stand-up comedian was the best job ever.

BOB PRIESTLEY
(SMILE ORANGE FILMS)

should be avoided at all costs. Instead, do what the Smile Orange Films team did — go to see a real Northern comedian and steal his jokes.

George 'Welly' Roper had been on the first series of Granada TV's *The Comedians*, appeared on *The Wheeltappers and Shunters Social Club* and was one of the more successful stand-ups on the club scene. Butler, Priestley and cameraboy Andrew Boldy went to see him perform at The Palm Cove Club, a low-end club in Manningham, Bradford. The pub was

a throwback to the seventies, despite having only just opened in the nineties.

The production team were writing down Roper's jokes as he said them. Roper noticed this and singled out cameraboy Andrew Boldy for ridicule. Boldy is deceptively good at arguing but he could say nothing to combat Roper's mockery. He could only grunt into his beer. But, as the Smile Orange production team spilled out onto the cold Bradford street, they knew they had their material. It was time for the team to write up their stolen jokes into a script and find a good movie set in which to film it. (Note to self: That is the most boring sentence so far in this book. Definitely come back and re-write this later).

WHAT IS THE FUTURE OF CAPITALISING ON SUCCESS?

As for what success might look like in the future, this is a hard one. I tried to call Malcolm in Cottingley, but he has had his mobile cut off. I don't know what he's up to but I'm sure it'll be a success.

FILM FACT

The secret to success is to set your aims incredibly low. Smile Orange Films often measure success as 'we didn't die'. Therefore all their projects can be seen as massive successes. So far.

CHAPTER ELEVEN
THE MOVIE SET

WHAT ARE MOVIE SETS?

A movie set is the enclosure in which a film scene is shot. There is an ancient Chinese myth about the origins of movie sets. The myth states that, centuries ago, during the Han Dynasty, people wanted to believe that kung fu was relevant to their lives so they desperately pretended to smash planks with their bare fists and take blows of incredible power to their chests. To hide the obvious sham of these demonstrations they built fancy little huts around these fighters to obscure them from view.

Sooty's head is blown off.

There are no actual pictures of that small water boy Lun Chi, so instead I went onto the internet and came up with this. Here is Lun Chi grown up. The world should be more grateful to this man.

SMILE ORANGE FILMOGRAPHY

THE HUNT FOR THE YORKSHIRE GRIMACE (1995)
Horror comedy / Directed: Drugsy, Tripsy and Tragedy / Smile Orange
Films / Fat Bald Cunt Productions / 73 mins / SVHSC / Colour

Northern comedians Dougie Rivers and Gary Rhodes suffer from numerous terminal diseases. Luckily they have just found their illegitimate son from whom they can extract the organs they need to live. Unfortunately the son has just been kidnapped. So Rivers and Rhodes set out to stop the kidnappers killing their son, so that they can kill him themselves. There follows a tsunami of cheap obscenities, for example, at one point, Rhodes hurls insults at a 'Sooty wanker!' from a moving car. The children's puppet Sooty then emerges and immediately gets his head blown off by a shotgun wielding Orville the Duck. Are you still with us Johnny Pigram? The film's conclusion obeys Smile Orange's first rule of filmmaking: Always end with a massive fight. After the fight it is revealed that Rivers and Rhodes have been fighting themselves all along. So they end up killing and then burying themselves on the moor.

After the film's credits there are several minutes of black screen before the film actually officially ends with a burst of coughing and a quick final shot of Rivers and Rhodes. This was designed to wake people up who had fallen asleep watching the film. Basically the plot of *The Hunt for the Yorkshire Grimace* is *Ransom* (1996) starring Mel Gibson, although Ransom hadn't been made at this point. Another case of Hollywood stealing ideas again? I suspect so.

Cast and crew and writers and editors and caterers of Hunt for the Yorkshire Grimace outside their 'live-in' set (clockwise from left: Priestley, Birdsell, Tennyson, Butler and Bousfield).

Over the centuries the owners of these huts became massively influential in the community and would invite people to peep through the huts' keyholes and watch as the fighters did their thing. The crowds became bigger and bigger but the keyholes were so small. So one day a small water boy, Lun Chi, became frustrated at these circumstances and in anger kicked one of the hut walls, destroying them completely. Now everyone in the village had a clear view of the fighting action and Lun Chi was heralded as the inventor of sets. No word of a lie.

WHAT SHOULD I LOOK FOR IN A GOOD MOVIE SET?

Hollywood movie sets contain huge lighting gantries, large backdrops and massive loading doors. But an even better movie set is a cheap terraced house in Leeds where the cast and crew can all live together in harmony, like a big family. This is what Smile Orange Films did when making their third feature film The Hunt for the Yorkshire Grimace.

WHERE SHOULD MY MOVIE SET BE SITUATED?

As a space to work in, film locations should be safe, secure and pleasant. Having said that, Smile Orange chose a

space with objects that give us insight into the psyche of a film's characters. With this in mind Smile Orange Films decided to dress their set as a place that *The Hunt for the Yorkshire Grimace*'s main characters, Dougie Rivers and Gary Rhodes, would feel at home in.

Hunt For The Yorkshire Grimace title sequence

Priestley and Boldy relax underneath various animal heads and an experimental Hitler/Orville hybrid puppet which was cut from the final film for not being weird enough.

> Butler and I lived constantly surrounded by props and obsessing over the script. We would be fixated on it. We had so many ideas and we had a hard time saying no to any of it. Sometimes we'd even go off on huge tangents and end up writing whole 'splinter-scripts' (see Glossary) for completely different films.

BOB PRIESTLEY
(SMILE ORANGE FILMS)

large red brick house located on Cardigan Road in Leeds, a road christened by the Daily Mail as 'the most burgled street in Britain'. In keeping with this tradition the Smile Orange movie set was, of course, burgled. Later on there was another attempted burglary which Bob Priestley fought off single-handedly by constructing a huge barricade against the door and using a strong Yorkshire accent.

HOW DO I DRESS MY MOVIE SET?

Dressing a set is the act of decorating a

Smile Orange Films got so distracted that they actually filmed one of these 'splinter-scripts' and sent it to the homemade film compilation show of Jeremy Beadle's *Hotshots*. A child

Rivers and Rhodes dressed as minstrels.

One of the advantages of living on your set is that, just like Butler here, you'll get to relax in splendour like a true gentleman.

We managed to make the lounge look really horrible. We stapled up garish wallpaper and put up framed pictures of monkeys in vivisection labs. It looked really, really awful. Then we had to live in it.

JULIAN BUTLER

(SMILE ORANGE FILMS)

SMILE ORANGE FILMOGRAPHY

DR LEECH'S FAMOUS TAPEWORMS (1994)
Short / 30 secs / VHSC / Colour
Spoof advert promoting the use of tapeworms as slimming aids. Rejected by ITV show Jeremy Beadle's *Hotshots*.

called Edgar Wright was working as a researcher on the show but refused to show the Smile Orange film due to its adult content. It's this kind of narrow minded thinking that made Wright the multimillion pound Hollywood director he is today. Smile Orange Films on the other hand, once again, had been snubbed by the evil Beadle.

I don't know what that Beadle's problem with us was. His logic seems totally fucked to me.

BOB PRIESTLEY

(SMILE ORANGE FILMS)

Having secured such a large set/home the last thing Smile Orange wanted were other housemates stumbling across them at 3am in the morning when they were filming themselves dressed as minstrels. So, despite the landlord (Mr Qureshi) selfishly trying to rent out the vacant rooms, Butler and Priestley had to make sure that the rest of the house remained empty.

Occasionally though some people were allowed to stay. Smile Orange actress Sue Wright asked if a friend, Tracy, could stay

One of the finest tongue gags ever filmed.

> Whenever any prospective resident came to view the house we'd show them the lounge set-dressed as Rivers and Rhodes' front room and they never came back. After a while Mr Qureshi gave up and we had the place to ourselves

BOB PRIESTLEY
(SMILE ORANGE FILMS)

in the house as her boyfriend had thrown her out. Smile Orange needed the rent money and so she moved in. One night she sat down with her tea and her new found housemates as they were viewing the rushes from an exciting film they were making. Unfortunately, during a scene of

> At the time we felt honoured that Sue would trust us to look after Tracy. Thinking about it now though, what sort of friend would recommend moving in with us whilst we are filming *The Hunt for the Yorkshire Grimace*? We welcomed Tracy with "Hi, yeah, make yourself at home. Just ignore us if you hear us going 'AAAAAGGGGGHHHHHHHEEEEEUUUUEEEUUUURRRHHH!!!!!!!' Oh and please don't touch that bag of offal, it has explosives in it." Tracy was in an emotional state and, in hindsight, the sincerity of their friendship has to be questioned

BOB PRIESTLEY
(SMILE ORANGE FILMS)

Butler getting his tongue cut off with scissors, Tracy vomited. It was pointed out to Tracy that the tongue was only a lightly broiled chicken breast in red food colouring but, as she was eating chicken at the time, her retching just increased. A few days later the producers came home and Tracy had moved out without saying goodbye. Or paying her rent. Or possibly even cleaning up her vomit.

WHAT ARE THE ADVANTAGES TO LIVING ON A MOVIE SET?

There are many advantages to living on a movie set. One of the main ones is that you can keep your budget down by drinking tea from your prop cups and wearing the film's costumes as your everyday clothes.

WHAT ARE THE DISADVANTAGES OF LIVING ON A MOVIE SET?

You end up drinking your tea from a tit-shaped mug and dressing as a minstrel.

The Edit V episode about Clive Baldwin is my favourite bit of Television ever made. What made it stranger was that Baldwin, who was from Hull, continued speaking in this fake American Al Jolson accent even when he wasn't blacked up.

JULIAN BUTLER

(SMILE ORANGE FILMS)

Edit V was a weekly show of Yorkshire based stories. I remember Butler went out one night and gave me the job of recording a funny looking episode about a school for bouncers. I was waiting until it came on to press record, but before it was a piece on Al Jolson impersonator Clive Baldwin. Baldwin is the last remaining blackface minstrel in the world. I was amazed that this still happened, so I recorded that part of the show as well.

BOB PRIESTLEY

(SMILE ORANGE FILMS)

ARE THERE ANY MORE ADVANTAGES TO LIVING ON MY MOVIE SET?

Another advantage to living on set is that filmmakers can constantly refer to video research material and develop their script to reflect these influences. Two videos that had an influence on *The Hunt for the Yorkshire Grimace* were the death film compilation *Traces of Death* and the Yorkshire Television local news show *Edit V*.

ARE THERE EVEN MORE FUCKING ADVANTAGES TO LIVING ON A MOVIE SET?

Yes, relentless as it seems there are even

PRO TIP

To survive living in your own set I would recommend as much as possible getting out to the pub and getting smashed.

GUS BOUSFIELD
(SMILE ORANGE FILMS)

The wanking off was real but no one knows who performed it. Really we don't, apart from Butler who knows everything and did it and liked doing it and wanted everyone to see him doing it.

BOB PRIESTLEY
(SMILE ORANGE FILMS)

more advantages to living on a movie set. Smile Orange Films found that they could also put a full music studio in Bousfield's bedroom and make songs for their film until the cows came home. The cows never came home. They stayed out. In fact they completely disappeared. So an endless stream of unlistenable songs were created.

WHAT IS A CLOSED SET?

A set is closed when the amount of cast and crew given access to it are restricted during nude or erotic scenes. When Smile Orange Films came to film Dougie Rivers masturbating over an image of Margaret Thatcher the set was the most closed in cinematic history: It consisted of just one crew member, who was also the actor. He also may have blindfolded himself so he couldn't see what he was doing. If he didn't blindfold himself he should have done. The scene climaxes with a real ejaculation shot.

WHAT IS THE FUTURE OF MOVIE SETS?

As cameras become more portable, movie sets are being used less and less. In the future there will be only one set left. This set

will be a parlour room from the sixteenth century and all films will have to be filmed in it. Period dramas where ladies wear their nice big dresses will have a field day. Sci-fi films will be fucked. But who cares anyway cos the aliens will land for real next Monday says Malcolm from Cottingley.

Meanwhile, Butler, Boldy, Bousfield and Priestley had been filming in their set for so long they'd forgotten what daylight looked like. They knew that at some point they were going to have to shoot some scenes outside and the thought filled them with terror. Soon it would be time to pull aside Priestley's burglar-proof barricade, unlock the door, and walk through it. And then close it. And then lock it. And then walk down the street. And then maybe see a tramp.

No, I didn't do it.

JULIAN BUTLER
(SMILE ORANGE FILMS)

CHAPTER TWELVE
LOCATIONS

A lion in Africa — the original storyteller?

WHAT ARE THE ORIGINS OF LOCATIONS?

For as long as man has existed he has told stories and those stories were set somewhere, usually where they were. Naturally, the first locations were situated where the first modern storytelling humans evolved. Africa. The cradle of civilisation. Or is it China? Not sure.

Kirkstall Abbey, Leeds.

WHAT ARE LOCATIONS?

A 'set' and a 'location' are two different things. I think? Locations exist before you arrive, whereas sets are built. To illustrate this let's use an example that everyone knows, the kung fu comedy film *Two Crippled Heroes*.

• **LOCATION:** *Two Crippled Heroes'* first battle scene, where the armless man and the legless man fight each other, occurs in what looks like a park. This is a great example of the use of a location i.e. a place that existed before the filmmakers got there.

• **SET:** On the other hand, in *Two Crippled Heroes*, the armless man's bedroom is a great example of a set i.e. the filmmakers built it. Or is it the legless man's bedroom? One of them anyway. What would I know?

WHAT IS A LOCATION MANAGER?

The location manager's job is to source locations, arrange location permits and make sure that when the crew is on location the shoot runs smoothly. Any filmmaker that does not think seriously about employing a good location manager needs their fucking head

Armley Jail, Leeds.

examined. Smile Orange Films never employed a location manager. Instead, whilst shooting *The Hunt for the Yorkshire Grimace*, the producers would drive around in an old Austin Rover Maestro panel van looking for places to film.

The crew trundled through Yorkshire, with no idea where they were going, with the actors, already dressed in costumes, sliding about in the back. When they finally did stumble upon a good location (somewhere nice like Bolton Abbey or Armley Jail) the filmmakers had to move fast. The lack of windows on the van meant that the first time the actors saw the location was when the van doors were flung open and they leapt out. The actors jumped from the van and immediately started shouting their lines, desperately hoping that the camera was rolling,

Filming like this, with no permit and amongst the public, caused problems. No matter where we went we always got shit from people. Children were the worst when filming. We once had to literally run from a group of braying delinquents

JULIAN BUTLER

(SMILE ORANGE FILMS)

Hunt for the Yorkshire Grimace's production office.

The producers also needed to film a scene where Rivers and Rhodes come out of a pub and throw up and they decided to use the exterior of the Woolpack pub

The first of many times that Smile Orange quite rightly (and quite righteously) fuckabout on the set of *Emmerdale*.

from UK soap opera *Emmerdale*. The Woolpack is right next to a large sewage works and it often reeked of human shit.

Back then the conspicuous use of a camera, even Butler's dad's camcorder, was seen as an event. We were often asked 'is this BBC?' or 'what are you going to do with what you've filmed?'. I often thought of asking them 'what are you going to do with this information once we've given it to you?

BOB PRIESTLEY

(SMILE ORANGE FILMS)

And, thanks to Smile Orange, it soon smelt of vomit too.

WHAT IS THE FUTURE FOR LOCATIONS?

Malcolm in Cottingley said this to me about locations: 'In the future all film locations will be created virtually by the Monochromatic Background Remover (MBR): Actors will be filmed against a monochromatic background and the MBR will then insert a different background behind the them. Unfortunately it won't make much difference though because, in the future, the majority of the world will be covered by massive alien motherships anyway. No, they didn't come round last Monday, the aliens postponed it. They're coming next Thursday now.'

For Smile Orange Films the gruelling *The Hunt for the Yorkshire Grimace* shoot continued. The team had been outside and found it hugely challenging. So they returned, through the barricades, into the safety of their living room set. Unfortunately their entry to the living

> For one scene we had this concept that we'd say each word of a line in a different location. We'd say one word walking down some railway tracks, then rush over to a cemetery and say one word there, then two hours' drive to Bolton Abbey to say another word there. Soon that wasn't even fast moving enough, so we decided to say each syllable of a line in a different location. Often a day's shoot consisted of driving somewhere to just say one syllable. Then we'd jump back in the van and be off. Back home. Check the footage. Missed the shot. FUCK! Do it again. Tomorrow. Skin. Up.

JULIAN BUTLER
(SMILE ORANGE FILMS)

Stills from the sequence where each syllable of dialogue was shot in a different location.

FILM FACT

Filmmakers often have problems finding the correct location for their shoot. Solving this problem is simple: Go outside, find a place that looks like the one you imagined in your script, you have now found your location.

room was blocked. By a big thing. A snorting, smoke-breathing thing. A thing that was begging for a huge naked body to be thrust underneath it. And what was the big thing? Find out in the next chapter.

But basically it was a papier mâché rhinoceros head.

CHAPTER THIRTEEN
ART DIRECTION

A collection of designer sex toys.

WHAT IS ART DIRECTION?

Art Direction is the control of props (also known as stuff, toys or bits). Props are objects used on screen by actors during a production. They can be divided into two categories:

CATEGORY A: Full-on props.
CATEGORY B: Nothing.

WHAT ARE THE ORIGINS OF ART DIRECTION?

Art Direction has its origins in design. Modern, cool design was invented in France in the 1950s by Philippe Starck. The Philippe Starck lemon squeezer dildo is a design classic. It is so well designed that the vibrate button cannot be found. Sometimes objects that are designed will be made out of coloured concrete for no reason. Things will pull out and

PRO RANT

These designers seem to have mislaid their sense of humour: Where's my kettle that looks like Hulk Hogan? I don't think I'm a Philistine but WHY can't I have an arse cleaning Jacuzzi bidet in the shape of Chris Eubanks' head?!!

JULIAN BUTLER
(SMILE ORANGE FILMS)

slide where they shouldn't. These things should delight you, if they don't then you're dead. That's design.

WHAT IS A PALETTE?

Art departments often use palettes when dressing a set. What are palettes? It's another way of saying colours. Here's how to use palettes: Imagine you are filming Ant and Dec and Ant is wearing bright orange. Then Dec will <u>NOT</u> be wearing shit brown. They will be in the SAME colours! Both in orange! Or shit brown. This matching of colours is called palletising.

WHAT IS THE ART DEPARTMENT?

A film is so much better if your actors are holding the object that they are saying they are holding. It is the art department's job to do this by finding things in shops, drains or cattle markets.

WHAT IS AN ART DIRECTOR?

An art director is a macroscopic multicellular neurotypical being in charge of an imaginary jumble sale on wheels. The best way to challenge your art director is to ask him, or her, to make a giant rhino head. Smile Orange Films' rhino head was made from papier mâché (French for mashed potato). It was enormous, without artistic merit and highly flammable when worn. But most importantly the team were incredibly

proud of it for no reason whatsoever other than it was totally finished.

Julian Butler fastidiously sticking little pieces of grit to Rhinoman's head. Detail like this is far too small to be seen by the human eye or a VHS camera. Therefore working at this level makes pointlessness look rational by comparison.

The rhino head found its way into *The Hunt for the Yorkshire Grimace*'s house/set and was dumped, festering in the hallway where it was later used as part of Priestley's barricade, blocking the front door against burglars. However, this utterly useless object became extremely useful when the filmmakers needed an idea to finish their film. So It was decided that a character called Rhinoman would conclude the massive fight scene at the end of *The Hunt for the Yorkshire Grimace* by bursting through Rivers and Rhodes' front door and, with powerful hairy legs and cock flapping, impaling the comedy duo. Two thrusts of the horn and the cinematic alchemists at Smile Orange Films had turned mashed potato into gold.

Ant 'n' Dec.

I don't know what to say about that really.

> "
>
> I liked the way the rhino horn came through Rhodes' chest, for something totally unconvincing it was quite convincing. We burned the Rhinoman head at one of Bob Priestley's regular 'I'm leaving for London. Again. This time for good. I hate you all' parties.

JULIAN BUTLER
(SMILE ORANGE FILMS)

WHAT OTHER SKILLS DOES AN ART DIRECTOR REQUIRE?

In the 1970s it was still common to see bits of porn magazines billowing across open stretches of the countryside like perverts' confetti. *The Hunt for the Yorkshire Grimace*'s script suggested that Rivers and Rhodes were the people who put it there. To get pornographic literature of the correct calibre the film's art department (managed by senior member Robert Priestley) hunted down a magazine called Sexual Oddities, in a proper adult shop

near Leicester Square and everything. After filming, the prop magazine was stashed in a hedge in a self-fulfilling pornographic prophecy.

Some mock-ups of fictional magazines were also made by the Smile Orange art department. One of these magazines was called *Lil' Baby Rape* and the mock-up featured a picture of children's TV presenter Jimmy Savile. This was twenty years before the true horror of Savile's crimes came to light. Another clear example of the Smile Orange art department's prophetic skills.

A further mock-up magazine in the film was called *Animal Fanny*. *Animal Fanny* was an imaginary magazine about bestiality featuring David Attenborough on the cover. In this instance, let's hope the prophetic abilities of Smile Orange's art department don't come true.

AS AN ART DIRECTOR WHAT PROPS WILL I BE ASKED TO OBTAIN?

One prop an art director will be asked to obtain on all Hollywood movie sets is offal. But beware: Offal procurement has its own economic rules, as Butler and Priestley found when they went into Mr Meats in Leeds Market and purchased a prop lung. There was a slight menace about the butcher, and not just because Butler and Priestley were off their heads. As the butcher pressured Butler and Priestley into

Lungs recently torn from a cow, massive and real.

FILM FACT

The Art Directors on When Harry Met Sally took seventeen years to choose cufflinks for Billy Crystal that were 'just right'. They then realised that cufflinks are really the wardrobe department's problem and dumped them down a drain.

taking a free bin liner of offal they didn't want, he seemed intent on showing the pair the opposite of capitalism — a world where you are given more goods than you have paid for. As Butler and Priestley left the shop the butcher again demonstrated his economic theory by clearing out the contents of his shit-rack and forcing them to take home a further seven kilo bag of unidentified animal scraps.

WHAT SHOULD I DO WITH MY PROPS AFTER FILMING?

In order to preserve goodwill, it is appropriate professional practice for an art department to keep props loaned to them well maintained and return them in the same condition they were acquired. *The Hunt for the Yorkshire Grimace*'s art department were kindly lent some electric wheelchairs when they lied to the manager of a mobility shop saying that they were making a film about disability. After the shoot, the wheelchairs were dumped, broken, with seats damp with canal water, outside the shop.

> The amount of money Smile Orange have paid charity shops over the years for props means that we should be seen in a similar light to any of the great philanthropists; the Good Samaritan, the Medieval flagellants and Lady Luck.

JULIAN BUTLER
(PHILANTHROPIST)

HOW ARE PROPS DELIVERED TO THE SET?

Currently props are driven to the set in an

The prop wheelchairs used in *Hunt for the Yorskhire Grimace*. L-R wheelchair one, wheelchair two.

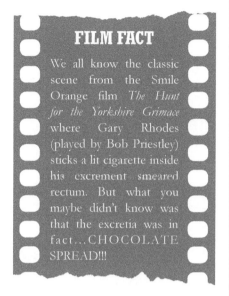

FILM FACT

We all know the classic scene from the Smile Orange film *The Hunt for the Yorkshire Grimace* where Gary Rhodes (played by Bob Priestley) sticks a lit cigarette inside his excrement smeared rectum. But what you maybe didn't know was that the excretia was in fact...CHOCOLATE SPREAD!!!

PRO TIP

Chocolate spread is far harder to remove from human ass skin than actual shit

BOB PRIESTLEY

(SMILE ORANGE FILMS)

art department van. But in the future, for ethical reasons, all props will be delivered by push bike. Bike riders in Yorkshire can be divided into two categories:

CATEGORY A: You get the full-on Lycra-clad Tour de France wannabe, sometimes a fatty too, someone who probably believes 'I'm eighteen stone but I'm aerodynamic.'
CATEGORY B: Nobody.

Actually that's not true, you also often see a slightly broken individual on a

Some cyclists.

bike with no lights. It's slightly less than suicide. Suicide is actually active. But this lot don't care whether they live or die. They think 'I'll ride to work on the bypass without lights. If I don't make it, I don't care. If I do make it then fuck it, another fucking day at work.' It's a vicious cycle. Great Pun. Those are the two categories of bike riders.

WHAT WILL PROPS BE LIKE IN THE FUTURE?

Future props will be spherical, smaller and white. Like the iPod. They will have Wi-Fi and be able to be used at a distance. Other props will be so ecologically sound that they will be deteriorating into inert sustainable compounds even before they are filmed, and therefore, in the soap opera *Emmerdale*, the Dingle family clock will be entirely made of methane. So says Malcolm in Cottingley.

CHAPTER FOURTEEN
MAKE-UP

WHAT IS MAKE-UP?

Makeup is composed of atoms arranged in crystalline structures and colourful shapes on the surface of something that is (or resembles) a living face.

WHAT IS PROSTHETIC MAKE-UP?

Prosthetic makeup is just one planet within

Applying make up (L-R) Gus Bousfield and Ricky leach (both looking really pissed off. In fact every member of the cast hated every single moment of the making of the film). Good picture though.

Ricky Leach fondly pushes his throbbing thumb into Bousfield's pouting, yet ripped, lips, in order to check the firmness of the latex. Another good photograph.

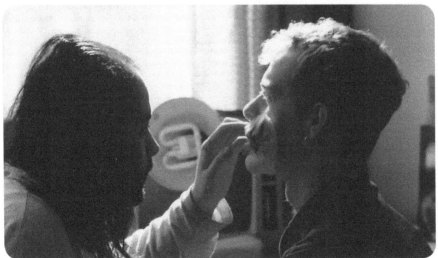

the makeup universe and consists of the creation and application of supplemental body parts including fake blood, burns, warts and big noses. Prosthetic makeup involves the use of that light rubbery stuff called latex. Latex mostly resembles human genital skin. This is because it is light, malleable, stinks of piss and can be found on the faces of actors.

Gus Bousfield with the final 'Yorkshire grimace'. Good picture that.

A model tortoise made especially for *The Hunt for the Yorkshire Grimace*. Not as good a picture that one.

PRO TIP

The monsters and the gibbons and the rubber hands that you and I love are not real! They're all glued together and then brought to set and put on the actors and no one knows they're not real. Many directors make the mistake of thinking the monsters and hands and gibbons are real and run off looking for them and disappear from the set for days and when they come back they are told that there aren't any real monsters and to stop being so silly.

NICKY HINCHCLIFFE

(TOP HOLLYWOOD DIRECTOR)

HOW DO I CREATE PROSTHETIC MAKE-UP?

To create prosthetic makeup correctly you should employ someone to do it for you.

WHAT IS A PROSTHETIC MAKE-UP TEAM?

Conjoined twins in *The Hunt for the Yorkshire Grimace* played by real women (a first for Smile Orange Films).

The prosthetic makeup team is the team you employ to apply the prosthetics for you. The script for *The Hunt for the Yorkshire Grimace* called for a gratuitous use of makeup including Siamese twins, squashed tortoises and scissored fingers. To deliver their cinematic vision the Smile Orange team assembled a makeup crew

far superior to any other ever seen in the Burley area of Leeds.

The actual 'Yorkshire Grimace' (see Glossary) was a key piece of makeup created by Richard Leach, the Tom Savini of Manningham. It is an amazing piece of sculpted art and was completely ruined by bad lighting from Smile Orange Films. Colin Wear created the film's dead tortoise and the finger slice effects. Wear is a Stan Winston-esque figure who has moved into digital film effects. His name can be found in the credits of Hollywood blockbusters along with the names of twenty thousand other digital slaves.

HOW DO I APPLY PROSTHETIC MAKE-UP?

The application of prosthetic makeup is a complicated part of the movie production. For one scene in *The Hunt for the Yorkshire Grimace* it was decided that Bob Priestley would have old man makeup applied. The process started with Priestley having his face entirely encased in alginate. It was like being immersed in a sensory deprivation tank and Priestley began an inner journey to the centre of his

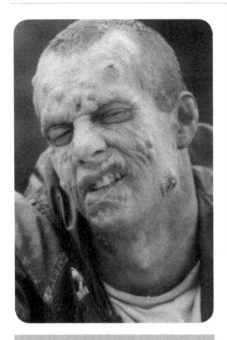

PRO TIP

For scenes involving melting skin, mutated faces and thalidomide limbs a cheap alternative to latex can be made by mixing flour and water into a stiff dough. Add food colouring for various skin tones. The dough can also be used as budget catering on set.

own mind. This completely freaked him out. Finally, when the cast was removed Priestley's inner demons disappeared. He then concentrated on being freaked out by his normal outer ones.

Next the makeup team made a plaster cast of Priestley's face and onto that sculpted a big nose, droopy jowls, baggy eyebags and a baldy baldhead — all the elements needed to turn a youthful

beauty into a ravaged mendicant. The team made another cast (yes, I know, this is getting boring now) The final makeup pieces were cast from this and they were ready to go.

Bousfield in properly good leper makeup.

On the day of the shoot the makeup was applied well in advance of turnover (see Glossary). After the bits were stuck to his face, Priestley had to make his way to the set. This involved him catching the bus at peak morning rush hour in his old man makeup. No one noticed.

> **"**
>
> I was on a busy commuter bus. I was wearing the standard twenty-five year old's clothes (raggy jeans, skate boots and *Shogun Assassin* tee shirt) but with one unusual addition; an old man's face. The prosthetics felt very strange and made me self-conscious, I kept thinking someone would have a go at me but no one gave me a second look. Testament to the makeup team's skills. Or the madness of Bradfordians.

BOB PRIESTLEY
(SMILE ORANGE FILMS)

Priestley as old man.

Butler with a tasche fully superglued to his face like a true professional actor and not just a man with a fake tasche stuck on his head.

PRO TIP

When using dramatic lighting effects on older actresses what you don't want is trouble. Therefore choose your older actresses by how easily convinced they are to have a full brow, chin and lip wax.

WHAT IS THEATRICAL HAIR?

Theatrical hair is fake hair that replicates real hair. Theatrical hair includes pubes, beards, sideburns, sideboards, mutton chops, breadboards, grass cheeks, chin sprouts and neck feathers. To play Dougie Rivers, actor Julian Butler wore a handlebar moustache applied with spirit gum. But, due to high blood pressure brought on by panic and aggression, Butler sweats profusely and the spirit gum didn't adhere. So in desperation Butler resorted to Super Glue to affix his tasche

A kidnapper covered in makeup played by Al Birdsell, one of Smile Orange's finest 'big man' actors.

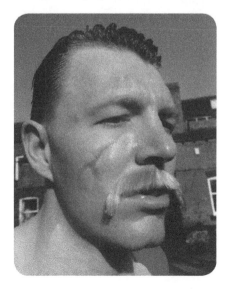

to his upper lip. Removing the tasche was painful and only caused Butler to be angry which caused more sweating which led to more Super Glue being applied. Subsequently Butler still has scars around his mouth to this day.

WHAT ROLE DO MASKS PLAY IN THE MAKE-UP DEPARTMENT?

Masks are often a much cheaper alternative

PRO TIP

Masks go all sticky if you keep them for too long, crumbly too, dry and wet like rubber porridge with raisins and gravel. Reverting back to the chaotic state from whence they came, before given form by human hand. For a short time obeying a shape given to them, but never tamed, always dreaming of reverting back to their wild state.

ALAIN DE BOTTON

(CONE PLACER & PHILOSOPHER)

A Prince Andrew mask worn by Tom Ashcroft.

A single joke shop mask can be very effective, especially if worn backwards, inside out or balanced on top of the head like a skin hat. My favourite mask was the one we had of American wrestler Hulk Hogan. It was massive, double the size of a normal mask. It was bought from Blackpool (the best mask town by far) and It looked really funny inside out too. Totally brilliant.

BOB PRIESTLEY
(SMILE ORANGE FILMS)

Some people say that this might be this but others say it might not be and it might someut else.

to prosthetic makeup and therefore play an important role throughout Smile Orange Films' work. Masks used by the team included: Zombie Vietnam veteran, a Prince Andrew mask, a chicken mask and a baby-man mask that resembled actor Keith Tennyson.

WHAT IS THE FUTURE OF MAKE-UP?

Dunno, but I'm sure Facebook will play a big part in it. So says Malcolm in Cottingley.

Augustin Bousfield with his head covered in papier mâché (French for mashed potato) in the early stages of 'masketry', before moving onto 'maskatronics and finally, of course, reaching the highest level of 'masking': A complete state of 'musk'.

There you go, that's that mask that was worn inside out, looks like they've added a couple of horns to its nose as well. They were like that Smile Orange. Next level.

CHAPTER FIFTEEN
SOUND RECORDING

HOW DO I ACHIEVE HIGH QUALITY SOUND RECORDING?

It can't be done.

CHAPTER SIXTEEN
OH, GO ON THEN. I SUPPOSE I'D BETTER EXPLAIN SOMETHING ABOUT RECORDING SOUND THEN

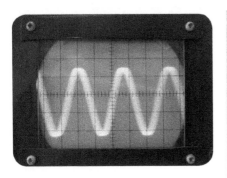

WHAT IS SOUND?

Sound is made by waves grooving through air and sound particles improvising with one another to create sonic fusion. The brain reads this signal and interprets it as sound.

WHY DO I NEED TO RECORD SOUND FOR MY FILM?

In a movie you need to record the sound of your actors because it helps your audience know what is going on and reduces the need to have a retiree sat to the side of your film playing the piano.

WHAT IS SOUND QUALITY?

In our last extensive chapter we dealt with every single aspect of high quality sound recording and we came to the conclusion that trying to achieve it is like pissing to the moon. You can't do it. You may have the best kit to come out of Germany ever but, time after time, your beautiful

PRO TIP

When a person is talking, if you can hear the words what is coming from the mouth then your film will be better. Sticking them onto the picture enhances the viewer's understanding of what the flipping heck's going on and meks it blumming knockout!!!

NICKY HINCHCLIFFE

(TOP HOLLYWOOD DIRECTOR)

imagery will be spoiled by badly recorded audio tracks engorged with farting, belching, coughing, humming, drilling, droning, crying, laughing, screaming, hammering and bat-squeaking (true story). On the other hand if you want to record piss-poor sound quality then that's do-able and the person who can just about do this, if they can keep their mind from wandering, is the sound operator.

These are sound waves that appear to be on something like an oscilloscope. Not sure if Smile Orange used oscilloscopes but it's sort of relevant to this chapter so bish, bash, bosh, it's in the book and that's another illustration and caption done. Ten more and I'm down the pub. Pie night.

Actually I can go down the pub and do the rest of these from here! Result. I just find the photos on my phone and use their own caption instead of having to write one myself. This is 'Densmore recording Mountain Chief2' apparently. Smile Orange never recorded a Mountain Chief. Right, steak and ale.

WHAT IS A SOUND OPERATOR?

The sound operator records all the noises the director and his mates want recording. These might include actors going to the bog, actresses coughing up grob or news readers having hissy fits.

WHAT MICROPHONE SHOULD I USE?

There is a huge variety of microphones used on movies sets. None of them work properly. To capture the best piss-poor sound quality for *The Hunt*

for the Yorkshire Grimace, Smile Orange Films decided to use the very worst in sound equipment: The Tandy Pressure Zone Microphone (PZM). The PZM is a cheap microphone that, due to its omnidirectional recording abilities, is still used by the filth today, in police interrogation rooms.

HOW DO I GET THE OPTIMUM RESULTS FROM MY SOUND KIT?

You will never get optimum results from your sound kit, all you can hope for is a hissy drone that makes dogs shit themselves. After buying their PZM,

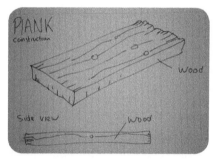

Oh, and a drawing of the plank that Smile Orange put the mic on, we need that. Done. Pudding. Should I go Sticky Toffee or Death by Chocolate? Maybe both?

Extra chips! They fucked up the order, they've given me extra chips and I never paid for it. This is the best night ever; on my own in the pub. Win win. PZM microphone drawn by me. Good drawing that.

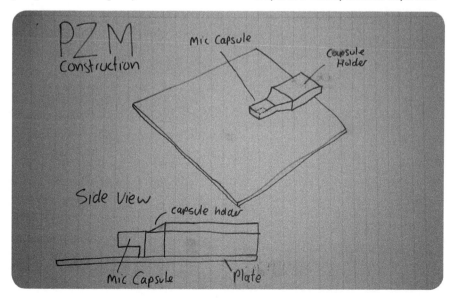

PRO TIP

Microphones are recording
devices that are very delicate
and mustn't be touched! Ever!!!
Without gloves on. Or licked.
Without mouth guard. Basically I
must keep away from them.

NICKY HINCHCLIFFE

(TOP HOLLYWOOD
DIRECTOR)

You think after
five pints I'm
drawing owt
now? This is a
downloaded
free picture of
someut to do
with the chapter
here. I might
just finish off
with a brandy
and go on
somewhere.

Smile Orange Films plugged it directly into Butler's dad's increasingly battered SVHSC camcorder. As there was no sound operator on *The Hunt for the Yorkshire Grimace*, cameraboy Andrew Boldy would drag the mic around on the floor and then throw it into shot just before pressing the record button. Later the mic got gaffered to a plank of wood so it could be thrown around even more. The Smile Orange filmmakers also constantly paid tribute to their beloved PZM microphone by carefully placing it in shot in as many scenes as possible.

WHAT SOUND RECORDING DEVICE SHOULD I USE?

The PZM microphone is undoubtedly a lovely piece of kit. Yes. But to get the best results out of your purchase then you should maybe consider also plugging it into a sound recording device of some description. Below is a

SOUND RECORDING DEVICE	PROS	CONS
SVHSC Sanyo Camcorder.	One less thing to worry about on set.	Big worries when you watch back the footage off-set.
Mono Cassette Recorder.	Will not crash.	Sounds squashed to shit.
Zoom Digital Hand-held Recorder (I think that's what it's called but check with your local moody Maplin's mentor).	Has a really big rcd button.	Every wanker has one.
Dad's massive 1960s reel-to-reel.	The best sound ever.	Angry dad.

I found this image on a flyer for a club here in the bogs of Porky's night scene. Can I say Porky's or do I need to change the club's name for the book? Fuck it, I've fucking done it haven't I?!! People need to understand what a great man I am. I don't get any respect. Shakespeare? He's alright, but no Roy Devon. I'm doing this, 3am, in Porky's, on the bog and I'm still a better writer than Shakespeare.

PRO TIP

My sound operator Paul is a quiet, rotund boy who is scared of heights. He is also partially deaf gauging by the results of his efforts. For God's sake! His dress sense is shocking too. It's OK wearing tight jeans but looking like a Tom of Finland illustration on set is going too far. I wash my hands of the lot. Ok that's sound done.

PETER WARD
(VETERAN FILM PRODUCER)

guide to help you make the right choice of recorder for your feature length video production, thrash band rehearsal, Primula Squeezy Cheese commercial or police interrogation interview.

WHAT IS THE FUTURE OF SOUND RECORDING?

Over time you will come to love your equipment. You will especially love your cheap Tandy PZM mic and its plank. But unfortunately your mic will eventually always find itself at the core of a massive hairball of leads. This hairball of leads will take about five years to reach its maximum circumference of about two feet. When it has reached this size there is no undoing it and it is best to throw the whole lot away and start again.

CHAPTER SEVENTEEN
VIDEOGRAPHY

WHAT IS VIDEOGRAPHY?

Videography is the art of capturing moving images onto a video based format. Videography is also known as Cinematography or Pressing Recordography.

WHAT IS A VIDEOGRAPHER?

The videographer is easily recognisable on set because they are the one holding the

Tripoding: No cameraman required.

camera. The director's relationship with the videographer is a symbiotic one: The director gives the videographer money and the videographer allows the director to remain aloof, unengaged and just an arty brain in leather trousers. Basically, the only reason videographers exist is because all directors are so fucking useless they are unable to operate the tools of their trade.

WHAT CAMERA SHOULD A VIDEOGRAPHER BUY?

Buy whatever camera you like, I don't give a shit. But just remember the nine stages of purchasing cameras:

- You need to buy a new camera.
- You go and buy one.
- Then you don't like it.
- Then a month later you forget why you didn't like it and you do like it again.
- Then it breaks.
- Then you can't live without it and you

Hugh Jackman cheerfully recognising some dust on a camera.

FILM FACT

Hollywood movie cameras always collect dust. At the end of a typical Hugh Jackman film 75% of the camera's weight is dust. After a Fields of the Nephilim video shoot 99.9% of the camera's weight is dust. Dust is dead skin. Which is horrible really.

PROCESS FLOW DIAGRAM: HOW TO FIND YOUR CAMERA'S RECORD BUTTON

Finding the record button is the main responsibility of a videographer. The process flow diagram below is a guide to the thought processes of a videographer as they try to find a camera's record button.

PLEASE NOTE: The main secret throughout this procedure is not to verbalise any of this, simply clutch your coffee cup like a monkey to a mango and smile and nod.

will do anything for it to be mended.
• Then you can't afford to have it mended.
• By the time you can afford to have it mended it's out of date.
• You need to buy a new camera.

WHAT VIDEO FORMAT SHOULD I SHOOT MY FILM ON?

When choosing the right video format you need one that will deliver the correct cinematic look required by your script. SVHSC is the ideal format choice for any up-and-coming filmmaker and was used to shoot Smile Orange Films' *The Hunt for the Yorkshire Grimace*. The picture quality was excellent and disgusting at the same time.

SVHSC is only one of a large selection of video formats, all of them easy to use and hideous to look at. The grid below is a handy guide to feeling your way through this complicated world.

WHAT PROBLEMS DOES A VIDEOGRAPHER HAVE TO OVERCOME?

Shooting *The Hunt for the Yorkshire* *Grimace*'s wheelchair chase scene was a seamless example of working together in a tightly knit, well ordered, cohesive unit and started with one of the main actors dropping out due to shitting issues. Diarrhoea affects all the best leading actors, George Clooney often kaks his kegs, Clint Eastwood wears a nappy and Julia Roberts once shat on

FORMAT	JARGON BUSTER	PRO NOTES
VHS	Video Home System	Unwatchable and truly essential for aspiring snuff movie makers.
SVHS	Super Video Home System	Unwatchable and costs you more for the privilege. Perfect for the high end snuff movie maker. SVHS also has the added advantage that it can't be played back on any system.
Hi8	High Eight	Beautifully replicates smearing Vaseline everywhere. Ideal for grainy hoax alien videos made in Roswell. Or pornographic rugby league films.
Low7	Low Seven	Grainy half-assed out of focus nonsense. Essential. Smile Orange Films developed this format for filming ghosts. They failed because of the first universal law of videography which states: The more important the thing is you are filming the more likely it is to be out of focus. Nothing come of it.
.8Betak	This is actually technically 8.8 abbreviated to .8. Therefore the format is .8 better than Hi8. Put a simpler way, the format is approximately 1.8 better than Low7.	When nothing came of Low7 Smile Orange Films upped their game and tried to develop this revolutionary format. But to be honest they didn't have a clue as to what even developing a format involved. Talking shit in pubs was as far as this got. Absolutely the worst format ever available. Perfect for mortuary corpse abuse videos.
Smak10	Unknown	Opiate based image capture format. Currently illegal. Made purely for the professional execution video market.

A picture of a camcorder (right) held by a man (left). Another man sits in the background (extreme right)

Natalie Portman. So, as a professional videographer, you will have to learn to overcome these problems.

Despite their actor 'crying off', the Smile Orange crew devised an ingenious way for them to deliver a world beating performance whilst remaining on the bog: The whole scene was filmed using somebody else's body, and the actor's close-ups were filmed on another day. Possibly whilst sat on the bog.

WHAT IS MAGNETOGRAPHY?

The famous wheelchair chase scene in *The Hunt for the Yorkshire Grimace* ends with Rivers and Rhodes trying to jump a canal in their wheelchairs. To achieve this effect Smile Orange Films pioneered their own animation technique called magnetography. This process was simple... yet brilliant... yet stupid:

- Print out a background image. Call it image 1.
- Print out the image you want to animate over your background — Call it image 2.
- Fasten something metallic to image 2 — a paperclip will do.
- Place a magnet under image 1.
- Use the magnet to move image 2 around on top of image 1.
- Film it.

The magnetographic sequence from *Hunt for the Yorkshire Grimace*. I think it is described in this chapter so I don't think I have to describe it here..

But for the shot of Rivers and Rhodes in their wheelchairs diving into the canal not even magnetography would suffice. So Butler and Priestley just jumped in. This were done and were good. The duo were very enjoyed (see Glossary).

WHAT IS A GAFFER?

A gaffer is a man, or woman, or mole who understands how to safely use electrical equipment on a film set. The Gaffer on *The Hunt for the Yorkshire Grimace* was called Nothing-Better-To-Do-Neil. Nothing-Better-To-Do-Neil was a long haired lad who was aimlessly killing time until his next trip to a climbing wall in Ilkley. He was also quite good at finding solutions to electrical problems. For example, at the end of filming the wheelchair chase

scene the camera's power cable kept overheating so Nothing-Better-To-Do-Neil's solution was to place the hot cable in a large freezer. Yes, the heat could have melted the ice in the freezer and the resulting water could have seeped out onto the floor and electrocuted everyone. But forget that, it were all filmed safely and they all did not all die. Once again, a successful shoot.

HOW DO I STRIKE A SET?

'Striking' is an industry term given to the clearing away of equipment at the end of a day's filming. It is called striking because at this point the chances of the director being punched are good. After shooting the wheelchair chase scene the Smile Orange crew celebrated with a Pot Noodle and the scene was struck. Or strook? Stroked? Whatever.

I don't remember any of this happening, I've just pieced it together afterwards from watching the film again recently.

JULIAN BUTLER
(SMILE ORANGE FILMS)

Having nothing better to do, Neil (right) had the time to paint pictures of Everest and the Universe on — and hang a homo-rainbow flag in — his Leyland Sherpa as well as trawl Camden for a prayer wheel and a jumper with ying yangs on it's sleeves. Whereas Bob Priestley (left) obviously had some serious business to attend to in his stolen wheelchair.

Them bombing the canal.

PRO TIP

Below is an extract from a poem I've written about Russ Robertson, my videographer.

Life's Too Short for Bland
Russ.
Robust.
Strong armed.
I'm carried
Baby-like
Onto set.
In beautifully veined forearms.
Plonks me down in front of TV.
I watch him at work.
Vermeer like projections
flickering through my retina
straight to my pig-like cerebral
cortex.
Transcendence.
Me.
He.
Man.
Got ctsuedh.
Functioning finger?
Yes.
My labial palps quiver.
Punch my button
and then to Nando's.
For massive chocolate biscuit
stack with ice cream and extra
chocolate sauce.

PETER WARD
(VETERAN PRODUCER)

WHAT IS TRIPODING?

Many people dream of having a successful career as a videographer. But, in this game, it's not enough to just master your camera, to proceed to the next level you will also have to master a tripod too. If you don't master a tripod then you may get killed. Then you'll have to press 'play' and start at the beginning all over again.

Tripoding is the utilisation of tripods for camera stabilisation. Whilst filming *The Hunt for the Yorkshire Grimace* the camera was often left recording on the tripod whilst all Smile Orange crew members stood in front of it and acted out a scene. This way the entire crew can do a cameo in the film as well as the director. Even Hitchcock wasn't that daring.

HOW DO I MEND MY CAMERA?
Leave it where it lies.

WHAT IS THE FUTURE OF VIDEOGRAPHY?

Videography is developing at an alarming rate. It's actually terrifying how fast it's changing. I can't keep up. It's left a crater in my brain. Why can't it just stay still for a second? So I went to see an expert, Malcolm in Cottingley, to get the low down on where all this is heading in the future. Malcolm had shat himself but after cleaning himself up he explained to me that the future lies in organic and brain based computers. He explained, I think, that there's hardware and software, but this new stuff is called wetware. It's basically living, in a grown stem cell sort of way. But how you programme it I have no idea. Just think, you could get your camera stoned, It'll take it to a whole new level. It might get depressed though, so watch it. Said Malcolm.

Oh, and the mothership WILL be here Tuesday.

CHAPTER EIGHTEEN
LIGHTING

WHAT IS LIGHTING?

Lighting is the illumination of the subject you wish to film. Common electrical lights include halogen, tungsten and LED (light emitting dildos). Smile Orange tried to ignore lights whenever they lit their scenes. Or should I say lighted the scene? Lit or lighted? One word means 'setting fire to something' and the other word means 'to illuminate'. But which is which? You would need to ask someone with a knowledge of words and writing but that's not me, I'm only the author of this book. Anyway, lighting your shoot is done by shining some lights in the direction of whatever stuff you want to shoot. Shot? Shooted? God knows.

WHAT ARE THE ORIGINS OF LIGHTING?

Light technology has progressed considerably and is now light years ahead of where it was. Good joke by me. Candles were used as the original stage lighting. Actually, no, the opposite, in Ancient Greece, the plays of Platypus were originally performed in daylight weren't they?

There's all that shit about lime too. Lime was used to light things in the past I believe. Lime is a white powder that is got from crushing rocks, I guess. Maybe they burned oil and lime together or something? Whatever, that's where the term 'the limelight' comes from.

In Roman times, big fires were used to light stage plays but this led to the melting of acting race the Thespians. During the Second World War searchlights were used as film spotlights and blinding actors became a big problem. Then in the seventies disco lights were used to light films but this led to questions such as 'why does Jane Austen have a glitter ball in her parlour?'

Ozric Tentacles: Better at lights than music.

In the late eighties acid house led to Fruit Salad light shows being used to light scenes and Ozric Tentacles, Megadog and Eat Static logos were projected over all films. Then in the 1990s mobile phone screens were used to light scenes and, of course, in Hollywood films today iPad screens light the way forward. Even better joke by me.

WHAT LIGHTS SHOULD I AVOID USING?

The one light you must avoid is the one used by Smile Orange Films during *The*

Artists impression of a nightmare dystopian Blaster World where beams of evil keep people from taking to the air and humanity Is forced to live underground without light.

Hunt for the Yorkshire Grimace, an evil home movie light called 'the Blaster'. The Blaster is a single, incredibly bright, blinding in fact, 1000W floodlight. Ordinarily this kind of super illumination would be used only as an effect to show some sort of bleached out religious experience. But ironically the Blaster was actually possessed by demonic sprites and constantly emitted vile smells, bellowed toxic smoke and gave the crew burns.

You won't find the Blaster in any shop. You cannot buy the Blaster. The Blaster buys you. One day you will look down and the Blaster will just be there in your hand, "ahhh, I need that" you'll think. But beware, this is the Blaster's parasitic hegemony already working on your feeble mind.

This is not thee Blaster. This is a Jessops faux-Blaster. It never blasted as well as the original Blaster. Fairly safe and professional.

Whilst shooting *The Hunt for the Yorkshire Grimace*, if the Blaster was turned on, the room was so brightly lit it was impossible to even open your eyes to find the plug to turn it off. It blinded and disorientated the whole crew, making everyone so hot that arguments started immediately. But the Blaster just fed off this human anger and misery, becoming brighter and brighter.

The Blaster worked for twenty years and never once needed its hideous 1000 Watt bulb replaced. The Blaster could not be attached to a light stand and was always resting on the floor giving all shots a horror film look. In fact everything the Blaster lit turned evil. Even if you lit an actor playing a good character with the Blaster, a twist in the plot would arise which would turn that character bad. Then, finally, the actor themselves would succumb to its parasitic legion and every shoot would end with slaughter on a mass scale.

And the evil just got stronger. Years later Smile Orange Films' Julian Butler used the Blaster near a window for a shoot, it melted the glass and nearly burned his house down. Even writing about the Blaster is dangerous. Beware, no one knows where the Blaster is now. It could be in YOUR video kit! Check your hands NOW!!!!

WHAT LIGHTS SHOULD I USE ON MY FILM?

Having said all that, you can use the Blaster if you want, I couldn't give a shit. And anyway, if you happen to be filming Smile Orange Films' thin and wriggly actor Bob Priestley, he will insist on the Blaster being used all the time, simply because it's heat will keep him warm.

FILM FACT

A typical Hollywood lighting set-up will use more than just one Blaster. There can sometimes be hundreds of lights used just to illuminate Sandra Bullock's crow's feet as she laughs at Tom Cruise as he takes a piss all over a gangster's back.

PRO TIP

Oh Fucking Lighting. I love those guys. You will be able to buy microdots, windowpanes, purple oms, laughing gnomes and Booby-Juice (see Glossary) from these guys. At <u>ANY</u> time. Whole sheets sometimes. They'll make you actually believe you're dead. Phenomenal chaps. You'll never know how long you were out for.

PETER WARD

(VETERAN PRODUCER)

WHAT DOES A LIGHTING TECHNICIAN DO?

Also known as the Lamp Operator, Electrician, Electric, Spark or Juicer, the lighting technician is responsible for setting up lights and listening to the instructions of the camera operator to enable them to capture the director's vision. The lighting department often work with highly specialised and very dangerous equipment and are often off their fucking heads.

WHAT IS THE FUTURE OF LIGHTING?

In the future the huge amount of energy needed for traditional film lights will lead to a more sustainable system being found: The use of animals as lights. The basic three light set-up will involve a firefly, a glow worm and an angler fish. In order to get these in place giant centipedes will

herd them about. The moths that are attracted to this will also be employed as barn doors. Stick insects will make great light stands and a dung beetle will roll shit everywhere. So says Malcolm in Cottingley, adding 'I shouldn't be telling you this but the mothership is coming tomorrow. This time it's certain.'

To sum up the lighting used on *The Hunt for the Yorkshire Grimace* we might say

PRO TIP

When I first saw the big men with the massive lights I were frightened out me wits, but I got chatting and they were really nice! A bit mumbly. But lovely. Little thrillers the lot of them. They gave me some purple pop called Booby-Juice!! Soon after drinking it I had to go home and I played the piano for eighteen hours straight, never had a lesson in me entire life!!!

NICKY HINCHCLIFFE

(TOP HOLLYWOOD DIRECTOR)

Fluorescent lights like this sometimes cause problems for semi-professional pro-sumers (and pro-end users) with 'strobing' and 'greening' caused by the 50/60Hz conundrum. Please bear that in mind.

they definitely had some and it was way too bright. And evil. Of course, the worse thing to wear in this hot environment would have been heavy, black woollen dinner suits. In the next chapter we will look at the wardrobe department and the heavy, black woollen dinner suits worn throughout the shoot.

MY MORNING

...I'm still up at 5am. I get distracted by some floating orbs which seem to hang in the air, goading me like a penetrating cursor. Two unblinking thought-eyes, piercing my mind, like the same effect you get from wireless atmospherics. Like a sinister warning from an outside universe, frankly frightening. Another realisation I have is that one is utterly alone, and then more thoughts of overpowering horror, then blackness, lastly decay.

I rouse myself and manhandle the lights into some form of assemblance. Simple tasks are confusing and take longer than they should. I crumple to the ground and feel sick. I fight the notion that my navel oozes a dark oil. I wipe my face with a handful of leaves torn from a nearby beach tree in an attempt to cool my brow but only manage to crush greenfly into my forehead. This loss of souls disturbs me beyond reason. I pull myself up and try to conjure the will to cease weeping. I cannot. Through my deep grief I manage to change a bulb and I feel I have nothing left to give. The sudden illumination of the whole sickening scene makes me believe I am on the brink, of what I cannot say, but I arrive on it amid a flurry of trumpets bathed in blinding electric light.

I blink away some of the blindness and find myself hugging several perfect strangers who implied the warmest and most unquenchable affection. I hold them close and feel them breathe through the thick, insulation of their North Face coats. I feel most secure. It was really rather a distinguished crowd. One of the men was a fat producer who looked at first sight like a piece of canned pork that has got mislaid too long in the summer. But the less he said the more he did; and what he did is one of the greatest treasures of mankind. He turned a... [continues ad nauseum]

RED BEARD
(VISIONARY LIGHTING TECHNICIAN)

CHAPTER NINETEEN
THE WARDROBE DEPARTMENT

FILM FACT

Finding costumes for your film is easy. YOU ARE ALREADY WEARING THEM!!!!

WHAT IS THE WARDROBE DEPARTMENT?

A wardrobe department can be found on most films sets and is responsible for buying clothes, bringing them to the set,

PRO TIP

Dressing up is fun and olden days' clothes feel nice against the skin. But beginners in the industry often forget that film costumes must never ever ever ever be worn whilst eating messy Nando's Chocolate Biscuit Stack!!!

NICKY HINCHCLIFFE
(TOP HOLLYWOOD DIRECTOR)

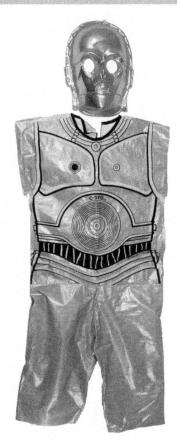

The only image I could find for free of a Hollywood costume was this really bad C3PO costume.

hanging them on hangers and helping actors to put them on.

WHAT ARE THE ORIGINS OF THE WARDROBE DEPARTMENT?

The first costumes were togas. The toga was invented by philosopher Platypus in Ancient Greece when he was late to

see one of his plays and he ran to the theatre having just got up, still wrapped in his bed sheet. Togas reappeared in the 1970s at toga parties. But why that happened no one knows? Is that the best we could do? Trying to get a glimpse of your neighbour's ass from behind a sheet? Fuck me, times were bad in the seventies. The entire population of the seventies were a bunch of fucking cunts.

HOW CAN I USE WARDROBE TO DEVELOP MY COMEDY CHARACTER?

In Hollywood when the Actor Jim Carey needs to dress up as a Lemony Snicket then the film studio will try to find him the world's most disgusting suit. They will hire a wardrobe department who gather many reference photos into mood boards and from these they will create an approximation of the ideal Lemony Snicket maniac. Although an easier way would be for Carey to simply look in his dad's wardrobe and bingo! There he will find the world's most disgusting suit and would have fucking done him well.

This has been proven because that is exactly what Smile Orange did when they wanted to find the world's most disgusting suits for their characters Rivers

PRO TIP

As a head of wardrobe on numerous British movies I am often asked how to create a realistic costume for the character of Henry the Eighth (Is that how you spell that?). It's easy. The skirt is made from a pair of your dad's work pants (unshat). Cut the pants off at the gusset to make a skirt. The codpiece is made from a milk carton with pink feathers attached. Get the feathers from a hen night pink cowboy hat found in the sludge on the floor of a nightclub in York. For the garter wrap a pair of your mother's knickers around the actor's leg. The ruff is made from toilet paper and finally, Henry's chain is simply a metal bath plug with gold chain effect from B&Q. You can find them halfway down aisle nine. Or is that aisle Q? Ask Darren or Pauline. Oh no Pauline's on lunch. Oh well, we're closing now anyway. Sunday hours. Come back on Wednesday and get 10p off if you bring a pensioner in with you.

MARION LIGHTHOWLER (HEAD OF WARDROBE / B&Q RETAILER)

BIG QUEENY AL., ANDRE

METCALF, WESLEY

Costumes which were later offered for sale during the credit sequence of *Hunt for the Yorkshire Grimace.*

and Rhodes. They were only sixteen-year-olds at the time so Bob Priestley simply went into his dad's loft and rummaged in some bin liners and minutes later came down dressed as a comedic 1970s child molester who had been thrust on stage at the London Palladium. Baffled and delighted Priestley immediately rang Butler to tell him to do the same. Butler had beaten Priestley to it and was already wearing a disgusting dinner suit, which he did to baffle teachers at school. From then on, these same black dinner suits were worn every time the duo played Rivers and Rhodes.

HOW DO I CHOOSE THE RIGHT COSTUME FOR A CHARACTER?

The wardrobe department is run by the 'head of wardrobe'. There are numerous methods that the head of wardrobe can use to dress a character. Smile Orange Films' technique is to chuck a bin bag in front of the actors, force them to pick out something to wear, slap any fat hanging out of the costume and laugh in the actor's face. Just look at the pictures

FILM FACT

Carry your costumes with you at all times. Then, if you see a good location you can put them on and film a quick scene. During the production of *The Hunt for the Yorkshire Grimace* Julian Butler and Bob Priestley would carry the Rivers and Rhodes black dinner suit costumes constantly whenever they were dragged unwillingly by girlfriends to do anything other than sit at home filming themselves.

Rivers and Rhodes in their dinner suits.

HICK AS SHIT BUILDERS

The Smile Orange wardrobe department.

above from *The Hunt for the Yorkshire Grimace* for proof of the startling results this technique obtains. These costumes are also an outstanding example of the creativity of stumbling fuckwits.

HOW DO I MAINTAIN COSTUMES?

Film costumes often get soiled during filming. A wardrobe department will therefore always keep several identical outfits for the actor to change into. Something that Smile Orange could have fucking done with knowing before jumping into the fucking canal wearing their only dinner suits. And so the sad-sack dickheads had to spend the rest of the shoot squelching about in two hundred and twenty-four years of stagnant filth from the Leeds and Liverpool Canal.

WHAT IS THE UNIVERSAL THESPIAN WARDROBE SYSTEM?

The wardrobe heads at Smile Orange Films recently discovered that every single costume can be created using different combinations of just five items of clothing. They've called it the Universal Thespian Wardrobe System (UTWS) and, for the first time in history, these five

items have been collected together in one glorious box and are available to be purchased by hopeless numpties like you.

The Wardrobe department? You should insist your shirts and trousers are ironed by this lot before you go on your impromptu set inspections/firing sessions. I always ensure they strip me to my pants, freshen up my creases and leave me feeling princey like Henry the Eightth (that spelling can't be right either).

PETER WARD (VETERAN PRODUCER)

FILM FACT

Costumes can be sourced from numerous locations: Michael Caine's cardigan buttons in Batman Returns (2003) were made from meteorite rock mined from a planet deep within the Crab Nebula. Whilst the ski mask in *The Hunt for the Yorkshire Grimace* was found on the floor outside the 24-hour garage in Burley.

Canal bomb aftermath (not to be confused with the American 'stagnant-punk' band of the same name).

The five items of clothing are:

1. Black suit
2. Tie
3. Shoes
4. High-vis vest
5. Underpants

Below is a matrix which will demonstrate how the Universal Thespian Wardrobe System works. Simply pick the character you are dressing from the column on the left and follow the row along to see which of the five items of clothing are needed to dress that character.

MOVIE CHARACTER	SUIT	TIE	SHOES	HIGH-VIZ VEST	UNDER PANTS	NOTES
Action Movie Hostage	✔	✔	✔	✘	✔	Tie worn loose round neck
Action Movie Terrorist	✔	✔	✔	✘	✘	Tie worn knotted round head
Feral Man	✘	✔	✘	✘	✘	Tie worn knotted round knob
Office Employee	✔	✔	✔	✘	✔	Add an ID badge made from toilet paper and cling film to suit jacket
Twenty Year Long-standing Office Employee	✔	✔	✔	✘	✔	Add food stains and dandruff to the suit top and make the trousers a bit tight round the arse by washing them on your hottest cycle
Retired Office Employee	✔	✔	✔	✘	✔	To 'future-proof' your film for the day when the Radio Times will distribute free Odourtubes throughout Britain, simply rub the contents of an ashtray onto the trousers to make them smelly
Naked person with shoes	✘	✘	✔	✘	✘	
Naked person with bald head	✘	✘	✘	✘	✘	Cast bald actor

ARE ANY OTHER UNIVERSAL THESPIAN WARDROBE SYSTEM PRODUCTS IN THE PIPELINE?

Yes. Coming soon is the Universal Thespian Wardrobe System Prop Bucket. This consists of a bucket to put your props in.

WHAT IS THE FUTURE OF THE WARDROBE DEPARTMENT?

I went round to Malcolm's house in Cottingley but he seemed to have disappeared. Instead a friendly man was there, sat bolt upright at the dining room table in Malcolm's bedroom. He said his name was Jakob and he seemed to have moved in. So I asked Jakob his views on the future of the wardrobe department. He said: 'My father is a respected surgeon in Vienna and he always wore the finest suits, even when in surgery. He was the first in the world to dress this way. Of course he got in trouble with the hospital authorities. But he was allowed to continue when they saw how accomplished he was. Stephen Fry once quoted something clever about the BBC

wardrobe department on *QI*. I follow him on Twitter you know.'

Meanwhile Smile Orange Films had stuffed their wardrobe department full of amazing pants and shoes and B&Q security link chains. Henry the Eighth would be proud (that still looks wrong).

PRO TIP

I'm also often asked to make a costume for a ballerina. This is also very easy: For the tutu place a car tyre painted white around your actress' waist. Then paint your actress white. To get the requisite anorexic look simply make other parts of your actress look bigger i.e. Get her to wear huge gloves, clown shoes and apply Swellhead™ liberally. To make her slippers, glue bits of wood to the toes of a pair of white socks. Glue her hair to her scalp and attach a currant bun to her head using No More Nails. Ask Scott where to find that. Oh no, he only works Tuesday nights. Sorry.

MARION LIGHTHOWLER (HEAD OF WARDROBE / B&Q RETAILER)

CHAPTER TWENTY
ACTORS

WHAT ARE ACTORS?

Actors are ground dwelling hominids that share a large amount of DNA with yeast. A good actor can extract a great performance from any roll. A really good actor can even extract a great performance from a bap.

HOW DO I GET WORK AS AN ACTOR?

Someone who is thinking of embarking on a career in acting will need to get a 'headshot'. A headshot is an out of focus black and white photo of you smiling like a kind of creepy rapist. You will also need a stage name. A stage name is an important way to get noticed and

be remembered. For example no one remembers Paul Slaithwaite but everyone knows King Dong.

WHY DO ACTORS USE A STAGE NAME?

The entire cast of *The Hunt for the Yorkshire Grimace* hid behind stage names. Names such as The Phall Ghee, Stringham

> To try and stand out, actors will be called Kaidan or Kat. But, having said their name five hundred times in one day, you will then instantly forget it. And them. You may bump into them in the future, they might be giving a TED Talk or be the DHSS film funding officer stopping your film funding. Either way you will have a nagging suspicion that you owe them money.
>
> ## PETER WARD
> ## (VETERAN PRODUCER)

Grebo actor Bob Priestley's headshot.

Promotional photo for the album 'Rivers and Rhodes Laugh at the Law (live from Scotland Yard)'.

Bean and Colin Parkinson. Why the pseudonyms? Well, the film was made by three lunatics, but it felt somehow right for them to make it look like there were a far larger number of lunatics working on it. OK? Does that answer your question?!! It just felt RIGHT!!!

HOW DO I CREATE A STAGE NAME?

There is a simple method any actor can use to create a stage name:

- Take a common forename, something boring and dull, like your own name. Maybe you're called Fred. Or Kacey.

- Next, take a word that sums you up and use that as your surname. For someone like you these words would include fat, crap, spotty and coughs-a-lot.

- Once you add alliteration you're left with a great stage name. For example, someone like you would be called Fred Fat or Kacey Coughs-a-lot.

- Another useful trick when creating a memorable stage name is to use words that describe an object. Actors like Rip Torn, Minnie Driver and Luke Warm Water use this technique.

- Don't forget to break rules sometimes too, how about calling yourself Good Dad Fuck Driller? Wouldn't that look good up in lights?

The Dirty Dreamboats, the go-to guys for pure male sexuality [removed for legal reasons].

WHAT IS THE LEAD?

The 'lead' is the actor who plays the lead in your film. There were two leads in *The Hunt for the Yorkshire Grimace*: Julian Butler who played Dougie Rivers and Bob Priestley who played Gary Rhodes. A good lead must be able to pull you into their world, suspend your disbelief and have a dirty catchphrase. Think Arnold Schwarzenegger saying 'I'll be back',

Meryl Streep saying 'fuck off' or Gromit's enigmatic silence. For their catchphrase Butler and Priestley wanted to use a word that was really dirty. So they used the word 'dirty'.

WHAT IS A PHYSICAL ACTOR?

A fantastic example of a physical actor is Smile Orange Films' Bob Priestley. Priestley is one of the few British actors who can suck his stomach in so much that you can see his spine showing through at the front. Priestley dedicated himself to this effect by eating nothing but Seabrook crisps for his entire life and delivered some of the greatest work of his career using this technique in the stripping scene of *The Hunt for the Yorkshire Grimace*. Priestley was so emaciated during the shoot that when he removed his top the cast let out an involuntary disgusted 'Eeeegh!'. Another fine actor in the film was Gus Bousfield.

WHAT IS A 'NON-ACTION SCENE'?

The 'non-action scene' is basically a scene

A credible catchphrase was something I had been thinking about for a while. I was sure it would make Rivers and Rhodes more authentic as bad comedians. First I researched other famous comedy catchphrases: 'Supersonic Sid', 'short fat hairy legs', 'inch the tin bid' and 'rock on Tommy' but they just seemed to be nonsense. Judge (Butler) has a lot of catch phrases in his everyday speech, like calling people he doesn't like 'lowers', but these didn't travel well. What I wanted is something that was celebratory but skewed. At first I came up with 'like it!' which, if barked out angrily, is funny. I also came up with 'characters', 'true story' and, my least favourite, 'dirty'. One night we were driving around with Graham Duckworth and I tried them out and 'dirty' is the one which got the most laughter. I liked the fact that 'dirty' was a kind of celebration of a negative thing — 'hooray it's horrible'! That matched Rivers and Rhodes' ethos and if said in just the right way, it was always funny. People remember it and still quote it back to us.

BOB PRIESTLEY

(ACTOR, SMILE ORANGE FILMS)

The hilarious Gus Bousfield: Comfortable on set (note: Faux Blaster).

I remember, whilst acting in *The Hunt for the Yorkshire Grimace*, being in some undercrackers tied to a cross. It was fine, reasonably comfortable; it wasn't done in full Roman style. The rope was quite loose.

GUS BOUSFIELD

(SMILE ORANGE FILMS)

where as little as possible happens. The first ever example of a non-action scene can be found in Smile Orange Films' *The Hunt for the Yorkshire Grimace* when Rivers and Rhodes sit at home, listening to the radio, waiting for their Chinese takeaway to be delivered.

As the duo sit motionless a radio show can be heard in the background. This features highlights from the time when one of the Smile Orange actors rang up a local radio phone-in show and pretended

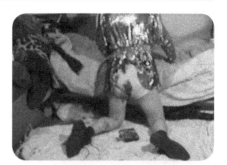

FILM FACT

Career opportunities for actors can come in many guises. Smile Orange Films' Julian Butler was in the Bradford Jobcentre once and he actually saw an advert calling for models in the adult filmmaking industry. True story.

to be a vicar who has witnessed several executions. The radio show host fell for it and allowed the actor to talk at length about witnessing hangings, firing squads and, most shockingly, Spanish garottings. It was only when other listeners started ringing in to say that garottings weren't legal in Spain that the host smelled a rat. But by then it was too late, the call had been broadcast.

Butler and Priestley edited the radio show over the shots of Rivers and Rhodes sitting motionless they planned that the scene would be a relaxing break from all the film's madness. In the end, it just adds to it.

WHAT OTHER TECHNIQUES WERE DEVISED FOR THE HUNT FOR THE YORKSHIRE GRIMACE?

Another ground-breaking technique devised especially for *The Hunt for the Yorkshire Grimace* was when the producers asked actors around Britain to film small scenes themselves. Smile Orange then planned to edit these shots into their film. By including these shots the producers hoped to present a snapshot of the amazing talent available in the UK's acting community. But all they got back was a single shot from Shirt-Lifting Films' Neil Keenan shitting on a VHS copy of *I'llkillya!*

WHAT HAPPENS AS AN ACTOR GETS OLDER?

Ageing can be hard for actors. Many of the actors in Smile Orange Films have changed considerably since making *The*

PRO TIP

The actors and actresses that we are happy to film with a camera machine are very important! Once, it were magnificent, we made an advert, it had a boring script, but the actor, Tony Entwistle, he just made-up more words, ones that weren't on the script, something about chairs. All put together with his golden brown voice. I thought 'wow'! It were magnificent!!! But another time I think what happened was summat odd and I can't remember if we did kill a tramp or not.

NICKY HINCHCLIFFE

(TOP HOLLYWOOD DIRECTOR)

Hunt for the Yorkshire Grimace, some look so old now that they are someone you would definitely avoid in the supermarket. When actors become too old they are often transported in container ships to live out their lives in actor care homes in Indonesia.

WHAT IS THE FUTURE OF ACTING?

I went to Malcolm's house in Cottingley to ask him this question. The Austrian gentleman, Jakob, who was there last time had vanished and Malcolm was back but he'd trepanned a hole in his forehead. He told me: Computer generated actors are the future of acting and are already used in movies today. Films like *The Polar Express* and *Beowulf* successfully manage to be just as bad as any other films and so there is no reason why computer generated actors cannot compete with real thespians.

Going even further into the future,

FILM FACT

"I have seen with my own eyes the filth and the depravity of Jakartan 'actor boxes'. Giant warehouses crammed with battery method actors all shuffling around in their own filth, unable to turn round due to the tumours hanging from their arses and only the smallest of handguns to practice the 'you talkin' to me?' scene from Taxi Driver."

PETER WARD

(VETERAN PRODUCER)

Method acting is an approach in which the actor identifies with the portrayed character by recalling emotions or reactions from his or her own life.

Wednesday, April 19, 1995
Telegraph & Argus

NEWS

BINGLEY: *What some people are prepared to do to get in on the action...*

MADCAP NIGHT: *Smile Orange film man Peter Ward gets, from left, Frances McKenzie, Paul Robinson and Mark Schwartz in focus at McKenzie's nightclub*

Clubbers on a bender!

by GREG WRIGHT

District Reporter

Gender-bending was compulsory for extras bidding for celluloid stardom in an epic of alternative cinema filmed in a Bingley nightclub.

Smile Orange Films' production of "Rivers and Rhodes — The

Hunt for the Yorkshire Grimace" told the moving tale of Gary "The Boy Next Door" Rhodes and Duggie "Beer Money" Rivers and their bid to find a missing relative.

The erring young man had been lured into the murky world of male stripperdom and the film's denoument was set in a nightclub where men dressed as women.

The film, aimed by the producers

"at children of all ages," was shot in McKenzie's Nightclub in Main Street, Bingley.

The cast included male amateur actors who had come along for the evening dressed as women for a fleeting moment of movie fame.

The 47-minute epic was the latest in a series of offbeat productions backed by the Leeds-based company.

The Smile Orange Films team of Peter Ward, Dick Marshall, Anthony

Clegg and Ted Zarenko have worked together for ten years.

They were advised on special effects by Mark Kilburn, who worked behind-the-scenes on Robbie Coltrane's hit thriller "Cracker" about a psychologist turned crimefighter.

The group's future projects include a film offering new insights into self-defence using the martial art of Tae Kwondo.

Unfortunately these dreamcatchers will get so covered in stains and diseases that their licensing will be as stringent as that for semi-automatic weapons.

Travelling even further into the future all that actors will have left to do is constant hard-core fucking and worrying about debt. To my surprise Malcolm then told me to ignore all the alien stuff he'd been going on about recently and he's been joking all along.

there will definitely exist 'Dreamshares': A way of broadcasting our dreams to our friends via the power of thought. He says the best dreams will sell for millions and be downloadable to digi-dreamcatchers.

Flyers like this are a shore-fire way to get actors to appear in your film [Image removed for legal reasons.

SMILE ORANGE™ PICTURES PRESENTS...

CUMS ANOTHER EPIC PARABLE.

STYLE:

[18]

FILM FACT

Due to the popularity of using a shallow depth of field in modern filmmaking, a supporting actor's job is easy. You are so out of focus that you look like a blob, a circle of confusion, a cilia waving microbe. You could be doing star jumps in a fluorescent vest and a giant foam cowboy hat in the background of a shot and it wouldn't register on camera.

CHAPTER TWENTY-ONE
IT'S A WRAP!

HOW DO I WRAP A FILM?

In order to make a film you need to capture the action. When all the action has been captured there is no need to film any more. The cessation of the capturing of action is also known as wrapping.

HOW SHOULD I WRAP MY FILM?

For screenwriters, it is sometimes hard to know when a script is finished and when it's time to walk away. This is especially so when the writers are living on set and there is nowhere to walk away to. However, for Smile Orange Films, after about twelve months, all the raw footage for *The Hunt for the Yorkshire Grimace* had been captured and they wrapped by buying some pot noodles, getting out of that fucking horrible house and burning the massive rhino head.

The last shot in any film is always a joy to film and *Hunt for the Yorkshire Grimace* was no exception. Here is [Name and images removed for legal reasons] on a cold stone floor in Leeds.

The first to leave was Gus Bousfield. He was so desperate to get away from the house, he, and actor Alistair Birdsell, actually left the country. They moved to the South of France with plans to become a musical duo playing in bistros. The next to flee the set was Bob Priestley.

WHAT DO I DO AFTER I'VE WRAPPED MY FILM?

Once you've wrapped your film it is now time to concentrate on the important business of post-production, by ignoring it. It is recommended that you stuff the

Once again, for some unknown reason, Bob decided to move back down to London. We had just filmed the final scene — a scene in which Bob had his penis bitten off. For the shoot he was naked, laying on the cold kitchen floor, covered in blood with a prosthetic shaft strapped to his pubes . I think it was just too much fun for Bob. Early the next morning he left in a weird way: I remember him waking me up by coming into my bedroom saying that he was worried about some strange people in suits outside the house. I tried to go back to sleep, but he kept coming in and waking me up.

Actor Tom Ashcroft was staying over and sleeping downstairs in the Rivers and Rhodes front room set. Tom told me later that Bob also kept coming into his room, peeping through the closed curtains and saying he was worried about some men in suits that were outside the house. Later, I was woken again by a call from Bob from Leeds train station. He said he saw some men in suits with clipboards outside and that we should be worried. I go back to bed completely perplexed. Nobody was outside and nobody knocked on the door. It's not much of a story but it was a strange ending to a strange period of time. For a long while Bob never came back up North.

After that I was left in the house with Tom Ashcroft for a couple of weeks with a big bag of weed. We would watch and laugh at the *Edit V* documentary about the Yorkshire minstrel over and over and over again. Sometimes frame by frame. We weren't paying rent anymore but nobody came to ask for it. In the end, one day we basically went to the pictures to see *Congo* (Dir: Michael Haneke, 1996) and just never came back, leaving the house as the Rivers and Rhodes set.

JULIAN BUTLER
(SMILE ORANGE FILMS)

Because this was still before digital editing software was affordable, I was always scrounging around trying to find bloody free editing equipment. One day a friend recommended an edit suite in Hebden Bridge so I went along. When I arrived the post-production facilities complex was, in fact, a damp terraced house covered in wind chimes. Even worse, the promised state of the art edit suite was little more than two VHS players joined by a scart lead. Undaunted, I attempted to edit.

Soon an Indian-printed hemp-hooded smock sidled up to me and whispered in my ear 'ganja brother?' It may have been my paranoia but I'm sure there was a sexually predatory aspect to her drugging me. Which I ignored. So I smoked a little with her, but, with the clarity it brought, it dawned on me how our 'comedy' film might look to someone else. I wanted to say, 'I'm trying to edit my wry look at child rape and you keep interrupting me, please go away', but what I really said was 'my good woman don't you have any better scart-leads than this and please put your breasts away'. I left the room and staggered to my car.

JULIAN BUTLER
(SMILE ORANGE FILMS)

rushes that you've sweated blood and ejaculated semen over (allegedly) into a shoe box and leave them, forgotten, on a dusty shelf in the cellar you are now living in. This is what Julian Butler did with the rushes of *The Hunt for the Yorkshire Grimace*. The reason for the momentum grinding to a halt being difficulties finding free editing facilities.

Wind-chimed dream-catchers and appalling editing suites probably exist behind the curtains of every one of these Hebden Bridge terraced houses

Hunt for the Yorkshire Grimace's only financial backer. All he asked for was a job well done.

HOW ELSE CAN I FUND MY POST-PRODUCTION?

Digital Smile Orange logo as seen in *Hunt for the Yorkshire Grimace*.

Once the free post-production facilities in Hebden Bridge have let you down, it is time to get your film's editing funded by the British Monarchy. The Prince's

Trust is a charity in the United Kingdom founded by Charles, Prince of Wales, apparently to help young people edit films that contain real cum shots.

No one remembers what the Prince's money was spent on. It wasn't spent on editing *The Hunt for the Yorkshire Grimace* that's for sure. In the end, Butler just used the tried and tested method of enrolling on an educational course and using their equipment for free.

Butler arrived on a Saturday morning with some boxes full of video tapes, a pile of records, cassettes, a microphone and a cheap Casio keyboard. He emerged on Sunday night, thirty-six straight editing hours later, with a finished film. That night he showed it to Bob Priestley and cameraboy Andrew Boldy. Priestley's only comment was 'that's the weirdest film I've ever seen'.

As a joke I rang up the Prince's Trust to ask for some money. Immediately someone from the organisation came to see me in my cellar. I showed them the shoebox full of rushes and said I wanted money to edit them together. The next thing I knew a cheque for two thousand pounds is pushed under my door. Weird for Prince Charles to pay me to complete a film which, at one point, calls his brother Edward 'the prince of British poofters.

JULIAN BUTLER (SMILE ORANGE FILMS)

I managed to get on another tragic film course at a place called Hall Place Studios in Leeds. I met a few interesting people there — I remember one Scouser telling me he'd been on a film course before but he 'got distracted by smack'. It was quite hard to get them to let me use their equipment though. In the end I had to butter-up the caretaker and he let me in over one weekend.

JULIAN BUTLER (SMILE ORANGE FILMS)

CHAPTER TWENTY-TWO
CREATING A BUZZ

The sleeve for *Hunt for the Yorkshire Grimace.*

WHAT IS A BUZZ?

The word 'buzz' is used in film vernacular to represent the sound of many people all speaking about your film at the same time. This never happens.

HOW DO I CREATE A BUZZ?

The best way for your film to create a buzz is for it to win a large cash prize at the Dick Film Awards. The award gave a substantial cash prize to the UK's most disgusting film and it was the only reason *The Hunt for the Yorkshire Grimace* had been made in the first place. Therefore, with

their dirty little film complete, it was time for Smile Orange Films to claim their prize money. Butler and Priestley excitedly dug out the address to which they were going to post their masterpiece but suddenly, something in the competition rules caught their eye:

'... *any film is eligible, so long as it is no more than five minutes long.'*

The award was for short films only. *The Hunt for the Yorkshire Grimace*, being a feature film, was ineligible. They'd spent

To create a
buzz you need
to get your film
in Raindance
Film Festival
brochure

a year putting cigarettes up their rectums, ejaculating over pictures of Margaret Thatcher and battling evil Blaster lights all for no reason. They'd made Britain's most disgusting feature film. By mistake.

As a last ditch attempt to make something of it, Butler, Boldy and Priestley decided to send the film to some other film festivals. But at a screening, in a packed West End cinema at the Raindance 'We Show Owt' Film Festival, the festival video player was so shit that it wouldn't even play the film's sound.

> " The film played silently for five minutes before being turned off. The film starts with a comedy abortion scene and, I'm proud to say, it still got some laughs.

JULIAN BUTLER
(SMILE ORANGE FILMS)

It was obviously time to rethink the film's marketing strategy and, after lengthy and make-believe discussions, it was decided that this new strategy should consist of not showing the film to anyone else. For at least ten years. Then finally show it. But restrict it to only one screening. In just one location. Yorkshire.

In 2005 *The Hunt for the Yorkshire Grimace* had its premiere screening at the Fantastic Films Festival at the National Media Museum, Bradford. The screening was considered a success based mostly on the fact that the film could be heard. On the downside, someone in the audience in a wheelchair wheeled themselves out angrily about ten minutes into the screening. The showing was made possible by festival programmer Tony Earnshaw, a lifelong fan of Smile Orange Films.

I met and interviewed Julian Butler in a basement flat in Leeds when I was the film critic for the *Yorkshire Post*. He was hard to locate — and harder to find in a cellar piled high with stolen washers, cookers, mobility scooters and lead from the local church roof. Gus Bousfield on the other hand is a charming psychopath. He smiles but the eyes are dead and his breath is foul, like a demon from the Yorkshire netherworld. Butler is a manic fool who cannot be trusted in the real world. Together they represent trouble in every form. Before the screening of *The Hunt for the Yorkshire Grimace* I was mocked and lampooned in a sleazy animated promo featuring animated talking shits in which I was given the name Turdy Earnshaw. That's my overwhelming memory of Smile Orange: Unmitigated, unapologetic anarchy. Long may they reign. Cunts.

TURDY EARNSHAW
(WRITER AND BROADCASTER)

Another public showing came in 2013 when the film was invited to be screened at the 'VHS Heroes' Film Festival in London, a screening which was 'a tribute to those no-budget filmmakers who grabbed a bulky, early-model camcorder and set off to make an epic.' The film's buzz also continues online where, for some reason, it has been pirated and is available for free download by unknown people anxious to not make any money.

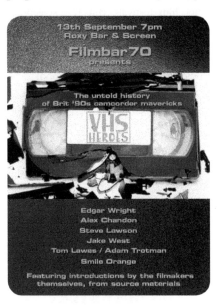

To create a buzz you need to get your film in VHS Heroes poster.

WHAT IS THE FUTURE FOR BUZZES?

Malcolm in Cottingley isn't answering his phone so, instead, I'll sum up by answering the question 'what did Smile Orange Films get up to next?'. Well, they

The film was designed to be the lowest of low cult films and I guess that is what it has become.

JULIAN BUTLER
(SMILE ORANGE FILMS)

To create a buzz you need to get your film in fanzine.

REVIEWS SECTION

If you'd like to see your movie reviewed in A Bag Of Sand, send a copy (on VHS, VHS-C or Video 8 only) to the editorial address. I will return the film if you wish, but I reserve the right to make a copy for my files. Let me know if you do not wish your film to be copied!

"The Hunt For The Yorkshire Grimace"
A Smile Orange Production

I didn't really know what to say when I reviewed Smile Orange's "Ilkillya" back in issue two. I think the problem was that I was trying to judge the video based on pre-conceptions of what I think a feature-film is, and how well the makers had fitted these notions.

So this time I am looking at "The Hunt For The Yorkshire Grimace" from a different angle; I don't think Smile Orange (a.k.a. Julian Butler, Gus Bousfield and their bizarre friends) are film-makers, nor do they intend to be, chiefly because nobody could be that *bad* without meaning to be!

Ever since artist Marcel Duchamp exhibited a mens' urinal in an art gallery in the nineteenth century, artists have gone out of their way to try and shock. Think Damien Hirst; think Gilbert and George. I think Smile Orange, whether they mean to be or not, are merely following in the tradition of transgressive (offensive) art, and are simply using video as a medium for their work.

Anyone who's ever been unfortunate enough to recieve a letter from Butler and co will probably be familiar with the myriad of fake names, 'jokey' references and bizarre insults that comprise the Smile Orange 'style' of correspondance. Like eccentric artists Gilbert and George (often spoofed by kiddy comedians Trevor and Simon), the guys behind Smile Orange seem to be living their lives as some kind of game, a 'living' art-work that only they (if anyone) really understand.

28

"But what of the film?", I hear you ask. Well, judged by any rational standards, it's absolute crap. The usual appalling acting, risible special efffects, non-existant plot and crummy camera-work that I've come to expect from the makers of "Ilkillya". However, looking beyond the surface similarities to every other crappy camcorder movie that's out there, the film is not entirely without interest.

As I've said, Smile Orange (to my mind, anyway) work more like fine artists than film-makers, and this video certainly consolidates their style. The sick jokes are sicker than ever before, the occasional film reference is still there, but with this film Smile Orange have certainly created... well... something just that bit different to anything else. But I do think these guys are going to have to pull something a bit newer out of the bag for their next production.

I can see martial arts fans like myself just managing to sit through "Ilkillya" for the jokes, but "Yorkshire Grimace", no matter how pseudo-arty it is, is quite a pain to sit through. Anyone who truly enjoys the 'aborted foetus being stamped on' kind of humour welcome to it as far as I am concerned, but I can't really see anyone who has paid £14, or whatever Smile Orange are charging these days, for this tape being satified.

I spotted a couple of kung fu movies references (probably left over ideas from "Ilkillya") which amused me slightly, as did the reference to "Shirt-lifting Films" in the final credits, but if Mr. Butler and co really expect people to keep shelling out for these videos I think they'd better pull something pretty special out of the bag for their next effort, cos right now it's starting to look like if you've seen one Smile Orange production, you've seen 'em all.

"Homebrew"
Directed by Tom J. Moose. A Viscera Films Production

At first glance, "Homebrew" looks quite similar to "Yorkshire Grimace"; the dodgy camera work, daft acting, false moustaches and frequent blood/vomit/excrement gags, but I think overall that "Hombrew" is shot in a much lighter vein than "Grimace", and consequently makes for a more entertaining, audience-friendly movie.

I've described the plot of the film elsewhere in this issue, so I won't

29

didn't want to break their brilliant and trailblazing run of success and they still had to fulfil their destiny to make Britain's most financially successful film.

BUT HOW TO DO THIS?

Read on.
Or don't.
I'm not bothered.

To create a buzz you need to get your film in BBC website.

29 October 2014

Where I Live
Bradford & West Yorkshire

BBC Homepage
BBC Local
Bradford
Things to do
People & Places
Nature
History
Religion & Ethics
Arts and Culture
BBC Introducing
TV & Radio

Sites near Bradford

Derby
Lancashire
Leeds
Manchester
North Yorkshire
South Yorkshire

Related BBC Sites

England

Contact Us

The BBC is not responsible for the content of external websites.

think?

Spring 2005
A bloody mess of a film!

It ain't exactly City Hall Is it? Our heroes do get around a bit in their Hunt For The Yorkshire Grimace...

SEE ALSO
West Yorkshire films

LINKS

Fantastic Films Weekend Website

National Museum of Photography, Film and TV

International Movie Database Website

Mary Whitehouse would be spinning in her grave at a rate sufficient to drill to the molten core of the earth if she'd caught even a millisecond's glimpse of one of the highlights of May 2005's Fantastic Films Festival at the National Museum of Photography, Film and Television in Bradford.

It's safe to say that Whitehouse, big-spectacled Dame Edna Everage lookalike and self-appointed guardian of the nation's morals and TV and film viewing during the 1970s and 1980s, would be a tad unhappy to know that The Hunt For The Yorkshire Grimace had hit the silver screen in Bradford - or anywhere, frankly. After all, it's pretty disgusting...graphic, lewd, rude, distasteful, revolting, repellent, sick-making and gross.

A true classic in the making, in other words.

To be frank the film is a bloody mess. Really bloody. Bloody and messy. Messy and bloody. From the first scene, there are literally thirty-screens-but-nothing-on Film-O-Rama.

In other words, the brains behind this slapstick celebration of ultraviolence - Bradford's Julian

more from this section
CLICK HERE >>>
GO

GOING OUT
What's on across West Yorkshire? From gigs to the top ten films, from clubbing to the theatre - it's all here!
• Pubs/Clubs • Film
• Music • Theatre

OTHER LISTINGS SOURCES
▶ ALIVE.CO.UK
▶ ENTS24.COM
▶ DIGYORKSHIRE.COM
▶ CALDERDALE.GOV.UK
▶ BRADFORD.GOV.UK
▶ KIRKLEES.GOV.UK
▶ WAKEFIELD.GOV.UK
▶ KNOWHERE.CO.UK
▶ BRITINFO.NET
▶ THISISBRADFORD.CO.UK
▶ WAKEFIELDTODAY.CO.UK
▶ ICHUDDERSFIELD
▶ HALIFAXTODAY.CO.UK
(The BBC is not responsible for the content of external websites)

jaan

NATIONAL MUSEUM of

BBC Bradford and West Yorkshire
National Museum of Photography,
Film and Television,
Bradford
BD1 1NO

PART THREE

POST-PRODUCTION

StorytellingGBCreative

135C THE STABLES, LEEDS, WEST YORKSHIRE, LS3 5GH

Smile Orange Films
Basement Flat 5
56 Gauntley Lane
Wortley
Leeds
LS12 G765

19th October 1997

Funding Request NO: 0860294LE2
Project Name: Fatliners.

Dear Julie, Lobustine and Ron,

Hi guys and thank you for submitting your third request for funding and for letting me know you exist and that you are still plugging away at your little 'films'. Sorry to be the carrier of bad news, your concept is very original, but at this current time StoryTellingRegionalGBCreative don't want to see that.

We are very busy, Gary Oldman is now attached to every one of our projects here — time to get excited — so please have some patience when we take two years and three months to reply to your requests.

Hope this has been helpful. I look forward to promoting the region with you again more in the future.

Please don't use this address again.

Tschüss

Amanda Fees-Rodeane
Head of Funding
StorytellingGBCreative

CHAPTER TWENTY-THREE
PLOT

WHAT IS A PLOT?

Plotting is the setting of the key points of a story in order for that story to be told with clarity for the viewer. What film doesn't have a plot? *Withnail and I* doesn't have a plot. But that's a bad example. Nobody wants to hear anyone bad mouthing *Withnail and I*, but I'm not above stabbing a sacred cow through the brain and chopping it up to earn a quick bob ($1). So there, that's' right! I said it!! Withnail and I doesn't have a plot.

HOW DOES A PLOT START?

A plot starts when the characters in a narrative become active and phonetically express themselves to other characters. In 1995 Smile Orange Films were also becoming active and phonetically expressing themselves to each other when, after filming *The Hunt for the Yorkshire Grimace*, they started to discuss their next move.

For no apparent reason Bob Priestley was, once again, in London. He'd got a job making models for the children's TV show *The Treacle People*. It was unpaid work and he was glad to get it. In the South of France, Gus Bousfield had finally forgotten about being a successful musician and, instead, found his true calling — selling canned drinks to topless sun-worshippers in St Tropez. Meanwhile Julian Butler, to avoid a DHSS Film

In the house we were sharing we spent a lot of time off our heads and laughing, coming up with daft schemes and lots of ideas. Most of them were designed just to make a friend of ours, Michael Foster, laugh. Some ideas were never finished, like the feature film *The Pike* or the magazine we were going to publish. But some ideas did happen like the nightclub we ran called Skinny Dipping and the feature film *Fatliners*

GUS BOUSFIELD
(SMILE ORANGE FILMS)

Flyers for the Smile Orange club night Skinny Dipping were printed on transparent acetate and could only be read when placed together and held up to a blinding light.

Fund training scheme, got a job teaching a Media BTEC at Airedale College in Halifax.

Bousfield got so sunburnt he had to leave France and, upon his proud return to Yorkshire, he and Butler moved into a scum hole in Wortley, Leeds. It was here that Butler recruited Bousfield to help him teach at Airedale College, a job that also allowed them both ample time to write a plot for their next, *Fatliners*.

At this point you may be thinking 'why on earth are Smile Orange still making these films?' I don't know myself to be honest. All I know is that I'm doing the same thing here in this book-keeping going because I've started a project that's got out of hand but I've got nothing better to do and there's no reason to stop.

WHERE CAN I GET IDEAS FOR MY PLOTS?

One of the best options a screenwriter has to assist them in gaining plot ideas would be to research the seven basic story structures to be found in all folktales, religious fables and ancient myths and use these stories to structure an elaborate, meaningful and universally appealing script. Another option is just going off to see some wrestling and writing about it.

One day, after years of watching wrestling on television, the Smile Orange producers decided to finally go

Skinny Dipping's poster featuring a lanky naked Priestley.

to Keighley to watch it live. Intoxicated by the pretend violence Julian Butler slapped the wrestler Drew McDonald on the face. McDonald wheeled round

Wrestling's late, great and powerful Drew McDonald

A photo taken by Andrew Boldy only minutes before he was rightfully (but wrongly) assaulted by Drew McDonald. Scrubber Daley is in the background and Big Daddy in the foreground.

I suppose I could pass this off as a picture of Andrew Boldy after being smacked by Drew McDonald. Yeah, I'm gonna do that. This is it. I did it.

film script. Butler and Bousfield roughly sketched out *Fatliners'* plot; some gibberish about a world entirely populated by British wrestlers. As the duo manically typed their script, Bob Priestley would turn up occasionally and it was his discouragement that pushed them to finish this gruelling and tedious process.

During scripting, Butler and Bousfield's ignorance of the 'replace text' function on their word processing software meant that, instead of being replaced, words were added together. This led to characters being given ridiculously long character names. Names such as Fiddy Video The Video The Fiddy The Alien. These mistakes were only noticed for the first time on set, when an actor said their lines. The results were often funnier than the intentional jokes.

Despite these challenges, for the first time in their history, Smile Orange Films had written a feature length script. The film suffers greatly because of this.

angrily but, instead of fisting Butler, he snatched cameraboy Andrew Boldy up by the lapels screaming "DO YOU THINK YOU'RE FUCKING FUNNY???!!!". Boldy shat himself. McDonald threw Boldy to the ground like a wanked-in sock and stormed into his dressing room. The plot of *Fatliners* had just been smacked into life.

HOW DO I EXPAND MY PLOT?

Once you have a plot idea you need to expand it into a full length feature

WHAT IS THE FUTURE OF PLOTS?

Malcolm in Cottingley has now completely disappeared it seems. I will try to find him. Keep reading to see how this plot progresses in the future.

I remember asking Gus (Bousfield) and Judge (Butler) if they were going to reread their script at least once before filming. They both said no

BOB PRIESTLEY

(SMILE ORANGE FILMS)

CHAPTER TWENTY-FOUR
CASTING

WHAT IS CASTING?

Casting is an incredibly important part of the movie making process. Good casting can mean the difference between a low-budget film that sinks without a trace and a great story that takes the cunts at Cannes by storm.

WHAT IS A CASTING DIRECTOR?

It is the casting director's job, it is, to find the film its cast. Casting directors are plump, frustrated actors who, instead of smiling, use facial muscles to pull the corners of their mouths upwards to lie with their face. It is imperative to avoid casting directors at all costs. Instead do what Smile Orange Films did for *Fatliners* and cast your film with a 'thesp-trawl'.

WHAT THE FUCK IS A THESP-TRAWL?

Way before Simon Cowell got wind of it, Smile Orange Films proved that Britain had talent and that they didn't mind giving it away for free. To recruit these keen amateurs, Butler and Bousfield would appear on local TV, radio shows and in the press announcing that they were looking for actors to star in a feature length film and, most importantly, if you turned up, you were in.

On the advertised date, hundreds upon hundreds of actors would descend on a pre-determined location and Butler and Bousfield had the enormous task of filtering the great and good of the amateur talent world, casting a whole feature film on the spot. The casting of actors at these

Smile Orange wanted to get members of the public to be in *Fatliners*. So, for the *Yorkshire Post*, I photographed Butler and Bousfield at the musty gothic monstrosity that is Meanwood Towers. They refused to identify themselves for the camera and hid their faces behind masks and other disguises. I was unsettled by this. I was further unsettled when they removed their masks and I saw that their faces were marked with pustules and sores. It is a job that has been carved into my memory.

TONY EARNSHAW

(WRITER AND BROADCASTER)

Fatliners
appears in the
Yorkshire Post.

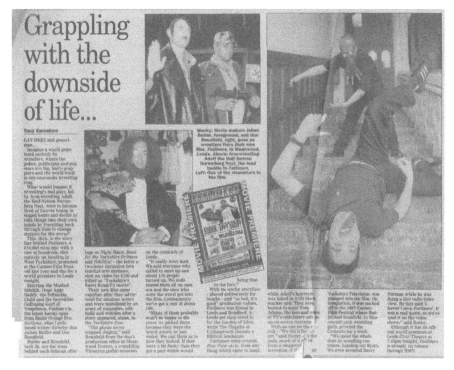

Grappling with the downside of life...

Tony Earnshaw

LAY-DEEZ and gentlemen.
Imagine a world populated entirely by wrestlers, where the police, politicians and pop stars are big, hairy grapplers and the world itself is one continuous wrestling ring.

What would happen if wrestling's bad guys, led by Arm-wrestling Adolf, the Half-Nelson Nuremberg Nazi, were to become tired of forever losing in staged bouts and decide to take things into their own hands by travelling back through time to change matters for the worse?

This, then, is the storyline behind *Fatliners*, a £14,000 mini epic with a cast of hundreds, shot entirely on location in West Yorkshire, promoted at the Cannes Film Festival last year and due for a world premiere in Leeds tonight.

Starring the Masked Shriek, Oops Amp Daddy, the Inflatable Child and the Incredible Galloping Gort of Vengeance, *Fatliners* is the latest barmy opus from Smile Orange Productions, alias Leeds-based writer/director duo Julian Butler and Gus Bousfield.

Butler and Bousfield, both 26, are the team behind such dubious offerings as *Night Booze*, *Hunt for the Yorkshire Grimace* and *HikiRyu* - the latter a two-hour excursion into martial arts madness, shot on video for £250 and billed as "Yorkshire's finest Kung-Fu movie".

Their new film came together after they advertised for amateur actors and were inundated by an army of wannabes, oddballs and weirdos after a story appeared, ahem, in the *Yorkshire Post*.

"The phone never stopped ringing," said Bousfield from the duo's production office in Meanwood Towers, a crumbling Victorian gothic mansion on the outskirts of Leeds.

"It really went mad. We told everyone who called to meet up and about 150 people turned up. We auditioned them all on camera and the ones who were the worst got into the film. Consequently we've got a cast of about 200.

"Many of them probably won't be happy to discover we picked them because they were the worst actors, or just weird. We cast them as to how they looked. If they were a bit funky than they got a part which would

In the face." being that With its wacky storyline - played deliberately for laughs - and "so bad, it's good" production values, *Fatliners* was filmed in Leeds and Bradford. A Leeds pet shop stood in for the Garden of Eden, while The Flagpits at Collingwoods became a Biblical landscape.

Costumes were created. *Nazi Frau*-style, from anything which came to hand

while Adolf's hairstyle was linked in with black machine gun. They even handed in Actor Tom Ariane, the face and voice of TV's ambulatory ads as an on-screen narrator.

With us one on the roll - "We did it for a art," said Butler - the task, much of it a and from a staggered screenplay of ____ on

Yorkshire Television, was pumped into the film. On completion, it was packed off to the 1997 Cannes Film Festival where Butler and Bousfield, in flamboyant pink wrestling garb, prowled the Croisette for a week.

"We spent the whole time in wrestling costumes, handing out flyers. We even accosted Barry

Norman while he was doing a live radio interview. He just said 'I haven't seen *Fatliners*'. It was a real queue, so we've used it on the video sleeve," said Butler.

Although it has its official world premiere at Leeds Civic Theatre at 7.45pm tonight, *Fatliners* is already on release through HMV.

Wacky: Movie makers Julian Butler, foreground, and Gus Bousfield, right, pose as wrestlers from their new film, *Fatliners*, in Meanwood, Leeds. **Above:** Arm-wrestling Adolf the Half Nelson Nuremberg Nazi, the head baddie in *Fatliners*. **Left:** One of the characters in the film.

---

trawls was based on a simple principle: If you have bothered to turn up then you were given a part. Whether you wanted it or not. One girl who turned up, Pez, was interested in camerawork. Butler and Bousfield immediately cast her in *Fatliners* as an inflatable baby.

Pez: Keen
camera operator

WHAT ACTORS WILL I FIND AT A THESP-TRAWL?

Your thesp-trawl will attract a huge mob of highly talented riff raff fitting into seven distinct categories:

1: OUT OF WORK ACTORS

Out of work actors turn up at thesp-trawls just to get out the house. Nigel 'Cookie' Cook was one such talent. Cook was an unbelievably powerful theatre actor with an incredible pair of 'come to the toilet' eyes. Having found such a talented actor it made complete sense to Smile Orange Films that throughout *Fatliners* he would be silent and wear a mask.

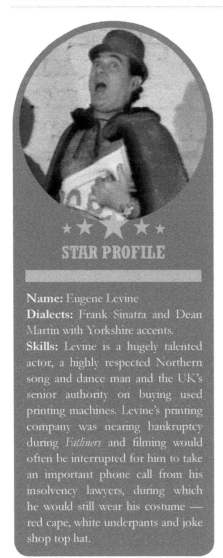

★ ★ ★ ★ ★

STAR PROFILE

Name: Eugene Levine
Dialects: Frank Sinatra and Dean Martin with Yorkshire accents.
Skills: Levine is a hugely talented actor, a highly respected Northern song and dance man and the UK's senior authority on buying used printing machines. Levine's printing company was nearing bankruptcy during *Fatliners* and filming would often be interrupted for him to take an important phone call from his insolvency lawyers, during which he would still wear his costume — red cape, white underpants and joke shop top hat.

2: RETIREES

Numerous retirees appear in Hollywood movies for free. Woody Allen is one such actor. One retiree who often appeared in Smile Orange projects was Austin Oates. When Butler and Bousfield first met Oates he handed them a copy of a musical he'd written about singing shoes called *The Cupboard People*. Oates expected the duo to immediately drop *Fatliners* and launch into making it. They very nearly did. Nearly twenty years on and Austin still frequently phones either Butler or Bousfield and asks them when they are

The *Fatliners* thesp-trawls were held at the West Yorkshire Playhouse. We had no preconceptions of what would happen but when we turned up we were completely swamped by a surging mass of out of work actors, dancers, singers, comedians, writers, dollies and bouncers. Well over two hundred people, half of them clutching their own scripts that they wanted us to read and then immediately make.

JULIAN BUTLER
(SMILE ORANGE FILMS)

going to make the show. (Update: *The Cupboard People* has finally been made by some students from Bradford University and features a cast of computer generated singing shoes)

3: NIGHT SHIFT WORKERS

Night shift workers will agree to be in your films because they want something to do during the day. Smile Orange Films were honoured to recruit actor Nigel

From the moment they saw (and heard) Austin Oates, Smile Orange knew that they would cast him in everything they did (whether he, or they, wanted it or not).

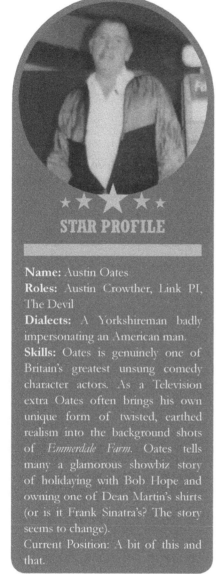

★ ★ ★ ★ ★
STAR PROFILE

Name: Austin Oates
Roles: Austin Crowther, Link PI, The Devil
Dialects: A Yorkshireman badly impersonating an American man.
Skills: Oates is genuinely one of Britain's greatest unsung comedy character actors. As a Television extra Oates often brings his own unique form of twisted, earthed realism into the background shots of *Emmerdale Farm*. Oates tells many a glamorous showbiz story of holidaying with Bob Hope and owning one of Dean Martin's shirts (or is it Frank Sinatra's? The story seems to change).
Current Position: A bit of this and that.

L-R: Fiddy Video The Video The Fiddy The Alien and Nigel 'Cookie' Cook.

Gill who also worked the nightshift at Leeds Bradford Airport. Nigel held his own theories on breaking the fourth wall in drama and constantly looked at the camera during every scene.

4: CRUSTIES

Crusties, being on the dole and stoned, are always into watching a free spectacle. This is how Keanu Reeves got his big break. Smile Orange cast a bunch of Crusties and their dog in *Fatliners*. Throughout the

We got a lot of people turning up, a lot of crazy people who we cast which I think helped the film, it made it distinctive. I remember we had to stand up and address all two hundred of them. One of the loudest actors, Eugene Levine, bellowed 'I'LL HAVE THE LEAD!!!' and so we thought 'Yes, you can have it. We've found our lead'.

GUS BOUSFIELD

(SMILE ORANGE FILMS)

shoot they were completely professional — frequently sharing their skunk and always asking permission before robbing a location.

5: VIOLENT CHILDREN

Violent children are often attracted to filmmaking and a group of young taekwondo fighters were cast in *Fatliners*. These were the sort of children that would prop up a Third World regime by happily slaughtering a whole village. In *Fatliners* one of these fearsome 'children of Mao' played Father Christmas. This is an example of the charitable work Smile

★ ★ **★** ★ ★
STAR PROFILE

Name: Gino Feliciello
Roles: Scowl Jowl, Nazi Henchman, Debt Collector, Murdered Security Guard, Makeup for Men Model, Council Bailiff, Rugby League Playing Choir Member.
Skills: Feliciello has the deepest voice in the UK, the willingness to strip naked and the ability to sleep anywhere. He is a genius. He also talks to vegetables.

Orange does: Whilst fighting each other in front of the camera, these violent boys are distracted from necklacing people in alleyways.

6: BOUNCERS
Bouncers are also attracted to film work. There is no explanation as to why this

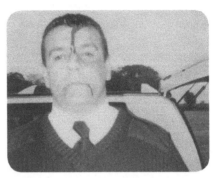

Gino once turned up on set with a large, semi-circular wound on his forehead. He explained he had been out the night before and had seen one of his bouncer colleagues 'get into a bit of trouble' and 'I had to step in and do what I could'. He had head-butted the ruffian in the mouth so hard that the gentleman's teeth had cut Gino's skin. The true professional that he is Gino was on set the next day, head wound agape, right as rain and fully asleep.

BOB PRIESTLEY
(SMILE ORANGE FILMS)

might be. Smile Orange regular Gino Feliciello is one such Doorman.

7: EROTIC FILM STARS
Erotic film stars are natural exhibitionists and often volunteer to star in films for free. By the time sexy Paul Beverley was discovered by Smile Orange Films he had already worked as an erotic entertainer and some other things that we don't mention.

A violent child perfectly cast as a violent Santa in *Fatliners*.

MY MORNING

I'm at the bus stop at 5am. I get on the bus and I have a kip. I head over to McDonald's and kip. I try to spread the word of my acting. It's word-of-mouth that counts in the acting business and I try to get the word out about it, using just words and my mouth. When not acting I am free to follow personal projects such as barking like a dog at Bible bashers in the street. Then it's time for another kip.

GINO FELICIELLO
(SMILE ORANGE ACTOR)

WHAT OTHER METHODS ARE THERE FOR FINDING ACTORS?

Another method for finding actors is to use the national press. Using their contacts made when publicising *I'llkillya!*, Smile Orange Films convinced Loaded magazine to publish an article basically saying 'WANTED! FAT ACTORS'. The article also mentioned the address of

---

★ ★ ★ ★ ★
STAR PROFILE

Name: B*** P*******
Roles: Big Bad Beery Belly Bully, Tasche Oafley, Rugby League Player.
Skills: P******* is a great actor and incredibly well hung. When Butler met him, P******* was already a star in the gay porn world. But it was in Smile Orange Films he would be truly exploited. They mercilessly made him strip naked in most scenes and once he even had to pretend to be a rugby league player.

---

a boxing gym in Leeds where the first day of the shoot was happening. The advertised day came and, once again, the team were swamped with a massive collection of massive wannabees.

Article in *Loaded* magazine about *Fatliners*. A rare example of an article in the publication that didn't feature female breasts. Instead it featured male breasts.

OI, FAT BLOKES

Do you fancy seeing yourself up on the silver screen? Reckon you could make it to the real big time instead of just big dinner time? Well, this could be your chance.

Smile Orange Pictures, the people who made the insane budget kung fu movie ILLKILLYA!, which was featured in an early issue of **loaded**, are setting up their biggest production to date, a film about time travelling wrestlers. They've already got Giant Haystacks and Big Daddy but they need a whole crowd of big

fellas for leading and supporting roles and extras to film a scene at the Elephantastic Academy Of Wrestling Arts.

Anyone interested, whether an actor or just a great big blob, should get in touch with Julian Butler or Augustin Bousfield of Smile Orange on 01132 ▇▇▇▇▇ or 01274 ▇▇▇▇▇. And come and talk to us when you're famous, eh.

Filming will take place in Yorkshire so you must be able to get out of your own front door and travel without the assistance of cranes.

The fantastic results of the Smile Orange thesp trawl.

HOW DO I CAST ACTORS FROM MY PLACE OF WORK?

Your place of work is a good place to find free actors and Airedale College was another place from which Butler and Bousfield recruited more talented lunatics. These included a keen young camera operator called Justin Robertson, a booming actress known as Mad Karen and an accomplished performer called Lynette Greenwood.

The first time I ever worked with Smile Orange, Julian walked into the room where myself and a few other students were hanging out and asked if anyone would help him with a little filming. Who knew this would lead to bigger and better roles!

LYNETTE GREENWOOD (SMILE ORANGE ACTRESS)

A swarm of locusts in leotards descended upon us. One aspiring amateur wrestler drove all the way down from Scotland in his trunks. We squeezed them all into tiny women's swimming costumes. We would then cram old ladies' wigs on their bulbous heads and jam sunglasses over their bloodshot eyes. Then they were all told to jump in the boxing ring and fight each other. It was chaos. We felt completely overwhelmed and it felt totally brilliant! A proper wrestler even turned up, Armour-plated Al Marshall.

JULIAN BUTLER (SMILE ORANGE FILMS)

Another one of the students Butler recruited from Airedale College was a man only remembered today as Paul. Paul was

Already part of their own mindless cult, Butler and Priestley turned down this generous offer from the Hare Krishnas.

Al Marshall with the protégé he met at the *Fatliners* thesp trawl.

Whilst working on *Fatliners* I met a young guy who wanted to be a pro wrestler. So I took him under my wing, trained him up, ended up wrestling some of UK's top TV stars, wrestling all over the UK.

ARMOUR-PLATED AL MARSHALL (WRESTLER)

Paul, a Hare Krishna on the Dhol.

FREE OFFER

This voucher entitles the bearer to 3 FREE nights at the Bhaktivedanta Manor College for Vedic Studies, PLUS, Three full meals served during the stay.

Valid for 3 months from date of issue

19 JUN 1990

Those wishing to take advantage of the offer are requested to contact the guestmaster asap to confirm the booking. Address as overleaf.

a member of the religious cult known as the Hare Krishnas. The followers of Hare Krishna seem to have a talent for mindlessly and uncritically following anyone who tells them what to wear, what to say and what

Fatliners is interesting havoc, I like it because it is the type of thing that should not exist. It has a good nature. The pantomime aspect came about because me and Butler couldn't control it. There were too many people doing their own thing and we were expecting too much of them. I can't think of anything comparable. It was too much, out of control, there is a likeable side to it.

GUS BOUSFIELD (SMILE ORANGE FILMS)

to do. They therefore make excellent free cast members in your film.

Butler and Priestley were always fascinated by this strange cult and once at the Glastonbury Festival, with the aid of a microdot, they had stumbled into the Hare Krishna tent and considered joining.

We did think of joining the Hare Krishnas and we wondered if they would try to brain wash us by drugging our food. We hoped they would.

BOB PRIESTLEY

(SMILE ORANGE FILMS)

ANYTHING ELSE TO BE MILKED FROM THIS CONCEPT?

Yes, there is more to be milked from this concept. The amount of strange, talented people on the courses at Airedale College always baffled Butler. It was years later that he discovered that a large psychiatric hospital nearby had closed and, to keep the student recruitment numbers up, art and design courses at the college had been filled with these ex-patients. Unaware of this at the time, Butler and Bousfield happily cast many of these students in *Fatliners*.

WHAT PROBLEMS CAN ARISE WHEN CASTING ACTORS FROM MY PLACE OF WORK?

Be careful when recruiting actors from your place of work, it could cost you your job! One day the Head of Airedale College called Butler to a tribunal where he was

I'd got to know Paul quite well over a year or so. But imagine my surprise when one day he turned up in orange robes and yellow paint on his forehead. He'd been a full practising Hare Krishna the whole time I'd know him and he'd never mentioned it!

JULIAN BUTLER
(SMILE ORANGE FILMS)

Nigel 'Gilly' Gill (left) being made more British by the stapling of a cheap plastic Union Jack to his tight-fitting crop top.

told that he was in serious shit. A Smile Orange short film called Mankillsport had been found in Butler's office and it contained footage of a student's naked penis, ball-sack and pubic region.

This was bad news and could possibly jeopardise everything Butler and Bousfield had worked so selflessly for. Almost half of *Fatliners* was cast from the college's students and they couldn't afford to lose them. This didn't look good. The duo began to wonder if their plans to make Britain's most financially successful film would ever be realised. That is the end of this chapter.

CHAPTER TWENTY-FIVE
DIRECTING

WHAT IS DIRECTING?

I will now write brilliantly about directing. Although of course the truth is if I did know anything about directing I'd be directing something wouldn't I and not sat here writing this book? Oh well, here goes. A director is the person in charge of a film. To be honest you should really know this by now as you are more than halfway through a book on filmmaking. If you need telling again then you're probably wasting your time here, someone like you is better off filling pies.

FUN FACT

Believe it or not Gustaf Brecht, the director of *The King and I* was actually a real king!!! On set, King Gustaf travelled by horse drawn golden coach, sat upon a royal cushion and had everyone call him 'your majesty', even Yul Brynner. After directing *The King and I*, Gustaf entered his political phase and directed a gritty kitchen sink drama about the problems of the owner of a country who accidentally gets pregnant.

WHAT IS A DIRECTOR?

As a director you must confront the human condition. In 1997 Smile Orange Films' Julian Butler was confronting his own human condition at a hideously corrupt tribunal at Airedale College. The reason for the tribunal was that the college believed that, whilst making a short film called Mankillsport, Butler had filmed the naked shaft and scrotum of students for his own entertainment.

SMILE ORANGE FILMOGRAPHY

MANKILLSPORT (1997)
Short / 4 mins / MiniDV

Film about a group of hunters whose human quarry is stripped naked from the waist down and hunted through the woods. We see the hunters as they chase a naked young man and as he runs his penis is often gratuitously and disgustingly displayed.

In the end Butler told the hearing not to worry because the flapping cock didn't belong to a student but instead to one of the college's lecturers. With the unfortunate misunderstanding

> The tribunal was a bit of a kangaroo court to be honest, they said Mankillsport was inappropriate so I asked them to define what was inappropriate about it. They couldn't. It was funny.

JULIAN BUTLER

(SMILE ORANGE FILMS)

cleared up Butler kept his job and the filming of *Fatliners* was GO, GO, GO!!!!! YEAHHH!!!!!

HOW DOES ONE DIRECT AN HISTORICAL DRAMA?

Many films are set in the past, these are called historical dramas. But how do you achieve that historically accurate look for your film? Well, it's all in the detail. Butler and Bousfield insisted that, for *Fatliners*, the historical locations would be accurate to the most microscopic detail. Then they looked at their budget of £0 and decided that they would just film in places that were free.

You know that BBC camo net we talked about earlier? Well here it is again. This time in *Fatliners*.

SMILE ORANGE FILMOGRAPHY

FATLINERS (1997)
Action Movie / 91 mins / Hi8, Umatic, 8mm, Betacam, SVHC / Colour / Director: Massive Faal Arse / The Bacon Messiah Company / The Watch 'n' Wipe Corporation / These credits are complete nonsense and nine minutes long FOR GOD'S SAKE! Just buy a copy and check them for yourself if you're that bothered Johnny Pigram.

Fatliners is an awful looking film with awful music and awful acting, but that's fine because the script is shit as well. The film is set in a world where everyone is a wrestler and follows a group of bad grapplers who travel back and forth through time trying to change history in favour of the bad guy. Their time meddling leads to Goliath beating David, Hitler defeating Churchill and Dracula killing Dr Van Helsing. Thankfully on their trail is our hero, wrestler Ooge 'Appy Daddy. 'Will the bad guys overthrow the natural order of the universe or will Daddy stop them?' is a question that you never ask whilst sitting through it all.

Every director's dream: Brian Turner as Van Helsing.

Butler and Bousfield direct two powerful men who are having a go.

Dracula's lair from *Fatliners*. On the walls are the torches that nearly killed the entire cast and crew.

One of these free locations was a school near Keighley where the film's vampire scene was shot. The scene is notable for the exciting return of the

Some actors on a set waiting to obey the command of the director.

Nosferatu looked good, monstrous.

GUS BOUSFIELD
(SMILE ORANGE FILMS)

stolen BBC camouflage netting. Another exciting moment was when some burning torches filled the cellar the team were filming in with carbon monoxide and nearly killed everyone.

FUN FACT

The country with the most directors is obviously the USA. But where in America is the biggest director? Answer: Alaska! Maybe it's the fried food!!!

L-R: Nigel Cook and Eugene Levine at Hyde Park Cinema, Leeds, about to be directed

WHAT IS THE FUTURE OF FILM DIRECTING?

I haven't seen Malcolm from Cottingley for many weeks even though I've looked for him everywhere. He did recently text me though, saying that, with the rise of cheaper and more reliable communication technology, it is now possible to direct films from home via Skype. Sadly this will hinder one of the more common Smile Orange directing styles, that of slapping actors and laughing at them until they do as they are told.

BRITAIN'S GREATEST DIRECTORS
BY VETERAN PRODUCER PETER WARD

KENNY LOACH: That lanky, specky Northern puff, constantly whines on about the dignity of being a scuffer.

NICOLAS 'STUTTERING' ROEG: Fit wife. Wish I'd streamed in there while he was stoned out of his tiny little mind.

LINDSEY ANDERSON: Girl's name. Girl's films. About young boys. *If....* is *St Trinian's* without the tarts.

JOHN BOORMAN: His son, Charley, is a drop out. Such an embarrassment.

BASIL DREARDEN: Poor old dreary Drearden and his frumpy old comedies. He had his mumsy on set with him at all times. Always had to be home to for his seven o'clock tea. I have a lot of time for the man, and his mum and his dad... all at the same time.

RICHARD LESTER: Went to Leicester in a sou'wester and shagged a jester until he got a blister. I could go on but I won't.

CHAPTER TWENTY-SIX
NON-LINEAR EDITING

John Bentham (right) often rubbed shoulders with living legends — people like Smile Orange Films. Unfortunately Bentham also occasionally lowered himself to talk to boring people — people like Muhammad Ali (left).

WHAT IS NON-LINEAR EDITING?

Non-linear editing is a computer based method of image manipulation which allows the editor to change images ad infinitum. Ad infinitum is Latin for 'adding up infinitely'. The symbol for infinity is ∞. The symbol for infinity In Hebrew is ב. Mathematicians tell us that there are an infinite number of infinities, the symbol they wanked out for this is ☺.

WHO WAS THE FIRST NON-LINEAR EDITOR?

In Ancient Greece, 412 BCE, the philosopher Platypus became unhappy with other people's memories of himself. So he got actors to re-enact scenes from his life but changed them in his favour. Platypus then got his friends to watch

these re-enactments insisting that they replace the old memory of the event with the new one. He became so obsessed that if someone in the village had an opposing memory of him he would kill them for the sake of continuity. There's no punchline here, that's it.

Fast forward to 1997 and Smile Orange's Butler and Bousfield finally finished filming *Fatliners*. Butler edited a promotional trailer and showed it, once again, at the Raindance 'We Show Owt' Film Festival. After the screening the duo was approached by a skinny, bespectacled man called John Bentham. Bentham ran a Punk and Oi! video distribution company in Lytham St Anne's called Screen Edge. Screen Edge were looking to distribute low-budget films and offered to pay for the post, mix and master of *Fatliners* in exchange for worldwide distribution rights. Smile Orange Films thought they knew what half of that meant and so they agreed. The next stage was to travel up to Lytham and start the edit.

FILM FACT

Non-linear editors collect small objects and take them back to their nest where they arrange them at the entrance in a manner that they find pleasing to the eye. They then dance around the objects to attract a mate.

WHERE WILL I FIND A NON-LINEAR EDITING SUITE?

The location of non-linear edit suites can be located in many varied locations. In 2014 when Will Smith directed the sci-fi fantasy film *After Birth*, starring his son Wally Smith, the edit suite was located inside the right heart ventricle of the Eastern religious figure, Gautama Buddha. When editing *Fatliners*, Smile Orange's non-linear edit suite was located in a similarly esoteric place: The stinky kitchen of a damp and mouldy office in a

As always, when we tried to mix Smile Orange with professional types the films always suffered. I had already edited a reference version of *Fatliners* at Airedale College and then I had to re-edit it on the non-linear editing suite. So I actually edited it twice. When digitising the rushes we ran them through a colour corrector which shifted all the colours an inch to the left. We had to stay up a whole night to re-correct the colour corrector. Coincidentally the scene I was editing at the time featured a futuristic version of *The Gladiators* called 'The Correctors'. It was a farce of epic proportions. Even if we went to Skywalker Ranch I'm sure they'd still fuck it up.

JULIAN BUTLER
(SMILE ORANGE FILMS)

John was a big advocate of low-budget filmmaking and when talking about Smile Orange John kept quoting his line 'It's the wine that's important not the bottle'. At first we thought that what he was saying about us was 'ignore their clothes, they've got beautiful bodies'. But then we realised he was saying that a film made on video could be just as valid as those made on film. I'd have preferred it if he was just on about our bodies.

BOB PRIESTLEY
(SMILE ORANGE FILMS)

terrace street in Lytham St. Anne's.

This was the first time Smile Orange had embraced the revolutionary technology of the non-linear editing systems. It made the whole process much longer and the film a lot worse.

WHAT DO THE TOILET FACILITIES IN A NON-LINEAR EDIT SUITE LOOK LIKE?

The toilet facilities in a non-linear edit

FUN FACT
A dusty indoor rubber plant is the closest an editor will ever see of nature for the term of their natural life.

suite are always of the highest standard. One time, when Butler enjoyed an all-night editing session in the building, the security system meant that he couldn't leave the room. This meant that Butler's empty cola cans became rudimentary toilets and, on one occasion, he forgot that the can next to him contained urine and thirstily drank from it.

PRO TIP

Drinking piss isn't too bad when you don't know what you're drinking. Urine does not have an unpleasant taste. But then when you suddenly realise what you've done some sort of psychological imprinting kicks in and you suddenly start retching with disgust.

JULIAN BUTLER
(SMILE ORANGE FILMS)

Butler and Bousfield take a break from editing and enjoy the seaside town of Lytham St Annes.

FUN FACT

When an editor wants to die they stop pissing in cans. The urine builds up and they are finally torn apart by an exploding bladder.

WHAT SKILLS DOES ONE NEED TO BECOME A NON-LINEAR EDITOR?

The non-linear editor is a pixel pusher, the ultimate shit-shiner and, as we know, shining shit is impossible. Luckily, being a non-linear editor also involves pissing in empty coke cans and, as we know, anyone can do this. If you can piss in an empty coke can you are halfway to being a non-linear editor. Ignore the shit-shining for now.

WHAT IS THE FUTURE FOR NON-LINEAR EDITING?

In twelve billion years' time the Multiverses will begin to end. Then will come the day of reckoning when all souls will rise and reclaim this fertile paradise. All editors will visit God whose edit suite will have its own built-in Mr Kipling French Fancy dispenser that will let an editor eat one every time they do a good edit. Like a trained rat. This will continue for eternity. That's what Malcolm in Cottingley told me. Via my dreams. He's still physically missing.

CHAPTER TWENTY-SEVEN
COMPUTER GENERATED IMAGERY

WHAT IS COMPUTER GENERATED IMAGERY?

Computer generated imagery (CGI) is the application of computer graphics to create or contribute to films, television programmes, commercials, videos, calculators, road signs, washing machine display screens and seemingly every other fucking appliance you can stick a fucking screen to. Nowadays every device needs to have a fucking squinting cat on a screen somewhere telling you that you're doing it wrong.

WHAT IS THE HISTORY OF CGI?

We all love the current batch of CGI movies like 漢字, 漢字2 and 字漢. But none of these cinematic wonders would even exist without the ground-breaking computer effects work by Smile Orange Films on *Fatliners*. According to Smile Orange Films, *Fatliners* was the first movie to ever use CGI and in the process they invented the industry working practices still used today: Farming out jobs to non-paid males working twenty-three and a half hours a day with a thirty-minute wank break.

WHEN SHOULD I USE CGI?

All modern films are 99.7% CGI. But back in 1997 CGI was completely unheard of and people would walk around constantly asking 'what the fuck is CGI?' The answer

Stinky Pudding: A man made entirely from dough.

to this question was, of course, 'Fatliners'. The film's CGI effects included the Earth in the shape of a wrestling ring and Heaven as a line of terraced houses. To make these remarkable images Butler and Bousfield recruited Miserable CGI Lad from a course at Bradford University and kindly promised not to pay him.

WHAT ARE THE PROBLEMS OF CASTING NON-CGI ACTORS?

One problem with casting real actors

An example of CGI from *Fatliners*: The Earth in the shape of a wrestling ring. That's what Smile Orange thought of. So that's what you can see.

Over-egging the pudding with another picture of Stinky Pudding.

Cameraboy Andrew Boldy on the set of *Fatliners*.

is the potential for them to create conflict. The most quoted example is during the making of Apocalypse Now when that fat actor wanted some more money. And that hippy one was full-on shouting constantly and at one point everyone just wanted to go home and they were all off their heads on drugs weren't they?

HOW DO I COMBINE CGI WITH LIVE ACTION?

Nowadays live action is shot against green screen, then the green is removed using Chroma key and the CGI is inserted. Here's how Smile Orange Films recommend using Chroma key when filming a scene involving a thirty foot high giant robot:

The giant robot as it appears in *Fatliners*: Proof that bigger is not always better. Unless you are Giant Haystacks (see previous chapter).

All I remember about the Miserable CGI Lad was he didn't want to do it. Thinking about it now the only reason he agreed to do it may have been that his tutor made him.

JULIAN BUTLER (SMILE ORANGE FILMS)

Giant robot at the Smile Orange club night 'Skinny Dipping'. This picture is here just to make sure you are in no doubt about how large the robot was.

Smile Orange Films are already planning a digital Austin Oates. Think the same but even slower to render.

BOB PRIESTLEY
(SMILE ORANGE FILMS)

• Make your robot in nine large Papier Mâché pieces, each big enough to fill your front room. This huge undertaking will take you many weeks, hundreds of newspapers, countless bags of wallpaper paste and roll upon roll of chicken wire.

• You will now need to transport your robot to a cheap warehouse in Bradford. The pieces will be so big that you will have to transport each piece, tied with household string, on the roof of your production office van. This will take many trips.

• At the warehouse, paint a thirty foot high wall in green paint.

• Reassemble the robot in front of the green wall and film the scene.

• Later, in post-production, use Chroma key to remove the green wall and superimpose the thirty foot high robot into your scene.

• Suddenly realise that you could have just filmed a tiny model robot and it would have looked just as big.

• Instead of feeling stupid, transport the whole robot, bit by bit, on top of your production office and set it up at a club night called Skinny Dipping you have foolishly decided to start running.

• At the club's opening night, ignore the fact that the robot is constantly threatening to topple over onto the loved-up heads of the ravers below and call the whole process a success.

WHEN SHOULD I USE PROSTHETICS INSTEAD OF CGI?
There are still moments in movies when old fashioned prosthetics are called for.

Juliet Uren and Gus Bousfield strap a robot torso to the Smile Orange production office's roof-rack.

An example of the ground-breaking work carried out by the *Fatliners* prosthetics team: A wrestling insect called Width Wasp.

An another example of the ground-breaking work carried out by the *Fatliners* prosthetics team: Tits in a jar.

Fatliners was no different and so *The Hunt for the Yorkshire Grimace*'s talented prosthetics FX team wee enlisted for the film. The team immediately set to work making numerous characters including one in particular; a man who was made entirely from dough. The FX team accomplished this by making a beautifully textured latex costume, Smile Orange didn't like it and threw a load of real dough over the top.

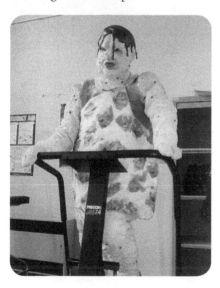

A year later Smile Orange Films were invited to appear at a glittering magazine launch party in a fashionable Leeds bar, dressed as characters from *Fatliners*. Many media players were in attendance and it was a good chance for the filmmakers to network with prime movers from the Northern media scene. On the evening of the event, moments before walking out

amongst the glitterati, the Smile Orange team took the dough bodysuit from its protective bin liner. To their horror they saw that, having been left forgotten in a car boot for a year, the dough had gone off and the costume was entombed in mould. With nothing else to wear and not wanting to let the event organisers down, Julian Butler marched into the bar head to toe in mould and stinking like a butcher's manhole. The team proceeded to delight themselves by clumsily wrestling each other for several hours, tipping over tables and spilling drinks.

At the end of the night the bar's manager revealed that he had been less than happy with the six foot Bradfordian in the dough costume who was infecting his bar with a crumbling snowstorm of contagious bacteria. He told Butler that 'your clowns weren't funny'. 'That's because the staff had no sense of humour' quipped Butler as he shuffled

More revolutuionary CGI from *Fatliners*.

Non-CGI props and costumes being made in the Smile Orange studio workshop (Butler's dad's garage).

Giant snake from *Fatliners*: Absolute proof that the right make up is more realistic than CGI.

proudly away dragging behind him a giant clod so mouldy it flaunted every kitchen hygiene rule in existence. And that is why you should use prosthetics instead of CGI.

WHAT IS THE FUTURE OF CGI?

After disappearing for days, Malcolm turned up at my house at 3am and told me that when considering the use of digitally created actors we will have to deal with the problem of the uncanny valley. The uncanny valley is a term given to something that tries to imitate a human but ends up just looking creepy. Smile Orange Films don't see this as a problem though because their actors have

always looked creepy anyway. Their actors grew up in the uncanny valley, they're at home there and so the coming of digital actors can only be a good thing for Smile Orange Films.

Fill the uncanny valley in with rubble and concrete it over, I say.

BOB PRIESTLEY (SMILE ORANGE FILMS)

CHAPTER TWENTY-EIGHT
SOUND DESIGN

WHAT IS SOUND DESIGN?

Sound design is the process of generating audio elements and applying them to the soundtrack of a production. The term 'sound design' includes the words SOUND and the word DESIGN. The definition of the word SOUND is obvious. Then there's the word DESIGN. Surely you can't design sound? What the fuck is being said here? How can you design something you can't touch, that's just taking all this stuff a bit too far.

WHAT IS THE HISTORY OF SOUND DESIGN?

In silent films the entire sound team was one man and a piano. This was never bettered until John Carpenter found a synthesiser at a car boot sale in Brooklyn in 1972. At that point the barrel house honky-tonk pianos fell silent across the land and cheap ominous noodling synth sounds echoed out across badly made

A fruit machine like this might have sounds coming out of it like 'WOOOOO!!! WOOOOO!!! WOOOOO!!!! and CHUKA!!! CHUKA!!! CHUKA!!! Sounds heard near the machine might include 'BASTARD!!!!'.

miniatures of the surface of Mars or communal living areas in the South Pole for eternity. Oh hang on, have I been talking about soundtracks instead of sound design? I might have done. Been a long week. Just got back from the Isle

"

PRO TIP

The noises made by the boys and girls or man or gran in your back garden that you filmed can be loud or can be quiet. They need to be all the same loudness so people, when they listen, aren't getting shouted at or whispered at by the boys and girls or man or gran in your back garden (or location as it's called in *Semi-Professional Filmmaker Magazine*. That mag is a beauty!).

NICKY HINCHCLIFFE
(TOP HOLLYWOOD DIRECTOR)

PRO TIP

Sound designers are the sort of guys who spend their time messing about with bits and pieces to make the most awful cacophony since Beyoncé stomped around on stage. This lot should be stricken from the budget immediately.

PETER WARD
(VETERAN PRODUCER)

of Man TT. Amazing burnouts at the end this year. When will Guy Martin win? He deserves it sooo much. And that is the history of sound design.

WHAT IS A SOUNDTRACK?

A soundtrack is recorded music accompanying and synchronised to the images of a film, television programme or fruit machine. Famous soundtracks include *Grease*, *The Singing Detective* and Lucky Winner$$$$. Soundtracks are often composed by great composers who spend years learning their craft and employ only the best orchestras

and musicians to record intricate and considered musical scores. On the other hand, like Smile Orange Films, you can knock it out in a makeshift studio in a kitchen in Lytham St Anne's on a cheap second-hand Atari.

WHAT IS A SOUND MIX?

One important part of the sound design process is the final sound mix. This happens in a sound studio where the audio tracks are mixed, mastered and finally synced (or 'jizzed') over the finished film. Essential equipment you will find in any good sound studio includes: Appalling lighting, primary colours everywhere for no good reason, a filthy kitchen, mouldy coffee in cups, cracked double glazed windows dripping with condensation, dust, dung, dark, pizza boxes that have tapes in them instead of food, broken Lucky Winner$$$$ machines, an old folded up bicycle, shop dummies and a vaguely tortuous feeling.

WHAT IS A VOICE OVER?

The voice over is a way of introducing

When I was writing the soundtrack to *Fatliners*, in the Screen Edge kitchen, people would lean across me to put the kettle on. Very distracting. My advice to people writing a soundtrack would be to do it as fast as possible if you are in the kitchen.

GUS BOUSFIELD
(SMILE ORANGE FILMS)

A modern sound recording studio.

the narrative or themes of a film with the use of the spoken word. Voice overs are usually recorded in a recording studio or under a duvet. The advantages of recording in a professional studio instead of under a duvet are that you can fit in a producer, the executive producer and the director to argue over every single syllable and pretend it actually matters. They're all stressed. It's all bullshit. But they still get to believe it's all so important. That is what a voice over is.

FILM FACT

If you want to get good quality, accurate and well recorded foley sounds then obtain them in the old fashioned, time-honoured way: Download them from Freesound.org.

sound effect for a scene where a cabbage is hit with a hammer.

WHAT IS FOLEY?

'Foley' is another word for sound effects. The word 'foley' actually refers to the inventor of sound effects who was a young horse by the name of Philip Richardson. There are many tricks of the trade associated with recording foley. For example: Chopping a dead man's skull in half with a large sword can be used as a

HOW DO I RECORD FOLEY?

Foley can be recorded in various ways. The producers of *Fatliners* cannot remember any of these ways. There is a sound effect whenever a wrestler flies down the time tunnel in *Fatliners* which sounds like a bog being flushed. So the film's producers can only deduce that this foley was created by recording the sound

A GUIDE TO FOLEY
BY VETERAN PRODUCER PETER WARD

• The sound of egg shells can be used as the sound of fingers cracking.

• The sound of banana peel slapped in the face of a neighbour can be used as the sound of dolphins mating.

• The sound of a champagne bottle being wielded by a large galloping Yorkshire man shouting 'LOOK, I AM EMPLOYED!!!' can be used as anything in a Ken Loach film. Whether set in Glasgow, Newcastle or The Wirral it doesn't matter, Ken Loach has discovered that where there's some poor sot being downtrodden, by some fucker you may have seen on *Emmerdale*, there's both pathos and bathos… And he's ready to exploit it in the name of socialism.

Gus Bousfield in his kitchen studio.

of a bog being flushed. In conclusion the job of foley artist is not one of the most important jobs in audio post-production but if used correctly foley can enhance the viewer's immersive experience a tiny bit, helping them to imagine that they are actually in some bogs.

FUN FACT

All the foley you will ever need can be captured in some bogs in the market in Wigan with a PZM tied to a plank. I did this on my film Big Trouble in Some Bogs in Wigan. But It doesn't have to be Wigan, there are plenty of other shitholes around.

PETER WARD
(VETERAN PRODUCER)

WHAT DOES A FOLEY ARTIST DO?

When the foley sounds have been recorded the foley artist syncs them with the picture and bang (or plop), your film is a tiny bit less worse than it was. It's still shit of course but then all your films are, aren't they? I mean just look at you.

WHAT IS THE FUTURE OF SOUND DESIGN?

Malcolm in Cottingley tells me: 'I've been watching the news recently and I'm seeing everything blowing up in the world. Not much hope for the future of anything, let alone people who bash turnips with a mallet for a living. It's inconsequential whether these people live or die. If we make it to 2050 alive, I'll fucking suck my own dick.'

CHAPTER TWENTY-NINE
CERTIFICATION

WHAT IS CERTIFICATION?

Certification is designed to classify films with regard to suitability for audiences in terms of issues such as sex, violence, substance abuse, profanity and farts. With soundtrack and foley added, *Fatliners* was now finally complete and ready to be certificated.

HOW DILIGENT ARE THE BBFC?

The BBFC have a reputation for being extremely diligent when certificating films. Smile Orange Films' Julian Butler and Gus Bousfield decided to test this diligence by inserting a personal insult, aimed at the then BBFC Director within their film *Fatliners*. It was one of the most offensive things the imaginative duo had ever come up with, involving not only the BBFC Director, but his family. The insult read:

The text was hidden in the middle of nine minutes of made-up names and nonsense which constitutes *Fatliners'* credits. Butler & Bousfield were keen to see if the BBFC would actually read every single word of this gibberish and, if the BBFC Director did find the insult, they hoped he would fly into a furious rage and retaliate, banning films in the UK altogether.

A typical BBFC employee.

FILM FACT

In Britain, film certification is carried out by the British Board of Film Censors (BBFC). A BBFC certificate must be awarded to any film that is released in the UK. Certification is obligatory and correct and It is important that our magnificent society is maintained by the diligence of an elite few that truly understand films and have been granted the right to protect the huddled masses from being harmed.

HOW MUCH DOES IT COST TO GET MY FILM CERTIFICATED?

It costs £500 to get your film certificated by the BBFC. Screen Edge agreed to pay for *Fatliners'* certification and for such a small company this was a big expense. What's more, if *Fatliners* was rejected then Screen Edge would have to pay for the re-editing and a further £500 re-submission fee. Because of this, John Bentham was very keen not to piss off the BBFC.

When Bentham came to hear what Smile Orange Films had written in the *Fatliners* credits he stormed up to Gus Bousfield in the Screen Edge kitchen/music studio and pushed him up against a wall. From his gritted teeth, red face and bulging eyes Bousfield surmised that Bentham wasn't happy. Millimetres from Bousfield's face Bentham screamed the words:

Bentham also said he was going to cancel the distribution of *Fatliners*. This was a disaster! But if you read the next chapter you will find out what the outcome of this was.

We were genuinely baffled by John's reaction. We honestly thought he would find it funny.

JULIAN BUTLER (SMILE ORANGE FILMS)

WHO PLAYED THE SHIMMERMAN ?
SHIMMERMAN PLAYED BY HOOPER

OH I SEE, AND WHO PLAYED HARDARSE ?
THAT GREAT THESPIAN, SPLITTY McCHEEKS

AND PLEASE TELL ME, THE WIDTHWASP
WHO INTERPRETED THAT BRILLIANT ROLE ?
OI FRANKIE

Just a small example from the seven minutes of the made-up names in the credits of *Fatliners*.

WHAT IS THE FUTURE FOR FILM CERTIFICATION?

Good.

THE BRITISH FILM CERTIFICATION SYSTEM CERTIFICATE CONSUMER ADVICE

'E' (OR EXEMPT)
Films that are educational or instructive about fishing.
'U' (UNIVERSAL)
Films that are available throughout the Universe.
PG (PARENTS AND GUARDIANS)
Films given as unwanted Christmas presents.
12 (NOON)
Films to be watched in the pre-lunch watershed.
15 (FIFTEEN)
Films to be watched by a minimum group of fifteen people.
80 (EIGHTY)
Films to be watched by eighty year olds.

CHAPTER THIRTY
THE PREMIERE

Guy Martin.
What a
great guy.

WHAT IS A PREMIERE?

A premiere refers to the debut of a finished body of work. The word comes from the French word première, meaning 'perm'.

WHAT IS THE HISTORY OF FILM PREMIERES?

When will Guy Martin win his premiere TT race, that's the real question? Guy Martin is a Superhero to me. Love Guy! LOVE GUY!!! He deserves it so much. He tries to make a tin of baked beans with his mate on TV but they had no real banter did they? They had their one joke, which was 'young man' didn't they? None of that taints his skill on the motorcycle though. Superbike, Supercar, Superstock and Supersidecars. All on that awesome Tyco Suzuki! Hang on, is it BMW now!??? AWESOME!!!

WHEN SHOULD I PREMIERE MY FILM?

Your film should only be premiered when it has been granted a proper certificate by the BBFC. Unfortunately this was never going to happen for Smile Orange Film's *Fatliners* because producers Julian Butler and Gus Bousfield had inserted a cruel insult about BBFC Director (and his family) (particularly his mother) in the film's credits.

Flyers for
the *Fatliners*
Raindance
screening.

Luckily, once the film's distributor, John Bentham, stopped throttling Bousfield, he realised that the film hadn't even been submitted to the BBFC yet. So Butler and Bousfield agreed to remove the offending paragraph and, with a massive blank space in the credits where the rude words had been, *Fatliners* passed with an 18 certificate. The film was ready to premiere.

WHERE SHOULD I PREMIERE MY FILM?

A film premiere should be held in a 21% oxygen environment with plenty of water and some form of energy source. The *Fatliners'* UK premiere occurred in such an environment: The 1997 Raindance 'We Show Owt' Film Festival and the Smile Orange producers had a good idea how to make the event go off with a bang. They were going to shoot the audience with a gun.

WHAT SHOULD I TAKE TO MY FILM PREMIERE?

A good producer will take business cards and a press kit to their premiere. A Smile Orange producer will take a gun. Nobody knew why, but Smile Orange's Bob Priestley had lived in London for a few years by now. On the night before the premiere, Bousfield and Butler stayed at Priestley's London council flat on the Ethelred Estate. Butler had his big black

sports bag that always terrified Priestley because he knew something scary was going to come out of it. This time a gun came out of it.

Butler and Bousfield wanted to test the gun and proposed firing it in Priestley's flat. The Ethelred Estate was no stranger to gun crime and Priestley was extremely anxious about causing any trouble. So Butler and Bousfield fired it anyway.

Having made sure the gun fired properly Butler and Bousfield put it back

Very loud it was. Deafening. Very small flat too. I'm not sure but, afterwards, I think I might have hit Bousfield on the head with a stick. As retaliation. Violence is always confusing.

BOB PRIESTLEY (SMILE ORANGE FILMS)

in the black bag along with some masks, costumes and flyers and set off to the glamorous showbiz premiere of their film at the Rex Cinema, Piccadilly Circus.

Fatliners in the Raindance 'We Show Owt' Film Festival programme.

Fatliners

Director: Brett Metcalf
Video, 4 min, trailer for feature film
Contact: Smile Orange Pictures, 29 Villa Road, Bingley, west Yorkshire, BD16 4EU Tel: 01274 568814 Fax: 01274 562656
A fantasy universe of wrestling and time travel, where Oooge Appy Daddy and his Sidekick are on the case.
Producer Julian Butler and Brett Metcalf are part of the new wave of British filmmakers who are attempting to forge a new visual dialogue with their audiences. Working with the most bare bones of budgets, they manage to create believable fantasy worlds which are shocking and amusing. Turning to the world of politics for their subject matter, their films are bold and controversial.

I can't remember the cinema specifically; to me every cinema is the same, just a maroon environment. A place of grotty exuberance.

BOB PRIESTLEY
(SMILE ORANGE FILMS)

Brian Turner, of film collective Ontolocide Uberbilde, was cast as Dr Van Helsing in *Fatliners*. Tuner was first to arrive at the film's premiere and greeted Butler by immediately attacking him. Butler threw him down some stairs and tipped all the flyers over him. Turner retaliated by farting and shouting 'GAS! GAS!' With this move he won the fight. Immediately afterwards the group dressed up as wrestlers and started handing flyers out.

Flyering was fun, you got to meet lots of other filmmakers, as well as angry waitresses. This was the first time we realised who the typical filmmaker was: Someone who had 'a good script' but 'just needed a good producer'. We didn't realise how lucky we were that we already had our own team. We never went to see any other films at any of these film festivals. We drank and got stoned. We didn't need anything or anyone else.

BOB PRIESTLEY
(SMILE ORANGE FILMS)

WHAT IS A TWELVE-DIMENSIONAL PREMIERE?
The flyers for the *Fatliners* show

Actor Brian Turner arrives at the *Fatliners* film premiere.

From Sundance to SXSW, film festivals seem to be magnets for the tragic. One bloke showed me a series of storyboards for a film he wanted to make about John Merrick, the Elephant Man. I kept telling him it had already been done but he wouldn't listen.

JULIAN BUTLER
(SMILE ORANGE FILMS)

announced a 'special twelve-dimensional screening' and the concept was simple: As the film was being shown the film's stars would act out scenes live in front of the screen. It was described as a twelve-dimensional screening as a reference to the point in the film when one of the characters talks about his belief in the

A lot of filmmakers get all sweaty about seeing their film on the big screen at some Leicester Square dive. I always thought that was boring. I didn't even want to watch our film ever again. I liked dicking about in a field with a camera then I liked to forget about it.

BOB PRIESTLEY
(SMILE ORANGE FILMS)

existence of twelve dimensions.

The flyering had worked and the screening was full. Lots of friends of Smile Orange turned up for the premiere and they were immediately recruited to dress up and perform. The film's distributor John Bentham was also in attendance and, as a special treat, he had taken LSD.

Behind the scenes at the *Fatliners* Raindance screening 2 (note: Pistol).

I was impressed because John was using the first digital camera I'd ever seen. I was doubly impressed because he was tripping at the time.

BOB PRIESTLEY

(SMILE ORANGE FILMS)

IN THE SCARY BLACK BAG THE GUN BEGAN TO GIGGLE

The film began and, to introduce the twelve-dimensional concept, a group of people dressed as wrestlers marched around in front of the screen. Next came the part in the film when we see a wrestler (played by erotic star Paul Beverley) naked in the showers. At this point Butler, Bousfield and Priestley jumped up onto the low stage in front of the screen and wrestled each other naked.

The gun was next. It was loaded and given to Smile Orange actor Richard Saint. Saint looked scary anyway, a 6ft 5 skinhead. But to exaggerate this he was dressed in an SS uniform. When the Hitler

I remember hearing my cock slapping on my leg as I ran down to the front in the darkness. I thought the noise would give the game away. I thought 'if we were going to do this then it might as well be good but this is working against me. Literally. Once we'd started wrestling I remember the video projector was either very bright or I might have been wearing a wrestling mask which had slipped over my eyes because I remember being blinded throughout. Having no visual record is a good way to get through things like this.

BOB PRIESTLEY
(SMILE ORANGE FILMS)

That nude scene at the premiere, that was genius that was. Just havoc. I was wrestling naked on the floor with Butler which must have been horrific for people down the front. But funny. Lots of people who didn't know me came up at the end and said they liked it. A girl I talked to after said that there are not enough cocks flapping about at film premieres.

GUS BOUSFIELD
(SMILE ORANGE FILMS)

After we'd been writhing on top of each other for a while I decided to look up into the faces of the audience. I remember seeing everyone in the packed cinema staring agog at us, mouths gaping involuntarily in complete disbelief. They were shocked and, of course, a little bit turned on. Who can blame them. This is the first recorded instance of the Human Windsock effect (see Glossary).

JULIAN BUTLER
(SMILE ORANGE FILMS)

Behind the scenes at the *Fatliners* Raindance screening 1.

paused, turned, pointed the gun at the audience and squeezed the trigger. The sound was like an explosion. It was an explosion.

Someone screamed. This is probably what made Saint laugh. He was now at the front of the theatre, the film flickering onto him as he faced the audience. He pointed the gun at them and fired again and again and again.

scene in *Fatliners* started Saint goose-stepped into the cinema. Halfway to the screen, with the light from the projector exaggerating his brutal bald head, he

I saw the flash go off and it illuminated Richard Saint's face. He was laughing cruelly. He did look like a real Nazi. Properly scary.

BOB PRIESTLEY
(SMILE ORANGE FILMS)

WHAT ARE THE RESULTS OF A TWELVE-DIMENSIONAL PREMIERE?

Of course good natured, sadomasochist Nazi enthusiast Richard Saint was only firing blanks at the audience. So when John Bentham finally stopped screaming and came down off his LSD trip he began wondering if this was just the sort of thing that an international audience would appreciate. As his mind cleared he started to ponder what would happen if he was to take *Fatliners* to the most glamorous film event in the Multiverses: The Cannes Film Festival.

CHAPTER THIRTY-ONE
THE CANNES FILM FESTIVAL

This is one of the badges distributed in Cannes by John Bentham. Note: It is actually impossible to physically fuck a production value.

WHAT IS THE CANNES FILM FESTIVAL?

The Cannes Film Festival is a festival held every year in Italy. The selection process for the world's largest international showcase of cinematic art is gruelling and only the most celebrated movies are chosen to appear at the glittering event. Or, like Smile Orange Films, you can just pay £400 to the organisers and you're in.

We knew that we were really going against the grain showing a no-budget shot-on-video movie. So we got badges made saying 'fuck production values' just to press the point home. As the week progressed these badges became extremely popular. It was almost like, the more successful people were, the more they liked to wear them. Very odd.

JOHN BENTHAM
(SCREEN EDGE)

I remember those badges, they were manufactured to a very high standard. The fucking irony.

BOB PRIESTLEY
(SMILE ORANGE FILMS)

HOW SHOULD I DRESS AT THE CANNES FILM FESTIVAL?

Successful networking at the Cannes Film Festival relies on great flyering, a well-honed pitching technique and dressing in a wrestling mask. Let's take a candid, or should I say 'Cannes-did' (good joke) look at the best way to dress whilst networking at the festival.

Just look at that, that's fucking weird. There's people laughing at them in the background too.

• Men: A cheap wrestling costume made from bright green, Bradford market leggings, pink fluorescent cape and mask stitched crudely from an old t-shirt. Wear your costume for the entirety of the festival and also clutch a Morrison's shopping bag full of cheaply photocopied flyers for your film which you should hand to every single person you meet. If you can't afford a good wrestling costume then wear what every other numpty does

Because I was dressed as a wrestler I saw the whole festival through tiny eye-holes stabbed through an old t-shirt I'd sewn into a mask. My view was quite restricted. I think I met Lloyd Kaufman, Sigourney Weaver and Barry Norman but I can't be sure.

**JULIAN BUTLER
(SMILE ORANGE FILMS)**

We gave out a lot of flyers dressed as wrestlers, we were putting out flyers over someone else's flyers and some men came over and menaced us. They told us to go with them and they took us to a hotel room. Inside was Lloyd Kaufman of Troma films. He just laughed. Another time there was a fashion show being staged on the red carpet. We were stood to the side watching these attractive models doing this fashion catwalk and a couple of them beckoned us up. And so, wearing our masks and Bradford market tights and in front of hundreds of people, we got up and joined them marching up and down the catwalk.

**GUS BOUSFIELD
(SMILE ORANGE FILMS)**

A flyer for the Cannes screening of *Fatliners*.

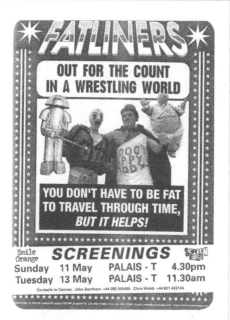

There were cameras everywhere, the lads of course proved popular in their cosies and got to do a fair few interviews. Live TV were struggling a bit trying to interview them in the bar of the Martinez Hotel. Their hand held mic was faulty and the camera-mic wasn't working too well with all the room noise. Julian [Butler]'s solution was to shout all the answers at the top of his voice. He then, of course, had the attention of the whole room and had everyone in stitches.

JOHN BENTHAM (SCREEN EDGE)

— a linen jacket with pink shirt tucked into white jeans and cowboy boots, maybe even a neckerchief. It's basically a fantasy version of yourself. You're saying 'I'm at work and I'm on holiday at the same time and both these things are glamorous'. Oh and, no matter what they say, a scart cable worn as a bootlace tie is acceptable dress.

• Women: Anything backless, but not arseless (DO NOT take your backlessness down as far as your rectum).

• Hair for men: Short, bobbed, thinning and dyed black is a must.

• Hair for women: Long, straggly, unwashed red hair with white roots is mandatory. Or a huge ginger mane with extreme fringe if you are a UK female filmmaker.

• Bags: Always carry one of the much sought after ugly looking bags that are given away free at festivals. The older the film festival bag the more respect gained. The most collectable festival bag ever is the Hastings 1066 Lesbian Shorts hessian sack.

WHAT IS INCLUDED IN YOUR CANNES SCREENING FEE?

Your screening fee also gives you passes for most of the big parties and premieres at the International Cannes Film Festival. This means you can walk, unchallenged and wearing your wrestling costume, straight into every red carpet event and stand, shoulder to shoulder, with the all the other A-listers.

WHERE SHOULD I STAY DURING THE CANNES FILM FESTIVAL?

If you are attending the Cannes Film Festival it is best to turn up with no money and nowhere to stay. Initially Butler and Bousfield slept on the floor of John Bentham's hotel room. But Bentham was also freeloading the room. Smile Orange were freeloading off the freeloader. This

At Cannes I tried to persuade Andie MacDowell to come to the *Fatliners* screening. She said I was very Freudian. I think that was the lycra tights that were part of my wrestler costume she was on about.

My cock was showing through the leotard, which is phallic and it ties in to being Freudian, I guess. Anyway she didn't come.

GUS BOUSFIELD
(SMILE ORANGE FILMS)

It was strange. We talked to various big shot Hollywood producers about our film but all they kept saying was that they were only here for European pussy.

JULIAN BUTLER
(SMILE ORANGE FILMS)

could not last and the duo were soon thrown out onto the street.

FILM FACT

If you find yourself on the street during the Cannes Film Festival start talking to random people you meet in the hope that they will agree to put you up for a night. You might then meet 'Mick' who will let you stay at his for a night or two.

Andie MacDowell: Failed to attend *Fatliners* premiere.

Bousfield and 'Mick'. Note Mick's razored spine. This is a typical injury aquired at the Cannes Film Festival.

UK filmmaker 'Mick' had his wallet stolen during a scuffling knife fight at The Petit Majestic. Luckily it was only a slight cut to his back and a ruined shirt. When attempting to report this to the local Gendarmerie, he, along with Smile Orange Films, were literally kicked out of the door and spat on by the police! He called the British consul the next day with thoughts of taking action, but was quietly told to forget it.

JOHN BENTHAM
(SCREEN EDGE)

BBC Radio 4's Dave Cohen: Great at following Smile Orange around.

Another free place to stay during the Cannes Film Festival may be provided by a BBC journalist who will be following you around for the whole festival. Journalist and comedian Dave Cohen somehow got to hear about *Fatliners* going to Cannes and decided to cover their trip with daily reports on *The Afternoon Show* — a second rate Radio 4 daytime magazine show for mums who iron.

Dave Cohen was making a kind of daily report. One night we didn't have anywhere to sleep and he took pity on us and let us stay in his hotel room.

GUS BOUSFIELD
(SMILE ORANGE FILMS)

HOW DO I PUBLICISE MY FILM AT THE CANNES FILM FESTIVAL?

Getting film critics to write a rave review about your film is a great way to gain publicity at the Cannes Film Festival. When Smile Orange Films learned that BBC film critic Barry Norman was at the festival they were keen for him to review *Fatliners* and whenever they saw Norman

Dave went everywhere with us, recording everything. He even came into the bogs where we changed into our wrestling costumes. I always thought that was a great interviewing technique.

JULIAN BUTLER
(SMILE ORANGE FILMS)

they would shout at him 'WHAT DO YOU THINK OF *FATLINERS*?' Strangely Norman would always slink away looking worried.

One day the duo saw Norman addressing a group of producers at a promotional stall. Norman was hemmed

I saw the whole thing. Dave (Cohen) steams straight in with the mic and is asking whether Barry will be coming to the *Fatliners* screening. Julian [Butler] accidently leans a bit too hard on a display shelf and the whole thing collapses around everyone. This causes Barry to raise his voice somewhat, but he was OK really and we did get it on tape!

JOHN BENTHAM
(SCREEN EDGE)

in by promotional material on all sides. Finally, this was their chance to get a response from him, there would be no slinking out of this one! So Smile Orange, with Radio 4 in tow, went over to get answers from him.

WHAT WILL HAPPEN AT THE SCREENING OF MY FILM AT THE CANNES FILM FESTIVAL?

You will get up late and miss it.

WHAT IS THE FUTURE OF THE CANNES FILM FESTIVAL?

The future of the Cannes Film Festival is to host film screenings at a nanoscopic level. The screenings will happen inside the human body for the enjoyment of the one hundred billion parasitic microorganisms that live there. One problem might be the promotional material of one hundred billion parasitic microorganisms being smashed to the floor by one hundred billion parasitic-micro-filmmakers and one hundred billion parasitic-micro-critics getting angry at them. So Tweets Malcolm in Cottingley.

L-R: Julian Butler, Doc Savage and Gus Bousfield on Cannes' Strip de Frottage.

"

An American wrestler called Doc Savage came to the *Fatliners* screening, he wasn't impressed by the fight scenes, he told us our wrestling was 'for pussies'. But oddly he loved the gag where Freddie Mercury battles AIDS.

GUS BOUSFIELD (SMILE ORANGE FILMS)

A disgraced pop star [Image removed for legal reasons].

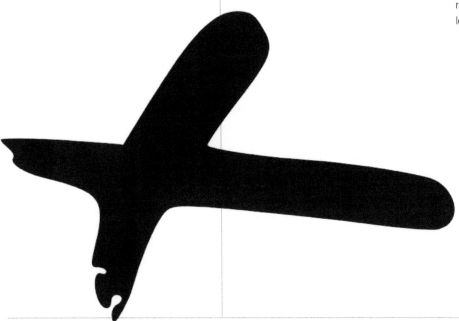

CHAPTER THIRTY-TWO
DISTRIBUTION

WHAT IS DISTRIBUTION?

Film distribution is the process of making a movie available for viewing by an audience. This means showing the film in a big, smelly, cold cinema where children flash laser pens onto the screen and take calls on their mobiles thus making it the worst environment in which to watch a film. Distribution is also putting the movie in shops and the uploading on the internet by humans for watching by humans. This chapter will be extremely boring.

WHAT IS THE HISTORY OF DISTRIBUTION?

Basically the history of film distribution is so boring that it might be the bit that finally makes you throw down this book, wipe your arse and walk away. The story of the distribution of Smile Orange Film's *Fatliners* started with Julian Butler and Gus Bousfield returning from Cannes to find the film's audio files deleted by the post-production house and so the film had no sound and Butler and Bousfield had to synchronise every line

Fatliners appears in The Times.

Fatliners VHS cover.

again. It was a massive job which they should never have had to do — working with professionals was turning out to be highly unprofessional.

WHERE ARE FILMS DISTRIBUTED?

There are many outlets in which filmed media is distributed. Screen Edge distributed *Fatliners* on VHS tape in the UK and US in shops like HMV, Virgin, Tower Records and Forbidden Planet. Only the most tragic of filmmakers would list every sale they're aware of. So here we go:

• Cameraboy Andrew Boldy stood behind someone in HMV Newcastle who was buying a copy.

• 'Roger', a friend of Bob Priestley, was bought a copy as a Christmas present by his boyfriend.

• A friend of Julian Butler, Andy Orr, runs the second-hand London record shop Music and Video Exchange, and a copy of *Fatliners* turned up there.

> " The fact that our film was for sale in proper shops seemed totally wondrous to us. We could go into any HMV shop and go to the 'F' section and find *Fatliners*, right there next to classics like *Father of the Bride*.

BOB PRIESTLEY (SMILE ORANGE FILMS)

Press pass made by camera operator Justin Robertson for the Leeds *Fatliners* premiere. Being the only cameraman there meant that Robertson really just made this to show to himself.

Fatliners in the Edinburgh Film Festival brochure.

FATLINERS

Set in a world where every single person is a wrestler and where life is filled so the good guys always win, *Fatliners* is a time-travelling, sci-fi comedy shot on Hi-8. God creates the wrestling world, but then throws out his revolting son — The Inflatable Child. It is this fallen angel who teaches the disgruntled bad guys of wrestling, who are sick of always losing, the secret of "Fatlining" — travelling through time to change the laws of the universe so they can win for a change. The film ends with a huge bout between the good guys of all times versus the bad guys of all times," says Julian Butler, who directed the film with Gus Bousfield. Press notes gave the following examples: "Hitler crotch-holding Churchill, Goliath splash-downing David and Dracula leaving Helsing with a case of the Boston Crabs."

The cast of 150 amateur actors were recruited through ads in the local and national press. "We got hundreds of aspiring and amateur actors and we stuck them all in — everyone worked for free," Butler says. As for the film design, the creators wanted to avoid the glitz of US wrestling and capture the essence of the "tragic British wrestling scene". If the production values and performances leave a little to be desired, the Smile Orange team is not disappointed. "If it looks crap, then it's quite funny," Butler says.

The project was picked up by John Bentham of Screen Edge, a company formed to seek out new independent talent. Screen Edge has funded post-production and the transfer to Beta SP.

Meanwhile, Smile Orange has Lottery funding for its next film — horror-movie meets Baywatch in The Pike "it is about a half-man, half-pike going crazy in the canal system of Britain." Longer term goals include trying to co-fund a genre picture with India's Bollywood.

Dirs: Julian Butler, Gus Bousfield

1996. Beta SP. 90mins.

SMILE ORANGE PRODUCTIONS
28 Villa Road
Bingley
West Yorkshire BD16 4EU
Tel: +44 1274 ███
Fax: +44 1274 ███

SCREEN EDGE
28/30 The Square,
St Annes on Sea, FY8 1RF
Tel: +44 1253 ███
Fax: +44 1253 ███

Exec prod: John Bentham
Prods/scr: Butler, Bousfield
DoP: Andi Boldt
Prod des: Peter Ward
Ed: Butler, Steve Robinson
Main cast: Tom Adams, Eugene Levine, Nigel Cooke, Gary Watson, John Hartley, Poz.

Budget: £2,000

Funding: Private finance, Screen Edge

DOES MY FILM NEED A GIMMICK TO SELL IT?

Publicity is easy to get for a film if you have an original gimmick; *Fatliners'* gimmick was that it was a film. In 1997 some UK film festivals would show any feature film as long as it was made in the UK and often *Fatliners* would be screened for this reason alone. A screening at the Edinburgh International Film Festival was one such event. Only one person attended, sitting silently on their own, all the way through to the end.

Smile Orange website flyer. Funny to have a flyer for a website. Nobody would do that nowadays.

But *Fatliners* wasn't unique and had reluctantly become part of a 'no-budget film scene', along with films like *Paperbag Man and Friends*, *Pervirella*, *Rhinobitch*, *Bad Karma* and *Fistful of Fingers*. The films were all inferior to Smile Orange's output but best of luck to them anyway.

HOW CAN I USE THE INTERNET TO DISTRIBUTE MY FILM?

The internet is very useful as a film distribution tool. Smile Orange publicised *Fatliners* with a brilliantly designed website made by graphic designer Juliet Uren. The only problem was that this was in 1997 and no one was online to see it.

FILM FACT

Everybody is shopping online now aren't they? I don't agree with online shopping because I can't control what the wife buys. If I see 'er going out t'shops I can at least say 'get back here now!'. But I never know when she's shopping online do I?

WHAT HAPPENS WHEN I GET ASKED TO LECTURE ON MY FILM?

When your film is successfully distributed you will be asked to lecture at prestigious film schools. Such was their standing in the cultural history of Europe, Smile Orange Films were invited to lecture at the prestigious National Film and

Now you can visit Smile Orange online studios at
http://web.ukonline.co.uk/smileorange/
Find out about all our Films and forthcoming distractions, get up to date with our news and Reviews, and leave your mark in the Visitor's Book.

Guerrilla filmmakers band in Britain

By SHEILA JOHNSTON

LONDON At a time when the local movie biz is raking in more coin than it has for decades, a new generation of Brit guerrilla filmmakers is shunning the system.

They don't spend any time in the industry's favorite watering holes like the Groucho Club, and don't bother filling out applications for lotto funding. Instead, they're spending their energy dashing off microbudget pics bankrolled by friends, family, neighbors and even welfare checks.

"I've sold everything I had to make this film — washing machine, bed, everything I didn't need," says Peter Tong, 45, who's just produced the comedy road movie "Gobsmacked!" He adds, "I even moved in with my girlfriend. But I've never been so happy. The film was fully funded by me and my friends. When I got stuck, I just asked for a few quid here and there."

Shot on DigiBeta, his maiden effort is officially budgeted at "well under half a million pounds ($850,000)." However, when pressed, Tong admits, "I've only spent 10 grand so far."

The band of wannabes are inspired by the Stateside school of just-do-it filming, which spawned indie stars such as Spike Lee and Quentin Tarantino.

A surge in disposable income in boom-time Britain has made an investment in a friend's movie more feasible for many people.

But if anything unites this new breed, it's their sense of exclusion from the mainstream industry. Paul Spurrier, 30, helmer of "Underground" (budget $170,000), says, "Broadcasters and film companies tend to use people they know. If you don't have a track record and are not part of their circle, you feel left out."

Rod Turner, 34, producer of urban comedy-thriller "Let's Stick Together" ($480,000), got tired of the slow-grinding wheels of the funding bureaucracies.

Turn to page 77

Television School for Rich Kids where they were paraded like noble savages in front of excited anthropologists.

HOW DO I DO INTERVIEWS?

A lot of filmmakers seem to think that we should give a flying fuck what their views are. On TV, in magazines and online they proclaim constantly about, not only films, but religion, philosophy, economics, politics, gender and rugby league. In truth a filmmaker is no more knowledgeable than the average man on the bus. Or the average man under the bus. When publications such as *The Times* covered *Fatliners* the Smile Orange interview technique was to laugh at every question and spout contradicting lies. That's how to do interviews.

WHAT IS THE FUTURE OF DISTRIBUTION?

The internet has transformed film distribution forever and ever and ever. What once looked like a puckered little anus squeezing out tiny rabbit pellets now looks like an ageing pornstar's gaping arsehole constantly leaking muck. *Fatliners* was one of the first films to dilate that orifice and we're all grateful for that. So why is the film completely forgotten today? Well, Malcolm in Cottingley predicts that in about fifty years' time complete global economic collapse will mean that all films will look as cheap as *Fatliners*. Only when every film is shot on hi-8, is set in Yorkshire and stars Scarlett Johansson in a bad leotard will *Fatliners* finally be recognised as the ground-breaking classic it is.

Appearing in trade papers such as *Variety* is a great way to raise awreness for your low budget crap.

Fifteen years after completing *Fatliners* and I am only just beginning to understand what we made. So God knows how long it will take other people to understand it.

JULIAN BUTLER (SMILE ORANGE FILMS)

JANUARY 12-18, 1998   *VARIETY*   FILM • 77

Guerrilla filmmakers band together in Britain

Continued from page 11

"We approached Channel 4 and British Screen but they said it would take up to a year to come to a decision," Turner says. "And my director, Viv Fongenie, had spent over three years on a previous project with the British Film Institute. The two of us first met in January '96, worked on the script of 'Let's Get Together' for about three months and shot it in August. If you can't do it in six months, it's probably better to leave it."

That shooting sked makes Turner's film the "Titanic" of Brit guerrilla cinema. Producer Julian Butler, who, at 27, has about 30 features and "quite a few" shorts to his credit, boasts, "We can make a feature in a week."

The catch

However, there's one major snag: Financed without pre-sales or great heed for the marketplace, these pics often languish without a buyer. Turner admits, "People are reluctant to pick them up because they haven't been involved from the beginning. And we haven't got the contacts or the skills to sell a film."

Josh Collins, 30, produced "Pervirella," a surreal time-travel comedy ($170,000) that has found a U.K. video distributor but no sales agent. "Making the film was

> ### 'We've never thought of (the establishment) as a career. We didn't approach the television companies or British Screen — they're not really our style.'
> Julian Butler, producer

almost easy compared with trying to sell it," he sighs.

The usual line is to lambaste the U.K.'s ultra-cautious theatrical distribs.

Sales agent Grace Carley of Stranger Than Fiction, a company specializing in "offbeat, low-budget" pics, liked "Strong Language" ($280,000), a first feature set in London's club scene, so much that she put up its completion finance.

But no buyer has yet taken the time to check it out. "It's like pulling teeth to get them to see movies like this," she says.

Yet Carley also admits that in some respects the caution is justified. "Many of the films made using the American 'credit-card' method tend to be pale imitations of movies made on much bigger budgets. And, however good your intentions, you're still competing with big titles on video shelves."

Creative marketing

Producers and directors have found ingenious ways around the distribution bottleneck. Many screen their work on the rapidly expanding club circuit, albeit without financial reward. Others employ ingenious scams to maximize profits.

One of Butler's no-budgeters, a $340 opus called "I'llkillya," was sold to latenight TV. The check? A paltry $375. "But," he adds, "we knew that, under the rules of the Performing Rights Society, you get a fee of about

£90 a minute each time your music is transmitted on television. So we made sure the film was plastered with our own music and earned about £12,000 ($18,000) from that."

Thanks to the precautions of adding his home phone number to the end credits, and of sending review copies to fanzines, Butler claims to have shifted about 1,000 units of "I'llkillya" by mail order, at $20 a throw. Filmmakers like him have no

ambition to strut the corridors of Blighty's media establishment: They're perfectly content to remain in what is fast becoming a parallel, underground economy. "We've never thought of it as a career," Butler says. "We didn't approach the television companies or British Screen — they're not really our style."

He adds, "We make exploitation movies — the Roger Cor man school of filmmaking. And the beauty of it is that we don't have to answer to anyone."

Duvall's 'Apostle' full of Indie Spirit

Continued from page 57

The Spirits also present awards for debut performances and first-time scripters. The most unusual nomination this year is a single entry for Phuong Duong, Eddie Cutanda and Tyrone Burton of "Squeeze" in the debut acting category for their semi-autobiographical roles as inner-city working-class kids involved in an acting workshop. An organization spokeswoman says the nominating committee

felt grouping the three into a single slot was most appropriate.

The annual ballot is determined by an 11-member nominating committee, with the IFP's 4,500 members selecting the winners.

The finalists in the foreign-film category are: "Happy Together" (Hong Kong), "Mouth to Mouth" (Spain), "Nenette et Boni" (France), "The Sweet Hereafter" (Canada) and "Underground" (Bosnia).

Until then, an ever growing herd of filmmakers are taking the tragic path of uploading their films onto badly made pay-per-view websites and using a hastily written book as a thinly disguised advert for them. All the films mentioned in this book can be downloaded for money at the Smile Orange Films website.

It was soon after completing *Fatliners* that Butler and Bousfield announced to Bob Priestley 'your next work will be a TV pilot about local news'. Things had been going unusually well for Priestley; he had just moved into a London flat for

fifty quid a week and New Labour had just got into power. Priestley remembers walking past Downing Street thinking 'I've got a new house, a new government, and new TV pilot. Maybe things really can only get better?' He couldn't have been more wrong.

PRO TIP

You can ignore all the advice in this book. Especially the pro tips.

PART FOUR

TELEVISION

StorytellingGBCreative

135C THE STABLES, LEEDS, WEST YORKSHIRE, LS3 5GH

Smile Orange Films

███████████████████████████

███████████████████

███████████

Leeds

███████████

21st May 1999

Dear Jubby, Gristle and Rope,

It has come to my notice that you now have a full TV series. Please come and visit me whenever you are free, it would be wonderful to see you. My PA, Always Texting Woman, can arrange the details.

Simply can't wait!!!!!!!!!!

Kind Regards

Amanda

Amanda Fees-Rodeane
Head of Funding
StorytellingGBCreative

CHAPTER THIRTY-THREE
TELEVISION

I'llkillya! soundtrack cassette cover. I'm just trying to think of some more words to put to this picture. But I can't think of any. I'm getting pretty laid back about this now.

WHAT IS TELEVISION?

Television (TV) is a telecommunicational broadcast medium used for transmitting and receiving moving images and sound. British television is a truly democratic medium that is watched by absolutely every single person in this great nation. Apart from the blind, and those people who don't own a television, and those people who are flocking to the internet in their millions.

A typical 1970s television. You can see a reflection of a bed in the screen. Televisions are often watched from bed. Is that a chair with washing hanging over it? The plug has been removed and, like a lot of people on it, this TV isn't earthed.

HOW DO I GET ON TELEVISION?

You will be told when you are required to go on television. In 1998 Smile Orange Films got a call from a producer at Yorkshire Television (YTV) called Nigel Clark who wanted to show *I'llkillya!* on his late night series *Flux*. Butler and Bousfield were delighted to oblige and couldn't believe their luck when Clark generously offered no payment at all. Instead Smile Orange were told to

record their own soundtrack, re-dub it over the film and then register with the Performing Rights Society (PRS) and claim thousands of pounds in music royalties. The *I'llkillya!* soundtrack was recorded in three weeks flat.

By listening to what Butler had edited into the film, I remade all the music. I did it on a four track cassette recorder and a sequencer. The music was very quick to make — it took only three weeks at twenty hours a day.

GUS BOUSFIELD
(SMILE ORANGE FILMS)

Butler and Bousfield took the completed music to the Yorkshire Television Studios, where an editor re-cut the show with the new soundtrack. Smile Orange's relationship with Yorkshire Television started, years earlier, when Butler posted a VHS of *I'llkillya!* to the YTV offices. A month later the tape was returned.

The tape was stuffed into an envelope with nothing but a compliment slip and 'NO THANKS' scribbled in big letters on it. No name or anything else. Ironically, a few years later, we were being rung almost weekly by YTV producers eager to show the film.

JULIAN BUTLER
(SMILE ORANGE FILMS)

Meetings in the YTV studios were now a regular occurrence. At one point Butler and Bousfield even took along journalist Dave Cohen, who was still following them around recording every bloody thing they said for Radio 4. Cohen sat in and recorded a meeting between Smile Orange and producer Nigel Clark, after which Clark said he thought the whole thing had been a practical joke.

I remember being interviewed for some YTV programme about low-budget films. We were mucking about and giving silly answers as usual, the sort of thing loved by shows we'd been on previously. But this time the producer was furious. At one point he screamed at us 'come on guys, please take it seriously!!

GUS BOUSFIELD
(SMILE ORANGE FILMS)

Eventually Clark came through and *I'llkillya!* earnt Smile Orange over £10,000 in music royalties when it was serialised, in its entirety, across the nation on ITV!!!! Always the ruthless salesmen, Butler and Bousfield decided to put their personal phone number in the credits of *Flux* in the hope that they would sell more tapes. But in the end this only resulted in drunk Geordies ringing the filmmakers at four in the morning to let them know 'that fucking kung fu is the funniest fucking shite like'.

After being shown on ITV, *I'llkillya!* made over thirty thousand times its budget back and it is, therefore Britain's most financially successful feature film.

Yorkshire Television Studios. There's a sign that says 'Reserved parking for *Calendar* and *Tonight* guests only'. So, if things are going really, really shit and you are forced to appear on local television and flog your product (e.g. a new book on how to make films) as well as your last atom of personal pride, then rest assured you will not have to walk far to do it.

Radio 4's Dave Cohen: Still following Smile Orange around.

Poster for ongoing Smile Orange project *The Pike*.

A comprehensive budget breakdown demonstrating how *I'llkillya!* became Britain's most financially successful film. Due to photographs of cancerous tongues the budget for Smile Orange's *I'llkillya!*'s had to be written on the inside of the fag packet.

Until someone hears differently.

Smile Orange Films now had to decide what to spend their money on. One idea was to make another film. Whilst making

Cliff Twemlow, writer, bouncer, filmmaker, full-on man.

> "
> *The Pike*, as a feature film, was going to be our masterpiece. The script was complete madness featuring underwater fight scenes, massive graphic sex scenes and something about apes driving around in a car. I'd still like to get funded to make it one day, but we've lost the script!*

JULIAN BUTLER
(SMILE ORANGE FILMS)

Fatliners, Butler and Bousfield had also been writing *The Pike*. Unofficially based on a novel by Mancunian bouncer Cliff Twemlow, *The Pike* featured a killer fish terrorising the Leeds to Liverpool canal's beach community.

HOW DO I GET LOTTERY FUNDING FOR MY PILOT?

Butler and Bousfield got some initial funding for *The Pike* from the National Lottery. No, they didn't win on a scratch card. Good joke. Instead, on a snowy night in Dewsbury, they joined a group of other hard-up filmmakers and listened to a presentation by a nice lady who said that if they wrote certain things in a certain way on a certain form and sent it to a certain address then you would get some money from the National Lottery. The scheme was called Arts for Everyone and it was a good idea, so, of course, the Arts Council soon put a stop to it. But not before Smile Orange Films got their hands on some pounds.

After securing their funding, Smile Orange Films immediately placed an advert in an actor's journal saying that they were casting *The Pike* but that, due to the sex scenes, 'some nudity was required'. From the two hundred replies one in particular caught their eyes: A photo of an actress squatting naked in front of a motorbike, urinating. Smile Orange had found their leading lady. Butler rang the number on the back of the photo but, unfortunately, the line was disconnected.

Despite never making *The Pike*, the PRS money and the Lottery funding wasn't wasted by Smile Orange Films. Butler and Bousfield purchased an Apple Macintosh computer

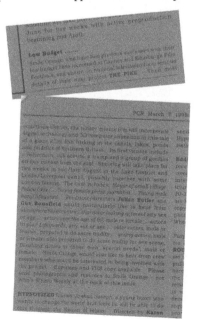

> The Arts Council was very insistent that their logo would appear at the end of the film and it should be the right size and colour and they sent us paperwork going on about this over and over again. They seemed so obsessed with their logo that they forgot to check that the film itself was made. We honestly did intend to make *The Pike* but our TV pilot just took over.

JULIAN BUTLER (SMILE ORANGE FILMS)

with non-linear editing software and a Sony VX1000, their first broadcast quality camera. With these tools they decided to make something that was truly momentous, the pinnacle of artistic endeavour and a mind-blowing thinkers spectacular. But instead they made a TV pilot.

Call for actors for Smile Orange Films' *The Pike*.

WHAT IS THE FUTURE OF TELEVISION?

No idea. No real wish to know really. TV is just one big advert now so there's no point in engaging anymore. Just like Bradford's laser-tag company, LazerNerdGamer, it's time to strike a match, claim the insurance and start afresh. So says Malcolm in Cottingley.

On the other hand Smile Orange were very excited. They had something that they never had before at the start of a project: Money. The problem was they didn't have a project. They were fucking fucked!

CHAPTER THIRTY-FOUR
THE PILOT

WHAT IS A PILOT?

A pilot is a one-off programme made to demonstrate how your television series will appeal to the dumb masses whilst earning you millions.

HOW DO I COME UP WITH IDEAS FOR MY PILOT?

From an Oxford-based academic serialising his latest book to a Cambridge-based academic adopting his latest biography; television pilots are based on an incredibly varied collection of ideas. One effective method of developing pilot concepts, used by both Smile Orange and academics, is going round the pubs and clubs of your suburban home town and writing down any old nonsense you can think of. There are ten basic stages to this process.

A Smile Orange ideas meeting [Image removed for legal reasons].

STAGE ONE:

Start your television pilot development meeting at an old man's pub, the peaceful atmosphere will allow the ideas to be introduced clearly. There will be a darts board but no pool table. This pub might be called The Star. Change pubs after three pints.

STAGE TWO:

Your friends/hangers-on who have a thirst for beer will be anxious to get to the next pub. As you walk across the supermarket car park, stop and smoke some marijuana. That's better. This will slow down everyone down. Hold their interest by keeping the ideas toing and froing to hold their interest.

STAGE THREE:

The next pub will be noisier so you will have to shout, but it's also more violent so you will have to keep your voice down. This pub might be called The Harvesters. The clientele of this pub will be rough-arsed and will eye you suspiciously; trying to work out if your artiness is gayness. Try not to look too arty or too gay. You will not succeed. You will be freaked out by the marihuana, paranoid by the impending violence and your beery friends will be shouting madness at you. Remind yourself you are having fun.

STAGE FOUR:

Next, the meeting will move to the high street. Smoke more weed, ignore people you went to school with and keep talking about ideas. Go to another pub where there are a great number of people who were in your year at school, feel bad that you ignored them in the street. This pub might be called The Brown Cow. Stay here until closing time.

STAGE FIVE:

The small town you're in closes at 11PM sharp so you will need to move your meeting to the nearest city. You should get the last bus 'into town' and you will bust for a piss the whole journey. When you get there you will have three options: The normal clubs, the student clubs or the gay clubs. The normal clubs are completely out of the question as they are far too violent so you might go to a student club. If you decide to hold your meeting in a gay club (called either The Sun or The Village) some of your colleagues will inexplicably decide not to come in. Do not protest too much, it will affect the harmony of the film collective. On entering the gay club you will undergo a transition period called 'queering up'. Note: If you are gay, ignore the above. After queering up, your television pilot development meeting will enter the dancing stage. Whichever environment you choose, it will be far too loud and confusing to communicate properly so suspend your talk in order to dance and thus develop further any visual gags or physical slapstick moves you may have discussed.

STAGE SIX:

This section of the meeting is over when the lights are banged on, whatever record is playing is ripped from the turntable and the transvestite DJ flinging her mic to the ground after barking 'NOW FUCK OFF'. You will not pull due to your dancing, or the fact that you are in a gay club. Note: if you are gay you probably will have pulled, whether you wanted too or not. Out on the street, smoke some more marijuana and restart your meeting. It will be cold and raining, you will be sweaty from the dancing and you will be freezing cold. This is normal. Become hypoglycaemic. Even your friends will consider this to be weak.

STAGE SEVEN:

It's about 4am. You relocate your television pilot development meeting to the cheap Indian restaurant which is next to the city morgue. This restaurant may be called The Kashmir. You will order the biggest naan in the world. You will feel cosy and warm inside and there will be much new inspiration for your pilot: Like a man face-down and fast asleep in a bowlful of curry.

Butler with Bradford's biggest naan.

The [pub removed for legal reasons].

STAGE EIGHT:

After your meal you will walk directly across the road to the cab rank to continue your meeting. Whilst you arrange yourselves into groups small enough to fit into cabs there will be some street theatre to inspire you: Maybe a fight or a domestic row. Or a domestic row in the form of a fight.

You might end up sharing a cab with a stranger/friend you bonded with last week because you laughed because he was walking, talking and pissing at the same time. He will be very drunk and act like he is your best friend. Throughout the ride home you'll continue to laugh about your television pilot ideas but the stranger/friend will take your laughter the wrong way and think you are laughing at him. When the stranger/friend gets to his home he will fall out of the cab and tumble angrily away into the night calling you all 'fuckinnn' bassstardsss'. He may be pissing at the same time.

STAGE NINE:
Walk home in just a t-shirt but chain smoke Silk Cut all the way in the belief that they will keep you warm. Meeting adjourned.

STAGE TEN:
The next day you will wake up and try to remember all the good ideas you had the night before but your mind will be blank. This is normal.

WHAT MAKES A GOOD PILOT?
The best television pilots should never attempt to appeal to a broad demographic. Instead, they should always be parodies of a late night

Tom Adams in the *Focus North* pilot.

PRO TIP
Notebooks are a good place to jot down your ideas. Notebooks can be purchased from a stationery shop. A stationary shop sells writing materials including notebooks. Notebooks are a good place to jot down your ideas. Notebooks can be purchased from a stationery shop. A stationary shop sells writing materials including notebooks. Notebooks can be... fuck it.

Yorkshire Television programme, more specifically, a single five minute segment within that show. This technique was utilised successfully by Smile Orange when they decided to spoof the Yorkshire Television series *Edit V*, specifically a story about the last remaining black and white minstrel in Yorkshire (a show you might remember them discovering whilst making *The Hunt for the Yorkshire Grimace*). Smile Orange called their show *Focus North*.

HOW DO I MAKE A TELEVISION PILOT?
Television pilots are filmed by production companies usually in a day and with a script that has been thrown together by half-bored girls whilst they wait to go to a free Gorillaz concert. This is ethically wrong. The Smile Orange way is to go to your doctor, pretend you've gone mad, get a six-month sick note, leave your cushy teaching job when the sick note expires,

After we had finished *Fatliners* we wanted to do something simple. We wanted the new format to be extremely straight. Copying local news programmes seemed a way to do this. We wanted to remove the responsibility for the way it looked so we could just concentrate on making it funny. Also viewers are already familiar with the way news stories are laid out and that reigned us in but also meant we could get away with a hell of a lot, as long as it was set up in the right way. It was a deliberate thing. We understood the problems we had with *Fatliners* and we wouldn't have done *Focus North* if we hadn't done *Fatliners* first.

GUS BOUSFIELD
(SMILE ORANGE FILMS)

sign on with the DHSS Film Fund and finally end up taking a whole year making your full length thirty minute pilot.

WHO DO I CAST IN MY PILOT?

Casting is probably the most important part of making a television pilot. Butler, Bousfield and Priestley decided to cast the face of DFS sofa adverts Tom Adams as the presenter of *Focus North*. The reasons for choosing Adams were:

• He looked 'very TV'.
• He had really big hands.

I was employed in a music shop called Spectre Sound (it was called that due to it being haunted) and me and Butler had been talking about who would be good and we thought of Tom Adams. I think he was in *Spotlight*, no, hang on he wasn't… I rang the DFS sofa company and they gave me the name of their advertising company and I got his agent from there. I finally rang Adams from work, no hang on, no I didn't…I… oh I can't remember now.

GUS BOUSFIELD
(SMILE ORANGE FILMS)

• He looked like he wore a wig even though he NEVER DID!!!!

It was the tenacious skills of Smile Orange's Gus Bousfield that got Adams on board. Bousfield worked in isolation, from home, for a whole day, phone-bashing and talent-tailing, only taking the very occasional break to practice on his one-string bass.

Finally Bousfield used his incredible negotiation skills to nail a deal with the actor by agreeing to pay whatever money he wanted. Tom Adams must have been desperate because all he asked for was a couple of hundred sheets.

HOW DO I FILM MY TELEVISION PILOT?

Filming a television pilot involves getting some people to pretend to be other non-linear editing system was slower than a dead tortoise. It was brilliant. But after a whole year using this time-devouring machine only ten minutes of the half hour pilot had been edited. So it was off to an edit suite in Sheffield, obtained for free by Airedale College student Justin Robertson to knock the rest out over a weekend.

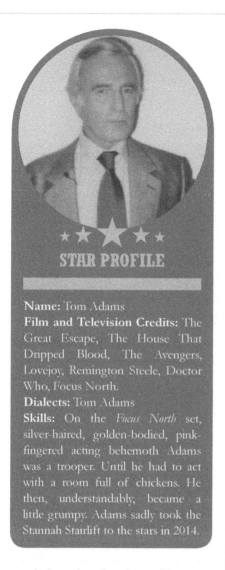

★ ★ ★ ★ ★
STAR PROFILE

Name: Tom Adams
Film and Television Credits: The Great Escape, The House That Dripped Blood, The Avengers, Lovejoy, Remington Steele, Doctor Who, Focus North.
Dialects: Tom Adams
Skills: On the *Focus North* set, silver-haired, golden-bodied, pink-fingered acting behemoth Adams was a trooper. Until he had to act with a room full of chickens. He then, understandably, became a little grumpy. Adams sadly took the Stannah Stairlift to the stars in 2014.

Justin also managed to get me some work in South Yorkshire on a cheap quiz show where I learned a lot about how the industry works. Especially when the company went bankrupt and I didn't get paid. I complained to the accountant who told me 'threaten the boss that you'll tell his wife about the affair he's having and he'll pay you'. Ironically I found out later that it was the accountant's embezzlement which was the cause of the company's bankruptcy in the first place. Good professional experience, all of it.

JULIAN BUTLER
(SMILE ORANGE FILMS)

people in various locations without any permission whatsoever. You will be constantly moved on by security staff. Remember, no matter what happens, you need to keep the record button pressed.

Try to keep production costs down, even if this means you won't be able to film everything you want. Butler and Bousfield desperately wanted to film someone wearing a pair of trousers that looked like realistic turkey drumsticks legs. But, for budgetary reasons, they were tragically forced to reject the idea.

Once you have filmed your pilot it is time to edit it. Smile Orange's new

It was on this same quiz show that Butler first met the talented camera operator Tim Peck. To amuse themselves Butler and Robertson had started a running joke where they would regularly ram each other's cars whilst driving to and from work. One evening, whilst driving

A typical day shooting the *Focus North* pilot: Priestley buttons up a tiger outfit and Bousfield (dressed as Freddie Krueger) leans into Butler's Ford Fiesta. The team are surrounded by their usual 'boxes of crap'.

FILM FACT

Getting a job within the media and any other industry is very easy: When being interviewed by prospective employers just claim that you are capable of doing the job. Then, once you have been employed you can learn as you go. This method works for every single job on the planet. Apart from cocktail waiter. That takes actual skill and going to college and knowing your drinks and learning the craft. And a wearing waistcoat.

to the pub, the duo rammed Peck's car out into the oncoming traffic at a busy T-junction. He was terrified. For some reason Smile Orange didn't see Peck for several years after that.

WHAT DO I DO WITH MY FINISHED TELEVISION PILOT?

Stick it up your arse. Only joking, it's now time to send your pilot to television channels. In 1998 Channel 4's late night broadcasting consisted of hours of entertaining shows all under the title *4Later*. Smile Orange sent the commissioning editor Olly Sharpe a copy of the first fifteen minutes of their pilot and forgot about it. Then, out of the blue, Sharpe rang Smile Orange to arrange a meeting. The future of Smile Orange was in the balance, they had to make the most of this meeting.

CHAPTER THIRTY-FIVE
COMMISSIONING

WHAT IS COMMISSIONING?

Television commissioning is the process in which TV shows are chosen for funding. Commissioning is led by commissioning editors. There are good and bad commissioning editors. The good ones are the ones who commission you. The bad ones don't.

WHERE WILL I MEET COMMISSIONING EDITORS?

You will meet commissioning editors in meetings and the only way to make these meetings run smoothly is to give the commissioning editors presents. Any old tat will do, from unbleached wrangler jeans to giant models of Stan Laurel, it's all good for making people think you like them and should easily get you through to the next level, I mean round... er... stage... er... meeting.

Basket of fruit and nuts. Oh, hang on, those are plums, not nuts. What's that spikey fucker? Star fruit? Guava? Anyway, the joy of fruit.

WHAT SHOULD I WEAR TO MY COMMISSIONING MEETING?

The type of clothes you wear to a commissioning meeting is very important. A friend of Smile Orange Films had kindly knitted the filmmakers three fluorescent tartan ponchos with massive orange smileys on the back. She also knitted them tartan kilts, leg warmers and arm warmers. The costumes were topped off with three giant foam cowboy hats purchased from Blackpool Pleasure Beach. The team considered wearing these to their meeting and even talked about arriving in a tartan knitted cart pulled by a pig, followed by donkeys, a cow, chickens and sheep. But in the end they chickened out. Good joke.

WHERE SHOULD I MEET MY COMMISSIONING EDITOR?

Where you meet your commissioning editor is very important. Channel 4's Olly Sharpe wanted to meet Butler, Bousfield and Priestley in the posh bar of his Leeds hotel. The trio were already out of their depth.

Whilst waiting for your commissioning editor to arrive you will become incredibly self-conscious. You may become acutely aware that you smell, have damp patches on the front of your trousers, or look like a giant. This is normal. When the

FUN QUIZ

You are a commissioning editor for a big TV channel. There are two companies promising that they can deliver you a TV series.

• **Company A** organised a fruit basket to be delivered to you then they arrived in a cab from their office in Soho's Golden Square saying things like 'after this meeting let's go for sushi, I know a wonderful place with fab square plates'.

Watch yer wallet!!!!!

• **Company B** has just stepped off the Megabus from Wakefield with pasty crumbs in their beards, wearing rags and saying things like 'I've seen more people down Oxford Street in the last ten minutes than I do at home in a week'.

It's a Megabus!!!

Which would YOU commission?

Correct answer: Company C: The one owned by your friend.

---

commissioning editor finally arrives (late of course!) try not to be baffled by what they are wearing. This is simply what people like them wear. It is not weird. 'It is I who am weird?' you will think. Ignore these thoughts. Everyone has them. But, actually yes, you are weird. Soz.

HOW DO I GET A COMMISSIONING EDITOR TO COMMISSION MY SHOW?

Commissioning editors are beholden to market forces and cannot just commission shows based on personal preference. Having said that, Channel 4's Olly Sharpe commissioned ten episodes of *Focus North* straight off the bat, simply because he had grown up in Yorkshire and got a perverse pleasure from seeing the area portrayed negatively. Sharpe

Priestley meets Channel 4.

offered a budget of £90,000 (€90,000) for ten episodes and very glad Smile Orange were for it too. They would be screened on Channel 4 on Friday nights, straight after Chris Evans' *TGI Friday*. For the Smile Orange team this meant that their ultimate dream would finally be fulfilled: They could now afford to make the pair of trousers that looked like realistic turkey drumstick legs.

The funny thing about getting commissioned was that I'd spent six months editing the second half of the *Focus North* pilot but we only sent Channel 4 the first half. Sharpey never saw the second half and we never used any of it in the show. I basically wasted six whole months of my entire life! Ha ha! Brilliant!

JULIAN BUTLER
(SMILE ORANGE FILMS)

WHAT IS THE FUTURE FOR THE COMMISSIONING PROCESS?

Malcolm in Cottingley tells me that soon the World Class Wars will begin. Elite Channel Exec Warriors will send insurmountable armies of commissioning editors to fight in endlessly epic battles against legions of low grade technical staff and some punks. Only Malcolm knows what the outcome will be, but, for now, he's keeping shtum.

Butler and Priestley celebrate a successful Channel 4 commission with Robbie the Rhino and his Challenge Cup.

For Smile Orange, production on *Focus North* began in May 1999. The first week coincided with a rare UK eclipse of the sun. This was seen by the Smile Orange team as an omen. It would have to wait to be seen whether the prophecy was good.

Or bad.

Numerous great shows never made it onto TV due to lazy commissioners. One of these was the musical drama series I wrote called *Stinky, Stinky, What Have I Done?* The musical was based on a true event that happened during the British BSE crisis when thousands of infected cows were being slaughtered daily. Two farm hands, Stinky and his mate, worked, day in, day out, destroying endless amounts of cattle using bolt guns. Soon the pressure mounted and they started to argue. Finally Stinky's mate took it upon himself to win the argument in the ultimate way — he bolt gunned Stinky in the head. Witnesses then heard Stinky's mate say "Stinky, Stinky, what have I done?". You could almost say he was 'herd' to say this. Good joke. Unbelievably, that's a project that never got commissioned.

PETER WARD
(VETERAN PRODUCER)

CHAPTER THIRTY-SIX
THE CREW

WHAT IS A TELEVISION CREW?

A crew is a group of people brought together so their abilities can create a television show: The camera operator operates the camera, the sound recordist records sound and the special effects loon makes a pair of wearable turkey drumstick legs.

SMILE ORANGE FILMOGRAPHY

FOCUS NORTH (1999/2000)
Channel 4 TV comedy series /
10x 30min Episodes / BetacamSP
/ Colour
Spoof of regional news programming. I've not attempted to describe the plots for each of these episodes because that would be just fucking ridiculous. No one would ever read that. Not even you Johnny Pigram.

Pennine Television

WHAT CREW MEMBERS WILL I NEED?

The first crew member important to the running of any television production is a production assistant. Daniel Kanyon was *Focus North*'s production assistant. He was priceless. And cost £300 a week.

Kanyon learned quickly to work in numerous strange situations: The production was initially run from Butler's flat within a dilapidated gothic manor house in Leeds called Meanwood Towers. Butler, Bousfield and Priestley

Inspired by Yorkshire Television, Smile Orange created Pennine Television — the imaginary producers of *Focus North*.

For those of you who don't have a clue, this is what the *Focus North* logo looked like.

A production assistant

lived there together, writing the scripts, sharing absolutely everything, including the one bed. Arriving for his first day on the series, Kanyon must have questioned who was employing him when he found all three of his employers fast asleep in the same bed.

WHAT DOES A PRODUCTION ASSISTANT DO?

The best production assistants will agree to do anything they are asked to do and yet are completely baffled as to why they are being asked to do it. One scene in *Focus North* required human faeces to be strewn over the street. The producers were now professional and therefore using real human bab was out of the question. So, instead, production assistant Daniel Kanyon was asked to collect a selection dog plops.

Turds in *Focus North*.

Smile Orange were already experienced crap collectors. As kids they had scooped poop and dead animals and mixed them up in a hole in the ground they called the Roxy Tox Box (See Chapter One). But, now they were professionals, they

Vague images swim in front of me but I try to drown them. I'm sure at one point a boy brought me different types of dog dirt and asked me which one I wanted to use in the next scene. I was young then and basically winging the whole thing, hoping that no one would know that I didn't have a clue. But this was it, this was the test. Nowhere to hide, no rock to climb under, no rock to smoke. I had no idea which piece of dog muck was suitable. I was about to be found out. I remember pointing to the biggest and brownest turd and staying 'that one?'. The boy walked away pleased with my decision. 'He never knew' I whispered to myself. 'My God. I think I may have cracked it'. I had suddenly realised that there is no right way. In fact everyone is doing it wrong. And if everyone is doing it wrong, so can I. 'Boy!' I shouted. The boy looked back, tired from thirty-seven hours without sleep. 'YOU! BOY! I've changed my mind. I don't want solid plop, I need dog's diarrhoea… you've got ten minutes. Chop chop'. The boy ran off, immediately scouring the gutters for watery canine squat. I was on my way. I had mastered my art.

JULIAN BUTLER (SMILE ORANGE FILMS)

I don't remember any of that.

BOB PRIESTLEY
(SMILE ORANGE FILMS)

could pay someone to do their dirty work. Good natured Kanyon brought the team a selection of dog dirt in a box with a happy smile. But, after *Focus North*, Kanyon decided to never work in television again.

WHAT IS A PRODUCTION COORDINATOR?

A production coordinator is vitally important to the running of any good television production. They must be the one person who can be relied on to keep calm when all around them is up in flames. Due to some fireworks going off in some Webbox. Steve Coote was *Focus North*'s production coordinator. Coote came highly recommended and the Smile Orange team took an immediate like to this witty little gentleman. Coote's small physical stature meant he claimed disability benefits and so, whenever Butler visited the DHSS Film Fund, Coote lent Butler his disability parking badge so he could park directly outside the funding offices, enabling him to get back to the set quicker.

WHAT DOES A PRODUCTION COORDINATOR DO?

For Channel 4 to pay them their budget Olly Sharpe told the producers to register Smile Orange Productions as a limited company at Companies House. The trio didn't know what any of that meant.

Focus North's live screening ticket: The only time Smile Orange Limited used their precious embossing stamp.

So they got production coordinator Steve Coote to do it. The only part of the process that Butler, Bousfield and Priestley paid attention to was when an embossed stamp with 'Smile Orange Productions Ltd' written on it arrived in the post. The team used this to stamp all paperwork, party flyers, posters and bus tickets they could find.

By law a limited company must hold annual general meetings where dividends are 'paid out'. The minutes of these meetings are meant to be kept and filed away. No one knows where. Smile Orange wisely ignored this very oak-panelled room way of doing things. Their efficient production coordinator took care of it all. Steve Coote also opened a Smile Orange

Tediously, the difference between the professional *Focus North* and the more amateur earlier films Smile Orange produced was simply money, management and experience. I suppose we had advanced

GUS BOUSFIELD
(SMILE ORANGE PRODUCTIONS LTD)

Productions Ltd company bank account. The show's budget was in his tiny safe hands.

WHAT DOES A TELEVISION SCRIPTWRITER DO?

Once you have employed a good production coordinator you can now concentrate on the important part; spending £100,000 on writing a show that is completely based on one in-joke.

Once you have finished writing five hours of scripts based on your one in-joke, these are delivered to your commissioning editor who will go through them meticulously looking for any issues. Or, if you're Channel 4's commissioning editor Olly Sharpe, you'll pass all ten *Focus North* scripts possibly without even reading them.

PRO TIP

I never want to lose any part of our precious in-joke so I back up everything onto three USB devices: USB1 is carried in my back pocket at all times. USB2 is kept in a chest of drawers at the front of my house in case of fire at the rear. USB3 is kept in a chest of drawers at the rear of my house in case of fire at the front. What's that? 'Ever heard of The Cloud?' you say. 'No, I don't want anything to do with that?' I reply.

BOB PRIESTLEY
(SMILE ORANGE PRODUCTIONS LTD)

Channel 4's contractual department told us that we'd written over ninety characters, the most characters they'd ever had in one series. They said that their actor contracts could not accommodate this and they asked if we'd made a mistake. We replied that we definitely needed all ninety characters. So Channel 4 had to change the contract that had served them well for over seventeen years, all because of a group of over-imaginative twats from Bingley.

BOB PRIESTLEY
(SMILE ORANGE PRODUCTIONS LTD)

WHERE SHOULD MY CREW BE LOCATED?

To stop three grown men having to share a bed, it is recommended that a television production crew move into what's known as an office. Production coordinator Steve Coote found offices within the sprawling Yorkshire Television Studios on the edge of Leeds City Centre. Being located within the studios that created *Edit V*, the very show *Focus North* paid homage to, was an inspired move and the team often gained ideas for their scripts from observing the building at work then taking the piss out of it.

WHAT IS A TELEVISION CAMERA OPERATOR?

A television camera operator is an invaluable part of the television crew. It is particularly important to find a camera operator who is able to shoot in a style which suits your production. *Focus North* was a homage to local news shows so Butler, Bousfield and Priestley decided to employ a cameraman with massive amounts of experience in animation. This cameraman was called Mark Something and it soon became apparent that Mark Something was highly skilled. At filming small bits of Plasticine.

Luckily Manchester cameraman-mountain Dave Stamford saved the day. Stamford had many hours of local news experience under his belt and easily made everything look like local news. Which is bad but was good.

WHAT DOES A PRODUCTION SOUND MIXER DO?

A production sound mixer records all sound on set. It takes years of experience to be a production sound mixer. So before Smile Orange offered their mate, Dave 'Dusty' Mundy, the role, they made sure he had never done the job before in his life. In fact, he'd possibly never done any job before in his life.

WHAT DOES A TELEVISION WARDROBE SUPERVISOR DO?

The wardrobe supervisor on a television set needs to be able to solve a large number of costume based problems, the main one being how to wear their

Mark Something worked differently, almost as if he wanted to move lead presenter Tom Adams frame by frame. So unfortunately we had to get rid of him. And, because Mark Something was Steve Coote's best friend, we decided that Steve Coote was the best person to fire him. Coote loved us for that one.

BOB PRIESTLEY (SMILE ORANGE PRODUCTIONS LTD)

Vivienne Westwood clogs convincingly. Smile Orange's wardrobe supervisor was a freelancer who also worked on the actual local news show *Look North*. She seemed obsessed with ensuring that *Focus North*'s costumes didn't 'strobe'. This gave Smile Orange the idea to dress their lead presenter, Tom Adams,

Dave Stamford: Cameraman genius. Generator novice.

A production sound mixer recording the dead.

A television make-up supervisor supervising make-up for telelvision.

in a suit, tie and shirt all made from material that strobed. This in turn gave the wardrobe supervisor the idea to walk out immediately.

A great example of the work of a wardrobe supervisor: Clothes on the legs of a man.

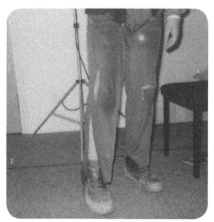

Smile Orange Productions filled the wardrobe supervisor position with runners Karen Hopkinson and Emma Dalesman. They were both brilliant despite their lack of experience. They also knew how to wear any Vivienne Westwood clogs convincingly.

WHAT IS A TELEVISION MAKE-UP SUPERVISOR?

A makeup supervisor (or 'makeup supervisor') is an artist whose medium is the human body. *Focus North*'s makeup supervisor, Kelly Burton-Downer, came to the show straight from doing makeup on *The Lion King*. Not the animated film but the West End musical.

WHAT DOES AN ART DIRECTOR DO ON A TELEVISION SET?

The art director is responsible for arranging the overall look of your television series. Unfortunately they sometimes fail to deliver this. *Focus North*'s art director was called Sam Dawson and he was immediately given the important job of making some human-sized turkey drumstick legs. The day when they were needed arrived and, as excitement mounted, Dawson brought the turkey legs onto set and unveiled them. Can you imagine the disappointment when the legs were revealed to be nothing more than hastily painted slabs of foam rubber with a pair of American tan tights over them?

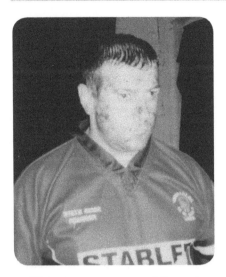

Focus North's Gino Feliciello about to lash out.

The team were crestfallen; they wanted perfectly crafted drumsticks, exquisite in every golden-fried detail, even including the tiny little white chef hats. The sensitive actor Bob Priestley wept and the large actor/bouncer Gino Feliciello began lashing out in frustration. Through tear stained makeup Priestley squeezed into the legs and goose-stepped around to wailing from the entire crew. None of them would really truly recover.

After *Focus North* was completed Sam Dawson went on to work on *Doctor Who*. Let's hope the show doesn't require any giant alien turkey legs. Otherwise they are fucked.

WHAT IS THE FUTURE FOR THE CREW?

Malcolm in Cottingley says that in the future you will be able to buy packs of dehydrated crews to which you just add water. Bit like those things, what are they called? Sea monkeys.

Big clip art picture of a crow. Baffling. Maybe in the wrong place? Or did I image search for 'crow' instead of 'crew'? Whatever I must remember to remove it later.

CHAPTER THIRTY-SEVEN
CELEBRITIES

I know a lot of famous people. Most of them in Armley Jail.

AUSTIN OATES
(SMILE ORANGE ACTOR)

Richard Madeley and his wife Judy Finnigan: A British married couple who are both celebrities.

WHAT ARE CELEBRITIES?

Celebrities are people who are recognised by other people who have never met them. But hang on, is the Yorkshire Ripper a celebrity? No, he's not and yet he is recognised by people who have never met him. Maybe you have to like the person for them to be a celebrity? That's not right though, surely, because what about that Max Clifford? Has anyone ever actually liked him? He's a celebrity isn't he? Let's try again. A celebrity is the sort of person a supermarket owner would think is a good person to open their shop. This is why John Wayne Gacy is not a good celebrity but Richard Madeley is. Hang on though, didn't Madeley get caught shoplifting though?

HOW DO I CAST CELEBRITIES?

A casting agent will find the celebrities needed for your television series. On the other hand you could just watch TV and cast anyone that makes you laugh. Now where was I? Oh yes! Tom Adams!!!! For Adams to agree to appear in the *Focus North* pilot meant he was desperate for work. So, when Adams heard the *Focus North* was to be made into a series, pound signs must have sprung up in his, and his agent's, fucking little eyes.

WHERE DO I FIND A CASTING AGENT?

Butler, Bousfield and Priestley employed

The way to direct Tom Adams was to tell him what to do and then leave before he shouted at you. We should have had a reinforced Punch and Judy box and just opened the curtains to give our directions and then closed the curtains and let him shout about Equity or whatever. In all fairness though, Adams did everything that was asked of him, even wearing silver hot-pants. I think some actors like to do this thing where they give directors' a hard time. Maybe it was important for him to do his 'Richard Harris' aggressive actor thing. Maybe he bought into those luvvie affectations. So, my one tip for working with Tom Adams would be to run away.

GUS BOUSFIELD
(SMILE ORANGE
PRODUCTIONS LTD)

a London based casting agent called Penelope O'Rourke and asked her to get Tom Baker for a cameo role in *Focus North*. After tireless work discussing contracts with agents, O'Rourke triumphantly announced 'YES!!! BIG SUCCESS!!!!' She had managed to book Stuart Hall. The crew were disappointed but later cheered up when they heard the rumours about Hall, who eventually went to prison.

Hall appeared as himself in *Focus North*, awarding the winner of the Pennine Business Awards their cheque. The team soon realised that he had a genuine ability to spout nonsense on any given subject so they also filmed him commenting on other stories in the series. These were then cut-up and dropped into every episode. This was Smile Orange's way of getting their money's worth out of Hall, spreading him throughout the show like a cheap meat paste.

★ ★ ★ ★ ★
STAR PROFILE

Name: Stuart Hall
Film and Television: It's a Knockout, Pub Quiz, Focus North.
Awards: OBE awarded in 2011. OBE removed in 2014.
Current Position: No longer in prison.

Tom Adams in hot pants. Now we're talking.

Celebrity Tony Capstick holding props.

At one point Hall was asked to comment on the story of a dole office that was holding a job-seekers Christmas party. Off the top of his head Hall screamed 'Booze! Fags! Tartlets! I want the wastrel life, not them! I deserve it!' Following the revelations of his private life these demands seem tame.

HOW DO I WORK WITH CELEBRITIES?

The date rape drug Gamma-Hydroxybutyric Acid (GHB) leaves its' victims enthusiastic and compliant and can be very helpful when working with celebrities. Another celebrity to appear in *Focus North* was Tony Capstick, the comedian famous for the 1981 hit single Capstick Comes Home. In his *Focus North* scene Capstick played a councillor informing viewers that a family should wash by licking each other. The script called for Capstick to demonstrate this by licking the torso of a rugby league player. The rugby player was played by an adult film star.

The drug GHB represented by a computer graphic,

Farmhouse interior, Yorkshire. Mid-wide shot of the actor Tony Capstick leaning forward, tongue extended, licking a rugby league player.

On the morning of the shoot Capstick insisted that he waited in the nearest pub where he immediately ordered the first of many triple vodka and tonics. The adult film star, on the other hand, was swigging from an unmarked black bottle which he revealed contained GHB. The adult film star also told anyone who would listen about the many 'good foursomes' he'd had on the drug. Butler and Priestley were

particularly awestruck by this knowledge, especially the fact that there was such a thing as a bad foursome.

Eventually the licking scene was filmed without a hitch and without Capstick and the adult film star having to get involved in a bad foursome. This was Capstick's last role before sadly passing on to the great tap room in the sky.

WHERE DO I FIND GHB?

GHB comes in plain black bottles bought from a large bodybuilder at a rave. I don't know how much it costs. If the bodybuilder needs lots of steroids then he will charge a lot, but if he is already huge then he will not need the money as much. Therefore always buy GHB from the biggest bodybuilder you can see.

SHOULD THE BODY BUILDER BE SHAVED?

Body builders are always shaved.

WHAT ARE THE RISKS OF GHB?

Bad foursomes. Stop asking me questions now, turn to the next chapter please.

WHAT IS THE NAME OF A BODY BUILDER IN LEEDS WHO CAN SELL ME GHB?

No.

HOW MUCH SHOULD I PAY FOR A CELEBRITY?

Celebrities cost a lot of money therefore they aren't usually worth bothering with. Instead, for most of the roles in *Focus North*, Smile Orange used their tried and tested method of getting free actors: The thesp-trawl. Once again they put adverts in the local press telling everyone to turn up at the West Yorkshire Playhouse. But this time they sent production assistant Daniel Kanyon to meet the actors whilst Butler, Bousfield and Priestley, like the cowards they are, watched from the anonymity of the bar.

After Kanyon had met and filmed over two hundred of Leeds' finest amateur talent the team viewed the tapes and cast the show. The trick was to cast someone who was almost identical to the character they would play on screen. For example a senile old woman was played by a senile old woman and a pompous ageing grey haired TV presenter was played by... you get the idea.

Smile Orange Productions also decided, once again, to use the gifted

Fatliners' lead actor Eugene Levine playing a politician in *Focus North*.

professional non-professional actor Austin Oates. Oates' had first starred in *Fatliners* and his spontaneous acting style relied on the fact he couldn't remember any lines. Or the names of the crew. Or the names of the producers. Or anything.

Butler, Bousfield and Priestley brought back numerous other actors from the old films to star in *Focus North*. The reason for this was that they were incredibly talented and incredibly free. Gino Feliciello, Lynette Greenwood, Eugene Levine and Al Birdsell all made an appearance and Smile Orange got so used to having BBC Radio 4's Dave Cohen following them around that they cast him in the series too.

We often encouraged people to play themselves because we knew we could never write dialogue as well as they could make it up. So the script would often just give the basic story outline and we'd ask them to say it in their own way.

BOB PRIESTLEY

(SMILE ORANGE PRODUCTIONS LTD)

We got really good results from the actors; you couldn't tell if they were pretending to be mad or actually mad. Maybe because they were both. It gave the show an unreal feel. To this day many people thought *Focus North* was a dream they'd had.

JULIAN BUTLER

(SMILE ORANGE PRODUCTIONS LTD)

Fatliners'
actress Lynette
Greenwood in
Focus North.

> I always liked to watch Tom
> Adams and Austin interact. They
> acted together many times but
> each time they met we had to
> reintroduce them to each other.
> I bet I introduced them to each
> other twenty times.

BOB PRIESTLEY
(SMILE ORANGE
PRODUCTIONS LTD)

Ozzy Osbourne
woman.
Christened thus
because of her
large eighties
hair which
resembled
Ozzy Osbourne
on the cover
of one of his
albums. Was it
The Blizzard of
Oz? Or Diary of
a Madman? I'll
go for Blizzard
of Oz.

WHAT ARE CELEBRITIES LIKE
IN THEIR PRIVATE LIVES?

Sometimes the real lives of the *Focus North* cast were odder than the characters they portrayed. Once Butler was driving to a shoot when he saw one of *Focus North*'s extras out of his car window. Nothing strange there. But, the thing was, she was calmly wandering down the central reservation of a busy rush hour motorway. And this was the day before she was needed on set.

To this day none of Smile Orange know the actresses' name, they only ever referred to her as 'Ozzy Osbourne'. All the same, Butler was worried. She didn't seem to know a) where she was or b)

> I'm sure that after working for
> us Tom moved on and forgot us,
> probably to cleanse his mind of our
> foul memory. But Austin forgot us just
> because he is genuinely forgetful.

JULIAN BUTLER
(SMILE ORANGE
PRODUCTIONS LTD)

what she was doing. Would she survive?

Luckily, the next day, the actress turned up on set and nailed the part of 'madwoman not knowing who she was or what she was doing' like a consummate professional.

WHAT IS THE FUTURE
FOR CELEBRITIES?

Malcolm in Cottingley says that the next big thing in the post-internet future will be non-celebrity celebrities. These are people who are famous for not being famous. The less famous you are, the more famous you will be. The problem will be that, as soon as you aren't famous, you then become famous and then nobody wants to know you anymore and then you're not famous anymore, it's a vicious circle.

CHAPTER THIRTY-EIGHT
TELEVISION PRODUCTION

A DAY IN THE LIFE OF A TELVISION PRODUCER

I'm up with the lark. I have a full English breakfast served to me every day by my invalid mother, my brother and my lover. They fight. I love this energy. This side of the cemetery we're respectable, so I put the bins out, and I make sure that I have an empty champagne bottle sticking out of the top just so the neighbours know I still have my career. Then I get my boy, Matamis Na Pula (It means Sweet Red Magic in Filipino), to bring round the Jag. As my boy drives I make some calls. Then stop off at McDonald's to feed the boy and collect my acting troupe. Whip out the camera and then, to put it simply, we make history.

PETER WARD
(VETERAN PRODUCER)

WHAT IS TELEVISION PRODUCTION?

Television production is the name given to the methods and practices required to take an idea for a television show from theory into reality. You don't have to be the sharpest knife in the drawer to work in television. Over the years some of Europe's most influential families have sent their most pinheaded inbreds to join the ranks of the television fluffheads (see Glossary: Prince Edward).

WHAT IS THE HISTORY OF TELEVISION PRODUCTION?

In 1932 John Logie Baird, the world's most famous Wishman, bounced radio waves off the moon in the hope of creating swingbeat. Instead he captured tubular waves in glass bottles. Fast forward to the present-day and his legacy lives on in jam jars which have been flattened into screens, the contents of which can be seen pretty much everywhere. You're probably reading this through one of his squashed jam jars now aren't you? So let's not

FILM FACT

On the British TV soap opera *EastEnders* there have never been any producers.

> Making telly-box magic is when the people who like the filming a lot have got tonnes of pennies between them they agree to make friends and share computers and pens and I'm not allowed in. When I'm older they say, but I'm old NOW I SAY!!!

NICKY HINCHCLIFFE

(TOP HOLLYWOOD DIRECTOR)

To get the free use of this van Smile Orange were duty bound to show it in the title sequence of their series. When I tried to get the use of this van for free by putting it in this book they told me to fuck off.

Pre-panic attack Priestley in makeup.

pretend you don't know what one is. Oh, hang on, by 'television production', you mean you want to know how television shows are made, don't you? OK. Got it.

WHAT IS PRODUCT PLACEMENT?

Product placement allows brands to advertise their products within films and television programmes. There are companies who will arrange product placement for you and Butler, Bousfield and Priestley decided to use one to keep financially solvent while Channel 4, like a dad who has spent his child's pocket money on tickets to the Isle of Man TT, hadn't paid them any budget.

At first, the trio were tentative about compromising their artistic integrity but, when they saw a catalogue of the free products that were available, they instantly solicited for as much product placement as they could get their dirty legs around.

There was an incredible amount of things they could have: From square crisps to sports cars, to a Boeing 747 covered

in FedEx livery (Smile Orange deduced that the last object was the entire basis for the making of the Tom Hanks film *Cast Away*). The producers didn't really need any of it but they greedily took it anyway and suddenly Bousfield was doing donuts in sporty Volvos, Butler was crashing Renault Espaces into walls and Priestley was eating lots of square crisps.

Of course In order to fulfil the contract with the product placement company these items had to be creatively shoehorned into the show. Therefore the *Focus North* opening credits featured a battered Renault Espace and a sketch about a dole Christmas party was hurriedly written as an excuse to film some square crisps.

WHAT MAKES A GOOD TELEVISION LOCATION?

As Bob Priestley found, whilst performing in *Focus North*, a good television location

Priestley:
Panic attack
imminent!!

should always be as far away from the public as possible. You may remember that, whilst shooting *The Hunt for the Yorkshire Grimace*, Robert Priestley had to catch a bus wearing old man makeup. Butler and Bousfield were inspired and wrote a sketch for *Focus North* about a boy with Clegghead Syndrome, a disease that leaves young people with old people's heads. So, Once again, Bob Priestley started a day's shoot at three in the morning in the makeup chair having old man prosthetic makeup applied.

The script called for the boy to train for the Paralympic Games, so a running track location was found in the grounds of a school. Priestley was filmed sprinting round the track, jumping hurdles and riding a bike. All whilst wearing old man's face makeup. For an Olympic athlete this would have been punishing. Priestley was no athlete. Add to this the early morning start and the relentless rain and Priestley started to crumble. A panic attack was imminent.

Despite hyperventilating Priestley somehow managed to crawl off and hide in the product placement Renault Espace. He just needed some peace and quiet to

I was alright in the end and we finished the scene and at least I managed to persuade Judge (Butler) that we didn't need to film the scene where I was going to try to swim down the overflowing River Aire.

BOB PRIESTLEY
(SMILE ORANGE ACTOR)

FILM FACT

Dealing with confusion, the daily terrors, squits, muscle spasms, frozen neck syndrome, goitres, stammering, Ventolin abuse, collapsing due to strawberry flavoured dry ice, fainting and more squits is all a part of being an actor. The trick is to think of your psychiatric episodes and illnesses in a positive way: Panic attacks are a good free appetite suppressant and hyperventilating and paralysis is like a long cigarette break.

That ostrich farm I was talking about.

pull himself together. But the Espace was parked in the middle of the school playground and when the school bell rang he realised his mistake. Hundreds of kids surrounded the vehicle, rocking it, laughing and screaming at the strange boy with the old man's head. It was horrendous torture for the already fragile Priestley.

To reiterate, a good television location should always be as far away from the public as possible.

HOW DO I PRODUCE A TELEVISION SOAP OPERA?

Television soap operas are long running serials that never seem to bloody end.

★ ★ ★ ★ ★
STAR PROFILE

Name: Stewart Mills
Skills: Seventy-two year old Stewart is an incredibly gentle and lovely retired Yorkshireman. Mills was so accommodating he would do absolutely anything the producers wanted and so Smile Orange exploited him mercilessly, immediately filming him snogging another male actor. All for no money whatsoever. And no expenses either. The strange thing is, no one can remember how or when he first appeared on set.

They are called soap operas because after watching them you feel dirty and need to wash. Smile Orange included a fictional soap opera within *Focus North* called *Three Peaks*. The show was set amongst a rural community of drug addled ostrich breeders and starred Stewart Mills, another one of Smile Orange's favourite actors.

HOW DO I SOURCE PROP VEHICLES?

Television production often involves the procurement of prop vehicles. One of *Focus North*'s sketches featured a van

We filmed the *Three Peaks* scenes at a real ostrich farm. At one point soundman Dave 'Dusty' Mundy was holding his giant extended boom pole and fluffy microphone cover above his head. If you squinted a bit then Dave looked like the biggest, weirdest bird ever. As he walked towards the ostriches they went completely berserk!

JULIAN BUTLER

(SMILE ORANGE PRODUCTIONS LTD)

with a pub in it called the Pub-a-Van. After many meetings it was decided that what was required was a prop van. Dave 'Dusty' Mundy delivered the goods again. He was a man with numerous automotive contacts, most of them from the Traveller Field of the Glastonbury Festival. The van Mundy procured was a stinking wreck with no road tax, no insurance and no owner documents. It was perfect.

★ ★ ★ ★ ★
STAR PROFILE

NAME: Sarah Ann Kennedy
CREDITS: Peppa Pig, Crapston Villas, Focus North.
SKILLS: Sarah played local journalist Emma Gelding brilliantly and hardly ever complained. But she is proper shamed by *Focus North* now, she's taken it off of IMDb and everything.

The Pub-a-Van segment was filmed in one day and a comedy acting masterclass from Sarah Ann Kennedy and Northern comedian Tony Piers ensured the scene was one of the best in the show.

After the Pub-a-Van was filmed the next question was 'what do we do with the van?' Unfortunately Smile Orange never asked themselves this question and the vehicle simply rotted in the Yorkshire Television car park.

The security department at the prestigious studios were a diligent squad who politely instructed Smile Orange to remove the van. They were ignored and suddenly, like a fly to shit, another dilapidated van mysteriously appeared in the car park next to it.

> It was completely our fault but also totally beyond our control. We'd tried not to wind up the security team at Yorkshire TV but it just inevitably happened.

BOB PRIESTLEY
(SMILE ORANGE PRODUCTIONS LTD)

Now, with now two clapped-out bangers to deal with, the security team stepped up their vigilance, nothing would get past them again. It was, of course, at this moment that the Pub-a-Van was stolen.

For months afterwards, the stolen van was spotted driving around Leeds, still painted up as the Pub-a-Van. It may still be around today; sad, past-it, angering most people but still strangely proud. In a way the story of the Pub-a-Van works as

A typical television prop vehicle.

The Pub-a-Van is a mobile drinking wreck and this is the celebrity equivalent.

a perfect metaphor for the career of ex-Take That singer Robbie Williams.

WHAT ARE TELEVISION BUDGETS?

The perfect plan B

Television budgets are the monies used in television to fund the creation of a television creative production. At the start of shooting *Focus North* Channel 4 hadn't yet paid any money into the Smile Orange bank account and Bob Priestley, who was paying for everything on his credit card, got the shits.

Therefore spending was kept to a minimum: On one day's shoot the location catering was bought from a local chippy. To keep costs down there was no fish allowed, everyone just had bags of chips. Priestley, being a vegan, didn't even have that. He possibly had a packet of product placement square crisps.

It was amazing what we made for that amount of money. The shows were too tight budget-wise but then they always are.

GUS BOUSFIELD

(SMILE ORANGE PRODUCTIONS LTD)

Actually, no, all the square crisps had been eaten by then. He had a packet of plain Seabrook crisps. Which he bought himself, along with everybody else's chips. True story. Invoices were already piling up and the producers began to wonder what would happen if Channel 4 reneged on their promise to pay up. Trying not to panic, Smile Orange Productions Ltd reassured themselves that if no money came through they had a Plan B. They would make the remaining shows entirely by filming Austin Oates knee-deep in a rural beck blathering on whilst catching crayfish with his bare hands.

But, before they resorted to that, Butler, Bousfield and Priestley just had to pray that the next shoot wouldn't cost too much money. Hopefully they wouldn't be filming anywhere expensive, like a studio or anything…

FILM FACT

If you have managed to read this far into this book then you are either mad, a genius or Johnny Pigram. Hi Johnny Pigram!

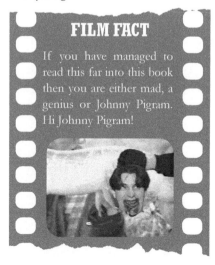

CHAPTER THIRTY-NINE
THE TELEVISION STUDIO

WHAT IS A TELEVISION STUDIO?

A Television studio, or studios, is, or are, a building, or buildings, which have been designed specifically for the creation of a television show, or shows, by a professional television production company, or companies.

HOW IS A TELEVISION STUDIO DESIGNED?

The design of a television studio is similar to the movie studio with a few amendments for the special requirements of television production. These amendments include: Audience facilities, live broadcast technologies and irate building managers who haunt you with endless amounts of guilt for the rest of your life.

WHY SHOULD I USE A TELEVISION STUDIO?

Television studios are used because they provide a controlled environment away from weather, noise and thieves trying to steal the camouflage netting that hides the portaloos. The producers of *Focus North* wanted to make the series look like an

The studios were full of antiques and props and everything. I really liked them. You know you've landed on your feet when you can have a free cup of tea whenever you want

BOB PRIESTLEY

(SMILE ORANGE PRODUCTIONS LTD)

The studios were full of antiques and props and everything. I really disliked them. You know you're being ripped off when you can have a free cup of tea whenever you want.

JULIAN BUTLER

(SMILE ORANGE PRODUCTIONS LTD)

A typical television studio.

We decided to have Rivers and Rhodes appear as guests in the *Focus North* studio and, during the break, I went to have a cup of tea outside the studio. I knew another show was being made in the studio complex because I kept seeing the runner taking tea into the editing suite. Soon the runner came out for a breather. As he stood next to me he took a long look at my costume: I was dressed in my full Gary Rhodes suit and looked like a psychotic comedian tramp. He then asked how our show was going. 'Yep all good, we're just doing a show for Channel 4' I say full of self-importance. I asked him what he was working on. 'A football show, teaching kids footie skills' he says. 'Nice,' I say, 'how's it going?' 'Not bad' came his answer 'but I haven't done this kind of thing before, I

Bob Priestley minutes before telling a multi-millionaire football star how to get on in the world.

don't know if it's any good'. 'Oh well,' I said like a seasoned pro, 'keep going at it and you'll get there.' 'Erm, yes, I'll do that.' He says, seemingly thankful for the advice. 'Oh yes, just don't give up mate…' I'm fully patronising him now, 'work at it and you might get a break.' 'Yes I'll do that.'

He finished his coffee and I watch him get into an expensive convertible car and drive off. Another runner rushes up to me 'what did he say?' she asked excitedly. 'Nowt much,' I reply. 'Don't you know who that was?'. 'No' I say. 'It was Michael Owen!' she says. 'Oh, he's fucking nowt.' I reply, 'now get back to fucking work you rancid piece of human shit'. True story, I say, true story.

BOB PRIESTLEY
(SMILE ORANGE PRODUCTIONS LTD)

authentically mediocre regional television show and so they deduced that they would need to hire an authentically mediocre regional television studio. The producers immediately hired the legendary Leeds studios whose name is synonymous with studio work. Unfortunately the name of these studios cannot, for the moment, be recalled by any member of Smile Orange Productions. Or Google.

WHAT WILL I FIND INSIDE A PROFESSIONAL TELEVISION STUDIO?

Television studios often have sets built within them. The set for *This Morning with Holly and Phil* attempts to recreate an average British living room; a welcoming environment in which you might relax, have a cup of tea and show the Prime Minister of Britain a picture of some paedophiles.

After studying *This Morning*'s set the Smile Orange production team dressed the *Focus North* set in the way that a regional magazine show would be dressed. Like a fucking disgrace. *This Morning*'s set contains many everyday objects that we all recognise from our own homes; a huge wooden box that looks like the biggest stash box in the world and pictures of paedophiles. But the *Focus North* team weren't simply content to use boring everyday pictures of paedophiles. Oh no. Determined to outdo *This Morning*, the *Focus North* set was dressed with a real <u>living</u> criminal: Stuart Hall. That's

what you will find inside a professional television studio.

A disgraced pop star [Image removed for legal reasons].

HOW DO I PREPARE FOR A STUDIO SHOOT?

Studios cost lots of money and working quickly is paramount when shooting in one. Therefore it is recommended that you meet your actors beforehand to address any issues that may arise. So, the *Focus North* producers met their lead actors, Felicity Pendle and Tom Adams, in the plush bar of an expensive Leeds hotel the night before their shoot. Over a drink the producers outlined their plans and asked if there were any problems. Felicity Pendle said she had learned all her lines and Tom Adams was happy. Unfortunately, on the first day of the shoot, Felicity Pendle had not learned her lines and Tom Adams was not happy.

[Image removed for legal reasons.]
Two lead actors prepare to say some words in a studio (L-R: Female actoress, male actorer).

SHOULD I USE AUTOCUE IN A STUDIO?

An autocue is a display device that projects a script in front of the camera lens so an actor can read his, or her, lines while looking directly into the lens. The device is an absolute life saver if your leading lady has not bothered to remember any of her lines. Smile Orange Productions had not bought an autocue and, when it became obvious that their leading actress hadn't learned any of her lines, they were so clueless that they didn't even consider the possibility of renting one.

"

On the day when Butler and Priestley were on set acting as Rivers and Rhodes they were running out of time because Felicity Pendle hadn't learn her lines. I remember them having serious discussions about it but part of Butler's costume was a prosthetic goitre attached to his face. So it just looked ridiculous. After filming the scene Butler just ripped it off. The goitre that is.

A great example of matching sofas in a television studio.

JUSTIN ROBERTSON

(SECOND UNIT, FOCUS NORTH)

Julian Butler as Dougie Rivers about to rip a Goitre off his neck.

WHAT ELSE SHOULD A PRODUCER BE AWARE OF IN A TELEVISION STUDIO?

As a producer you should be always be aware that the television studio can be a dangerous place. Especially if everyone is running around panicking because your lead actress has neglected to learn her lines. Things will get even tenser when your lead actress questions the safety aspects of using a chainsaw in one of the scenes and requests that the sketch is dropped. However, you love chainsaws and will refuse. This will then escalate into a full blown argument between your lead actress and you. Screams and insults will fly in all directions in front of the cast and crew and it will end with you bellowing asthmatically "WHEN YOU GET YOUR OWN BASTARD TV SERIES THEN YOU CAN DROP SKETCHES. UNTIL THEN DO AS WE FUCKING WELL SAY!!!". The situation will in no way be helped by Tom Adams threateningly revving a chainsaw and waving it inches from your lead actress's face.

Eventually the shoot will all end happily when your terrified and bullied lead actress will do what is demanded of her and another mediocre comedy skit will be in the can. And so, with your studio shoot complete, you can move on to exploit other people, this time a second unit camera crew.

CHAPTER FORTY
THE SECOND UNIT

WHAT IS A SECOND UNIT?

The second unit is a small team that works in addition to the main camera crew. *Focus North*'s second unit captured some compelling shots for the show: Close-ups of a hammer, some crumbs and a mole in a G-string hammock.

WHO MAKES A GOOD SECOND UNIT?

Your second unit should consist of people who are willing to do the tasks

MY MORNING

I usually wake up with my runner girlfriend Holly. We jump in her Mini Metro and drive the hundred metres to work. The offices are very busy; big piles of useless shit being moved in and out and crap being built. It's like a second-hand bric-a-brac shop because everything the producers buy is from charity shops. Some days I might be asked to film something like close-ups of a rugby league player's crow's feet. So I'd use the old Smile Orange Sony VX1000. It is usually broken.

JUSTIN ROBERTSON
(SECOND UNIT,
FOCUS NORTH)

Classic examples of objects a second unit will be asked to film.

that you don't want to do. The producers of *Focus North* were extremely immature and had problems dealing with members

The quintessential television second unit: Joel Levack (centre), Justin Robertson (right).

of the general public, therefore they utilised second unit member Joel Levack to communicate with the boring Lumpenproletariat. People like you. In

I think I met up with Julian Butler not long after finishing A-levels and expressed an interest in working on the upcoming project *Focus North*. Then I met with the production coordinator Steve Coote at those towers in Meanwood. And then got the job. I also sorted out some crew fleeces and I organised the wrap party screening of *Focus North* live at the Wardrobe.

JOEL LEVACK
(SECOND UNIT, FOCUS NORTH)

return Levack was encouraged to sleep with as many members of the crew and cast as possible.

The technical aspects of filming the great unwashed was left to second unit cameraman and ex-Airedale College alumnus, Justin Robertson. Robertson, like Levack, also showed great ability for someone at the start of their career.

HOW SHOULD A SECOND UNIT DISPOSE OF PROPS?

The needs of a production are constantly in flux and therefore props should not be disposed of unless the production has definitely finished with them. Therefore, just in case it was needed again, *Focus North*'s second unit left their mole on the window ledge of the YTV offices. The mole started to decompose and smell quite badly. Then somehow it dropped down onto the security hut below. The security team were quite angry. At least it distracted them from worrying about the Pub-a-Van.

WHAT ELSE DOES A SECOND UNIT FILM?

Second units often have to film things

One day Joel and I were sent off to film a shot of a mole reclining in a G-string hammock. Strangely we were confident we would find a mole, so we went and bought the G-string first. We then headed out into the countryside and stopped in a good place to shoot the scene. We looked down and there was a mole. It was just waiting for us. It's true. I've never even seen a mole before that day or since and it was just sat there. I grabbed the mole, filmed the shot and returned to the offices proudly. Julian Butler was not impressed.

JUSTIN ROBERTSON
(SECOND UNIT, FOCUS NORTH)

that happen unexpectedly and during a shoot at an agricultural show *Focus North*'s second unit managed to film, by accident, a news-worthy event when they spotted a kebab van with a huge plume of black smoke coming from it. Bob Priestley, dressed as the regional

I was just a bit pissed off that they had used a ladies G-string and not a man's. It took me a while to get over that. They did bring me a dead mole though, that was nice.

JULIAN BUTLER
(SMILE ORANGE PRODUCTIONS LTD)

Mike Plimmer

Chips are stranger than fiction: Shots of the fire that became a real case for the imaginary presenter Mike Plimmer.

reporter Mike Plimmer, described what he saw to camera, keeping in character throughout. The deep fat fryer was fully ablaze and the van owner was about to pour water on it. If he had there would have been a huge explosion, possibly killing him. Priestley shouted for the van

Justin thought that we shouldn't have tried to stop the van owner pouring water onto the blaze and then Justin could have filmed the man burning to death. I believe it's this kind of thinking which made Robertson the fine international news cameraman he is today

BOB PRIESTLEY
(SMILE ORANGE PRODUCTIONS LTD)

owner to stop, but he was ignored.

Luckily, at that moment, the fire brigade turned up and extinguished the fire, saving the van owner's life. Robertson captured it all on film and a whole new sketch was written around this footage completely misrepresenting the situation

Changing the meaning of real footage like this is probably against all laws of consent but Bob, Julian and Gus didn't seem to care. Or probably know.

JUSTIN ROBERTSON
(SECOND UNIT, FOCUS NORTH)

WHAT IS THE FUTURE OF THE SECOND UNIT?

I tried to ask Malcolm in Cottingley but he was too busy collecting golden frogs for the opening of his cryptozoological reserve.

Second units consist of the best of women and the worst of men. They should always shut the fuck up and get the work done, the best always do. But don't forget to still get your production coordinator to sack them at the end of it.

PETER WARD
(VETERAN PRODUCER)

CHAPTER FORTY-ONE
TELEVISION POST-PRODUCTION

WHAT IS TELEVISION POST-PRODUCTION?

Television post-production is the bit where you go indoors after you've been outside, switch on more monitors than are good for you, watch your footage and see where you have gone wrong.

WHAT IS THE HISTORY OF TELEVISION POST-PRODUCTION?

Television post-production was invented during the shoot for an episode of *Minder* when George Cole was punched in the face for real by Dennis Waterman. Not happy with this actual violence the BBC decided to 'remove' or 'edit' the shot out. It was at this point that television executives realised that not everything they shot had to be included in their shows. It is also interesting to note that the ruddy cheeks of Detective Chisolm's sidekick Jones were the first example of colour correction when they were made redder to make him look more of a pig.

HOW DO I SCHEDULE MY TELEVISION POST-PRODUCTION?

The post-production schedule of a ten-part series sometimes necessitates editing to happen twenty-four hours a day.

Your standard TV edit suite. Not the one Smile Orange used. Just a free shot taken from the internet.

As we toured the hallowed Yorkshire Television corridors we drank in the history. We could almost see producers discussing documentaries about minstrels or writing teams earnestly debating the nuances of a Jobfinder script.

JULIAN BUTLER
(SMILE ORANGE PRODUCTIONS LTD)

Focus North singing editor Justin Robertson.

Sometimes by the same editor. Second unit cameraman Justin Robertson, aided by Julian Butler, took over the late night editing of *Focus North* and, during breaks, the duo couldn't resist the temptation to sneakily explore the YTV studios.

WHAT SHOULD I DO DURING BREAKS IN TELEVISION POST-PRODUCTION?

Down periods during television post-production should be used to familiarise yourself with your editing software and equipment. Or, if you are Justin

One night when we were supposed to be editing we went into the Countdown studio. It was all open and there was no one there. We climbed on the set and then onto the lighting rig. The security guards came in. We just waited for them to leave and then carried on.

JUSTIN ROBERTSON (SECOND UNIT, FOCUS NORTH)

Purple, clocks and shagging were popular in the Countdown studio.

Robertson, you could steal precious DAT tapes of the *Through the Keyhole* theme tune or sneak onto the *Emmerdale* set and move props around so that the continuity is broken.

WHAT IS THE FUTURE OF TELEVISION POST-PRODUCTION?

The future of television post-production is an exciting one: It is called The Edit Suit. The Edit Suit will be a double breasted work suit with shuttle controls built into elbow patches and multiple monitors built into the shiny buttons. An editor will just have to walk to the bogs and back and his suit will edit his rugby match highlights video for him. And all the DVD extras too. So says Malcolm in Cottingley.

One day the *Focus North* producers were approached by Yorkshire Television's livid-faced Head of Security. He informed the producers that a crime had been committed that was far worse than the dumped Pub-a-Van or the rotting mole. To make matters worse the scene of the crime was within the hallowed *Countdown* studio. Smile Orange Productions were now in danger of being thrown out of the building altogether and, the Head of Security told them, it was all because of something Justin Robertson had been caught doing. The offence was so indescribably awful that it will hopefully work as a way to get you to turn the page and read the next chapter.

CHAPTER FORTY-TWO
THE TV SPECIAL

WHAT IS A TV SPECIAL?

From *Minder on the Orient Express* to 'Jobfinder: Bullying in the Workplace', the TV Special is an absolute favourite of anyone who has ever had nothing better to do than watch a television programme.

WHAT IS THE HISTORY OF TV SPECIALS?

Let's not bother with that. Instead let's reveal the unspeakable act that second unit cameraman Justin Robertson committed in the *Countdown* studio. He was, of course, found having sex in the ladies toilets with his girlfriend Holly Whitaker. Smile Orange's producers felt extremely disappointed. Disappointed that Robertson didn't wipe semen on the clock hand of that big stupid Countdown clock. He then could have made a nice clock/cock wordplay type joke of some description. Dirty.

Years later Butler bumped into two of *Focus North*'s runners, Jason Denning and Mark Graham. They had both gained full time employment at Yorkshire TV and they'd heard that the Head of Security had vowed that Smile Orange would never be allowed in the YTV building ever again. Ironically Butler was in the

It is unquestionable that Robertson is in possession of a massive talent, but not everyone saw it this way. I explained to YTV's Head of Security that there was simply nothing I could do. If I'd reprimanded Robertson he would have continued to muck around just to spite me. If I didn't reprimand him he'd have considered this as complicity. I wanted to help the security team but Justin was too far gone.

BOB PRIESTLEY
(SMILE ORANGE PRODUCTIONS LTD)

Jason Denning and Mark Graham with Gus Bousfield as Lucky Pierre.

My attitude to this was let romance blossom and seed be spilt. YTV probably wanted us to reprimand Justin further but at that point we weren't even paying him so he technically wasn't even our employee. So I ignored it all. And maybe laughed at it a bit too. I can't really remember.

JULIAN BUTLER

(SMILE ORANGE PRODUCTIONS LTD)

YTV building at the time they told him this.

HOW DO I GET MY OWN TV SPECIAL?

Moving, at last, onto the actual theme of this chapter; the TV special. *Focus North* was mildly successful when broadcast on Channel 4. So commissioning editor Olly Sharpe suggested re-editing the ten episodes down to five and re-broadcasting them. Sharpe also decided that a new sixth

When we left the studios we were like 'we've left rubble through your foyer and there's dog food rotting over in the shared area and you have been very kind, thank you very much.'

BOB PRIESTLEY

(SMILE ORANGE PRODUCTIONS LTD)

episode should be made and this would be the *Focus North* TV special. Smile Orange's producers weren't too keen on the idea but when Sharpe offered them a further £70,000 Smile Orange's producers were then very keen on the idea.

HOW DO I MAKE A TV SPECIAL?

A TV special should not be an excuse to find bits of old unused footage and link them together with jokes. Having said that, the *Focus North* TV Special did find bits of old unused footage and link them together with jokes. In fact most other TV specials do this too.

Chapter filler: *Focus North* in the press.

INSIDE TELEVISION: UP AND COMING

Northern lights

TOBYN ANDRAE charts the rise of comedy group Smile Orange and their latest project Focus North – a spoof regional news show on Channel 4

SPOOF news shows have become something of a comedy staple in recent times. On Channel 4, The 11 O'clock Show is back for a new series, revisiting the turf first ploughed by Chris Morris's The Day Today, while on BBC2 Chris Langham's brilliant send-up of current affairs documentaries, People Like Us, came to an untimely end on Monday. Even the granddaddy of them all, Not The Nine O'Clock News, was dredged up for a run of repeats earlier in the year, looking magically dated alongside the young talent of today, talent such as Julian Butler, Bob Priestley, Gus Bousfield and Mat Wardle, the team behind the latest offering of news satire, **FOCUS NORTH**.

Buried away in the night time schedules of Channel 4, Focus North is to regional news shows what Alan Partridge was to the chat show. Once viewed, it will be hard to look at those oh-so-sincere reports of local traffic accidents, cats stuck up trees or minor local celebrities with anything except utter derision.

"Basically, I was haunted by childhood memories of shows like Calendar and Nationwide, with their jumbla stories and patronising approach, and yet hundreds and thousands of people across the country tune into them every week," explains Mat Wardle, one of Focus North's four writer/producers.

"We just wanted to get something back. It's not high drama, it's not a sketch show, it's really a rebuff against the mind-numbing nature of regional TV."

Typical examples of a Focus North investigation include a report on the local council evicting a cemetery to make way for a new 5,000-seater fairground ride, a chef who serves nothing but road kill (including puddle shark and peas) or tonight's Hallowe'en special on a woman who is, quite literally, away with the fairies.

"When writing a spoof on parochialism, small mindedness and insular attitudes, we are all highly qualified, having lived and worked in Yorkshire for most of their lives," explains Wardle, 26. Yet despite their cramped offices, ridiculously low budgets and a costume department the likes of which most good charity shops would reject, the group, known collectively as SmileOrange, have already made quite an impact.

After starting out as a wedding video company, selling dreams to the lovestruck and accidentally pregnant, they diversified into making low budget horror films with names like Nightbeast, Hunt For The Yorkshire Grimace and Fatliners – the story of a group of overweight wrestlers whose belly-bashing transports them into a time warp. Falling into the category "so bad they're good", the films became

cult classics, getting shown at the Cannes film festival and earning their makers a certain kind of notoriety. Not a bad return on the £350 budget the films each cost to make, a sum that makes The Blair Witch Project seem the height of extravagance. So it was that Channel 4 talent-scouted the company and signed them up for a 10-part run of Focus North.

"In order to gain an authentic edge, all 10 scripts were knocked out in the space of four weeks," says Wardle. "We all had to live, work and sleep in the same room, which was hell, and really it was just a question of producing a very low budget comedy series that looked like it wasn't made for favours up on favours which, of course, it was."

With a cast that includes a strange mixture of ex-Eldorado actors, former regional news presenters and ex-convicts from the Yorkshire area (apparently so), Focus North's impact has been slow to build up. "We're very popular with the security guards and cleaners at Yorkshire Television," says Wardle, optimistically, but for those Friday night, post-pub viewing moments, it has a definite appeal. The future, it seems, could be SmileOrange.

● Focus North is on C4 at 1.45am.

ROAD KILLING JOKE: Fancy a slice of puddle shark?

FILM FACT

Yorkshire Television's *The Gaffer* has never had a TV special. But if *The Gaffer* ever did have a TV special it might involve the Gaffer and Ginger riding a canal barge down the Leeds to Liverpool canal. Or, here's another brilliant idea: Maybe The Gaffer and Ginger could go to the TT races and meet Guy Martin!!! Oh, hang on, would Guy do a TV special though? Especially *The Gaffer*? Would he lower himself that far? Never. So, no, that wouldn't happen.

To hide this fact, Butler, Bousfield and Priestley decided to set the *Focus North* TV special in the future. And to suggest what television might look like in the future they filmed Tom Adams' links with him standing in a studio lit only with a strobe light. The flashing looked amazing and of course Channel 4 refused to broadcast it because it would induce epileptic fits. The producers then spent many days and thousands of pounds in a post-production studio in Soho removing an effect that cost twenty quid to make.

HOW SHOULD I END A TV SPECIAL?

The end of a TV special should be spectacular and so Smile Orange decided to end their show with a massive fight between the cast and some chickens.

To give the impression of a chicken attack the poultry were physically thrown, in great numbers, at the cast. Everyone stayed professional whilst shooting the scene but special praise goes to seventy-

As soon as the chickens arrived on set Tom Adams was on the phone to his agent. I admit, making the TV special was a bit weird — the studio was sort of dark, with a strobe going and there were crates of chickens clucking throughout the shoot. But I had half a mind to say 'well you read the script Tom, you knew what was going to happen.'

BOB PRIESTLEY
(SMILE ORANGE PRODUCTIONS LTD)

two year old actor Stewart Mills who sat unflinching throughout the whole thing. This may have been due to his years of acting experience or possibly because his eyes were covered with two eye patches and his arms and legs were strapped to his sides.

HOW DO I WRAP MY TELEVISION SERIES?

The most important part of wrapping

Alien chickens massacring the entire cast is the only correct climax for a TV special.

BIZARRE **visuals** Edited by Mark Blacklock

Bizarre Jan. 2000

Focus North

Not the only fruitcakes

Smile Orange's new Channel 4 show *Focus North* ridicules the sofa-driven world of regional TV. STUART WRIGHT dons his brown cardigan

SMILE ORANGE (aka Julian Butler, Gus Bousfield, Bob Priestley and Matt Wardie) are an independent production company from Leeds with a taste for the foolish and strange. They cut their teeth making hommages to the heroes of trash cinema and now they've hit the big time on Channel 4 with *Focus North*, a show that does for smarmy regional TV what Alan Partridge did for Radio Norwich.

What are you like?
MW: We're like the loony at school that just loses it and spits and kicks until it kills the biggest kid there.

Tell us about your humble beginnings, and the film Nightbeast...
JB: *Nightbeast* originally came out as a really shit 1980s horror thing, made by a guy called Don Dollar, who is like the Ed Wood of video nasties. It was just the sort of thing we were watching when we were growing up. I wouldn't like to say we even thought of it as a film – it just so happened that it was feature length. We did the covers for it to carry on the pisstake. It looks like sort of thing you would take to parties or whatever."

Then came the Yorkshire kung fu flick, Ilikiliya...
JB: We just wrote this kung fu film because we always used to laugh at kung fu films. We'd search out ridiculous films like *Two Crippled Fighters* which

has a guy with no arms and one with no legs teaming up. Really bad kung fu, obviously.

Is that why you did The Hunt for Yorkshire Grimace, a tale of two Bernard Manning types in search of their kidnapped, Tourette's-suffering brother?
JB: We got a bit of success from *Ilikiliya* – it was shown on late night TV and the trailer got on the *Big Breakfast* – then we thought, fuck it, let's make the most offensive film we fucking can. No morals. I watch it now and I cringe and think we couldn't have done that. Really obvious stereotypes, but you're not supposed to do it. It's like children blowing a raspberry. It's all very childish.

Next came Fatliners, a film set in Ring World, a place populated entirely by British wrestlers.
JB: That's the one we had the biggest budget for (£2,000) and a cast of about 200. Massive amounts of work went into that one. We went to Cannes with it and we got into *Variety*.

And now regional magazine programme spoof Focus North, starring Tom Adams, an actor semi-famous for doing DFS (furniture showroom) ads.
GB: I think one of the things is that the stories are

independent of the local news set-up. It's just a device to get into each story. It's not meant to be sharply-observed satire.
BP: There's a pisstake of *Emmerdale Farm* called *Three Pigs*. Which is really badly-acted and influenced by Dylan Thomas, while being on the set of an ostrich farm.
GB: There was a character on Yorkshire TV called Hanna Hawkswell who they used to take to places like New York, and she wouldn't like it. She'd say: "it was crap and I want to be back on my farm." We've got a pisstake out of that with this woman called Millie Tarnwell. Basically, the *Focus North* crew corrupt her completely and introduce her to various vibrators and things.
GB: All the characters come back for the Christmas Special. The sort of voice of rationality that's been hanging around through the thing disappears. The scientist character, Dr Miles Ashcroft... well, he ends up being butchered by the whole crew of *Focus North* and then burned. So it's sort of a cross between *The Wicker Man* and *North By North West*.

Focus North will be repeated by Channel 4 in January 2000

Housewife's choi: babes in *Focus N...*

a television series is making sure that your production coordinator manages the final balancing of budgets, signing of contracts and paying of invoices. By the end of *Focus North* the show's production coordinator, Steve Coote, had becoming a close and trusted friend of Butler, Bousfield and Priestley. Coote

understood their humour and was the fix-it person they'd always needed to guide them through their own chaos. Coote was also in complete control of the company's bank accounts, budget and tax records. There was just one little fact that Coote hadn't fully disclosed to the team: He was a complete fucking liar.

CHAPTER FORTY-THREE
RUNNING A TV PRODUCTION COMPANY

NOTE: Some of the information in the following chapter is revised and updated from a previous edition of this book. The original text is based on interviews made with Smile Orange Productions during the shooting of *Focus North*. The updated text comes from interviews a year later.

HOW DO I SUCCESSFULLY RUN A TELEVISION PRODUCTION COMPANY?

The company directors of Smile Orange Productions Ltd suggest that the successful way to run a production company is to completely trust your production coordinator, Steve Coote, to deal with all administrative and budgetary duties.

(UPDATED TEXT:) It might be an idea to keep a little eye on your production coordinator. At all fucking times.

WHAT ARE INVOICES?

An invoice is a commercial document issued by a seller to a buyer relating to a sale transaction. You can leave the boring task of paying these to your production coordinator whilst you concentrate on making the creative decisions needed to successfully film a mole in a G-string hammock.

(UPDATED TEXT:) Production coordinators should NEVER EVER be trusted with the payment of anything unless you want an endless stream of unpaid invoices to arrive after you wrap.

HOW CAN MY PRODUCTION COORDINATOR HELP WHEN A PRODUCTION WRAPS?

After your production wraps the production coordinator will always be easy to contact to help sort out any loose ends.

(UPDATED TEXT:) Your production coordinator will be impossible to contact after your production wraps: Even when you go round to their London flat where, despite the curtains being drawn and the lights being on, they will never answer the door.

WARNING: Do not pay this bill yourself, It is just a picture in a book.

WHAT DOES A PRODUCTION ACCOUNTANT DO?

A production accountant deals with production finances on a daily basis. At the start of production on *Focus North* Butler, Bousfield and Priestley were informed by Steve Coote that an accountant was constantly monitoring the production's budget.

(UPDATED TEXT:) Soon after completion of *Focus North* Butler, Bousfield and Priestley observed that the production finances were in complete disarray. Below is a transcript from a phone conversation Bob Priestley had with Smile Orange's production accountant when, after discovering the financial discrepancies, he contacted him for the first time.

Priestley: Hello, production accountant. Please can you tell me why we are fucked?
Accountant: Hello? Who is this?
Priestley: This is Mr Bob Priestley.
Accountant: Who?
Priestley: Mr Priestley? From Smile Orange?
Accountant: Smile what?
Priestley: Smile Orange Productions Ltd.
Accountant: Ha ha, that's a stupid name for a company.
Priestley: Silence! You are our accountant.
Accountant: I'm not your accountant.
Priestley: But I've been told by Steve Coote that you have been dutifully tending to all our accounts for the entire series.

This is the type of calculator always used to calculate how much shit there is and the speed of the fan.

Accountant: Oh, has Steve been telling his lies again?
Priestley: Ah, of course I should have known.
Accountant: (More laughter)
Priestley: Kind sir, please help us out of this mess.
(Phone goes dead)
Priestley: Hello?

Smile Orange Productions Ltd began to wonder what the fuck was going on. The producers were about to investigate further when things got even more exciting. A large tax bill arrived from the Inland Revenue for £45,000.

DOES RUNNING A TELEVISION PRODUCTION COMPANY INVOLVE PAYING TAX?

No, don't bother with any of that.

> ❝
>
> Unimagined stress levels, shivering, skin loss, alcoholism, finding yourself curled up in a ball having a breakdown on a recreational site and handruff (see Glossary) are, apparently, all part of the exciting world of television.

BOB PRIESTLEY
(SMILE ORANGE PRODUCTIONS LTD)

(UPDATED TEXT:) It may seem odd but when you earn money you have to pay tax on it. Not doing so is a fucking moronic act of financial suicide which, funnily enough, will lead to actual thoughts of suicide for frailer members of your group.

WHAT HAPPENS ONCE I GET A REAL ACCOUNTANT?

When you finally get an accountant that actually exists you need to go to their office, explain your situation as logically as possible and then try the razzle dazzle. Like Smile Orange Productions

you should tell your accountant that this £45,000 tax bill nonsense is just a small downward blip in an otherwise upward trajectory. Tell your accountant that huge budgets are not uncommon in television and that your millions are just around the corner.

(UPDATED TEXT:) For some reason when you talk to your our accountant they will just rub their brow and sigh a lot.

WHAT WILL MY ACCOUNTANT ASK ME TO DO?

Your accountant won't ask you to do anything. Instead they will do all the work for you and you won't have to think about any of it.

(UPDATED TEXT:) Your accountant will explain that the Inland Revenue

> ❝
>
> I remember once, when we were all living across from Yorkshire Television in a rented house, Steve Coote used his newly awarded position of authority to try to convince my girlfriend, Holly, NOT to sleep in my bed but to 'keep warm' by sleeping in his bed, with him. But hang on, we filmed *Focus North* in the summer didn't we? So, he was cunning as well as a cunt.

JUSTIN ROBERTSON
(SMILE ORANGE FILMS)

A typical reaction whilst running a production company.

are investigating your company for serious financial irregularities and they are demanding to see all your company paperwork. You will realise that your disappearing production coordinator has taken all your paperwork with him and you cannot prove in any way how you spent nearly a quarter of a million pounds. To prove where all this money went you will then have to hunt down every receipt, bank statement, cheque stub, IOU and cum-stained bill for potato wedges for a romantic meal for your production coordinator and one of the production runners at TGI fucking Fridays.

HOW SHOULD I MANAGE THE COMPANY BANK ACCOUNT?

You can happily leave management of the company bank account in the reliable hands of your production coordinator.

(UPDATED TEXT:) Maybe check a bank statement every now and then. At least the Smile Orange [name of bank removed] bank account stipulated that a cheque must have at least two signatures for it to be cashed. But, after checking all the cheques (excellent joke) Butler and Priestley discovered that [name of bank removed] had been cashing cheques with only Steve Coote's name on them. The duo went to complain and after a lengthy meeting with the [name of bank removed] legal department the matter

was resolved when they were shown the door. The duo were crying all the way from the bank. Funny joke.

HOW DO I DEAL WITH LIARS IN TELEVISION PRODUCTION?

Impossible.

(UPDATED TEXT:) Really Impossible. After analysing all the bits of paper and the numbers and the computer screens with the numbers on them the truth was emerging for Smile Orange. That truth was they were fucking fucked.

CHAPTER FORTY-FOUR
BANKRUPTCY

WHAT IS BANKRUPTCY?

Imagine a huge boa constrictor wound loosely around a crab. You are the crab. The snake can crush you at any moment but it does not. It doesn't actually kill you but it is the eternal threat of being crushed that gets you in the end. This is bankruptcy.

HOW DO I FIND A GOOD INSOLVENCY PRACTITIONER?

Insolvency practitioners are licensed to advice people on all formal bankruptcy procedures. When you owe £45,000 to the tax man it is recommended that you get a good one of these very, very quickly. There are two ways to test whether an insolvency practitioner is good or bad:

1: CHECK THE SIZE OF THE ARM JEWELLERY.

At the very start of a meeting with your prospective insolvency practitioner always ask to check the size of their cufflinks. Smile Orange's manically brow-rubbing accountant recommended one insolvency practitioner in Halifax but when Butler and Priestley went to his offices they were confronted instead by a monster. The monster tried to charge for their initial consultation but Butler reminded him that this was meant to be free. This seemed to anger the monster who told them the insolvency would cost them £10,000. Priestley asked 'what is the £10,000 for?' The monster replied 'fo' adverts in t'papers'. Priestley said 'What, £10,000 worth of adverts?' The monster was now furious and ejected the duo from the building shouting 'YOU WHAT!!? ARE YOU BEING

Avoid all insolvency practitioners who wear anything resembling this.

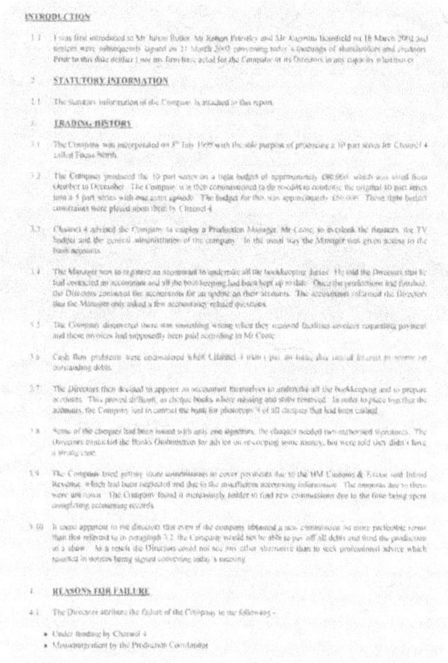

INTRODUCTION

2 STATUTORY INFORMATION

2.1 The statutory information of the Company is attached to this report.

3 TRADING HISTORY

4 REASONS FOR FAILURE

4.1 The Directors attribute the failure of the Company to the following -

- Under funding by Channel 4
- Mismanagement by the Production Coordinator

Smile Orange Production's boring bankruptcy report.

CLEVER WI' ME OR WHAT? GET OUT YA CLEVER BASTARDS, KEEP GOING…THAT'S RIGHT…ALL T' WAY OUT'. But what really freaked Butler and Priestley out was the size of his massive arm jewellery. Again, always ask to check the size of the cufflinks.

2: GET THREE QUOTES.

You've tried recommended insolvency practitioners and that didn't work so now it's time for you to cold-call licensed insolvency practitioners from the *Yellow Pages*. After endless phone calls Butler and Priestley finally got three wildly differing quotes from three separate firms: One for £2000, one for £5000 and one for £15,000. Guess which one Smile Orange chose to go with?

WHAT WILL MY INSOLVENCY PRACTITIONERS BE CALLED?

Your new licensed insolvency practitioners will be called Rhodesy and Townhouse. In every meeting they will seem to have just walked in from an all-night Leeds City Centre boozing session. They will insist that you do not mention to their boss that you are paying them only £2000 for their services. They will then openly mock your names. If one of you is called Augustin Bousfield then you will be laughed at the most. But the names Julian and Bob will be laughed at too. Do not try the razzle dazzle on them, they have seen it all before and they know you have failed.

WHAT ADVICE WILL MY INSOLVENCY PRACTITIONER GIVE ME?

Rhodesy and Townhouse started earning their £2000 with one sterling bit of advice: Because Smile Orange Productions Ltd had more than two company directors they were able to claim redundancy pay at the same time as going bankrupt.

> "We owed the government money and yet we could claim redundancy money from the government. That seemed illogical to me.
>
> **BOB PRIESTLEY (SMILE ORANGE PRODUCTIONS LTD)**

What everybody fears.

Rhodesy and Townhouse then proceeded to arrange an insolvency hearing. At an insolvency hearing your company's creditors are invited to come and discuss how the last of the company's savings will be divided amongst them. In other words, this is the day when the people you owe £45,000 can turn up and tell you off. HMRC don't usually turn up to insolvency hearings so you stand around for a couple of hours in a strange office somewhere near Batley and then sign a few papers, swear on a Bible a couple of times and BINGO, like a cheap video effect, your company is dissolved.

The Holy Bible. For no known reason this must be gripped tightly at your insolvency hearing.

I remember going to the insolvency hearing I think? Why did we go that day? Oh yes we were waiting for the taxman to turn up. I was the company secretary, the financial guy, so it was my fault (laughs nervously).

GUS BOUSFIELD

(EX-SMILE ORANGE PRODUCTIONS LTD)

HOW DOES IT FEEL TO BE BANKRUPT?

At this fascinating point in the TV production process you may never laugh again. On the bright side you will become incredibly skilled at harbouring bitterness, keeping it fresh but hidden, deep inside. You will also become highly critical of all TV/films/comedy. Even watching your own productions will be hard and the irony that you filmed a sketch about a school for debt collectors and then went

PRO TIP

When you owe money the bailiffs will come round and take your props off you! It can get right exciting! Lots of loud noise and shouting. Sometimes there's one, sometimes two, sometimes a van full, and another empty van to put all your props in!! They wear black bomber jackets, all shiny. The acting becomes very good and fast and action-based like a movie with Bruce Lee in.

NICKY HINCHCLIFFE

(TOP HOLLYWOOD DIRECTOR)

into debt yourselves almost makes you laugh. Almost.

FILM FACT

Indiana Jones and The Temple of Doom was the second Indiana Jones film.

Focus North [Image removed for legal reasons].

PRO TIP

Bailiffs can act better than most and they make great villains. For God's sake put them in front of the camera!

PETER WARD

(VETERAN PRODUCER)

With the mocking laughter of Rhodesy and Townhouse still ringing in their ears Smile Orange Productions Ltd were now financially and creatively bankrupt, burned out and broke. Like Jenks, the mighty Yorkshire Icarus, launching, firmament bound, towards the gods themselves, in a bin, finally,

FUN FACT

The company name Smile Orange Productions Ltd is now available to be used again as a company name.

inevitably, plummeting back to Earth with a bone-splintering snap and not even a cheque from Beadle to show for it.

They'd played themselves.

WHAT IS THE FUTURE OF BANKRUPTCY?

Bankruptcy is where the best company directors have a chance to shine. So if you own a company then why not plan for your inevitable decline now and, instead of going to the gym, practice swearing on the Bible whilst crouched in a ball. Oh and the mothership is back this Thursday. Apparently they're taking Malcolm in Cottingley on board again.

CHAPTER FORTY-FIVE
POST-BANKRUPTCY

WHAT IS POST-BANKRUPTCY?

Post-bankruptcy is the period post-bankruptcy.

WHAT HAPPENS POST-BANKRUPTCY?

Post-bankruptcy is a good time, for producers who have failed, to look at other career options. But for idiots like Smile Orange there was another choice: If your company goes bankrupt as a result of making a television show then simply try to make another television show.

HOW DO I MAKE ANOTHER TELEVISION SHOW?

The best chance you have of making another television show is by keeping in close contact with your commissioning editor. Unfortunately the last time Smile Orange saw their commissioning editor, Olly Sharpe, he was setting off across the Atlantic in his boat. He was never seen

again by Butler, Bousfield, Priestley or Google. Sharpe was replaced at Channel 4 by a man called Darren Bender. Bender wanted to commission shows of a better quality than *Focus North*. So he brought late night poker to Channel 4. Smile Orange were in trouble.

WHAT SHOULD I DO IF THE ONLY COMMISSIONING EDITOR THAT EVER LIKED ME DISAPPEARS IN HIS FUCKING BOAT INTO THE SETTING SUN OF THE ATLANTIC FUCKING OCEAN?

When your commissioning editor disappears into the setting sun you should definitely NOT pitch an endless list of desperate and unsuitable ideas to blank-faced strangers at TV channels. So, of course, Smile Orange pitched an endless list of desperate and unsuitable ideas to blank-faced strangers at TV channels.

Typical workplace of ex-TV company director.

Production design from the proposed show *The Fantastic Screw to the Bowels of the Earth*. Just one of many shows that were, for some reason, never picked up by major television channels.

DHSS Film Fund fraud investigators interview ex-TV company directors here (Note PZM microphone on table).

During this process you will end up feeling like a clan of samurai warriors trying to impress some otters.

WHAT SHOULD I DO WHEN IT ALL GOES TO SHIT?

If it all goes to shit you have several other exciting career options open to you:

OPTION 1: If you have excellent communication skills then learn to ignore them and, like Smile Orange's Bob Priestley get a job at a call centre. Priestley's years on location had taught him how to hold in his urine, this skill was useful at the call centre because every second he spent pissing and shitting was logged (good joke). These logs were then used to criticise, or squiticise (another good joke) his working practices during his weekly stats-review. Whatever that is.

OPTION 2: Do what Smile Orange's Julian Butler did after *Focus North* and rent an office intending to run a production company but really just sit about smoking all day. Unfortunately the DHSS Film Fund will find out about this and summon you to an interview, under caution, where two fraud officers will threaten you with a possible prison sentence. You will find it ironic that the interviews are taped using a Tandy PZM mic. You will be disappointed that they haven't tied it to a plank. Afterwards you

will ask for copies of these tapes but, by accident, you will be sent copies of interviews with people that have similar surnames as yours.

This is a challenging part of the filmmaking process as you will find it almost impossible to convince the DHSS Film Fund fraud officers that, due to your complete lack of business acumen, you run a pretend production company. Smoke high-grade skunk throughout this period to keep you relaxed and not at all paranoid.

When the DHSS Film Fund Fraud Department have got you then you'll need to contact Legal Aid and lawyer-up. This will scare the fraud department off your scent… er… I mean prove that you are innocent.

JULIAN BUTLER

(SMILE ORANGE FILMS)

OPTION 3: Do what Gus Bousfield, the third member of Smile Orange, did after *Focus North* and sit alone in a freezing little recording studio pumping out an endless stream of trashy TV theme tunes, endless avant-garde cacophonies.

OPTION 4: Ignore the fact that your production company no longer exists and make another television show. This is what happened to Smile Orange Productions when finally one of their

TVAM's Mike Morris in *Best of British*.

pitches was accepted and they were asked to make a one-off show for Channel 4 called *Best of British*.

SMILE ORANGE FILMOGRAPHY

BEST OF BRITSH (2002)
Channel 4 Comedy Lab / 24 mins / BetaSP/ Colour

Best of British is a sports show featuring events like 'Competitive Bullying', 'Lost Property Find' and 'Webbox Dog Food Chuck'. The show spoofs sporting programmes like *It's a Knockout*, *Superstars* and *We are the Champions*. These were some of the most appalling sports shows in the world and were actually very good.

This time around Smile Orange weren't leaving anything to chance and decided to assemble the most professional team they'd ever employed. They hired an accomplished crew and an expert director and as a result the finished show was a piece of shit.

DOG MEAL SAUSAGE

Factual Breakdown

Despite some of the professionals not being professional, there was one professional who was incredibly professional: Old Smile Orange contact Tim Peck. Peck had impressed Butler years earlier with his work on a shoddy Zee TV quiz show. Peck spent the whole *Best of British* shoot up a tower. No one really knows what Peck was doing up the tower, maybe he was just avoiding being smashed into by Butler's car. *Best of British* was broadcast on Channel 4 and then forgotten. It was the last thing the Smile Orange team made together.

But, ten years later, Channel 4 showed a trailer for a serious documentary about the British Paralympic team, also called *Best of British*. The trailer's voiceover was suitably serious and the music was uplifting but, hilariously, someone had, by mistake, edited in footage from Smile

Exploding Webbox was the first and last thing that Smile Orange ever filmed. Some say they shouldn't have bothered filming the stuff in the middle. But those same people say that pictures of exploding Webbox alone wouldn't have made much of a book. But I think it would. I for one am glad there is a picture of it in this book. So there.

Image mistakenly claimed to be of the British Paralympics team.

PRO TIP

After your film career is finally flushed away then a rewarding career as a car park owner is within your grasp. Simply tarmac a field and charge car owners £18 per day for the privilege of having their cars sinking into the badly tarmacked mud. When you have enough cars in the field install a homeless person in a bin to hand out his used heroin foil as an entry ticket. After a while you can move up the career ladder and become a safari park owner. This is the same as a car park owner but you release a mandrill to run around fucking the cars. Charge people an extra £20 as this huge simian bonobo ejaculates onto the bonnet of their motor. I think that's me done then.

PETER WARD
(VETERAN PRODUCER)

Austin Oates as Satan in *Best of British*.

Orange's *Best of British*. The whole thing was preposterous and a triumphant, but brief, return to form for Smile Orange.

WHAT DOES POST-BANKRUPTCY FEEL LIKE?

Post-bankruptcy is a time for film and television professionals to reflect on their strengths and weaknesses and plan how to move forward. Or at least backwards. Smile Orange had spent, in total, £175,000 on making just themselves laugh. But a whoopee cushion eventually deflates. And, in the end, none of the team got anywhere near what they were expecting.

I thought we were going be like Peter Jackson: Start by making local stuff, gain a cult following and then take Hollywood by storm.

JULIAN BUTLER
(SMILE ORANGE FILMS)

WHAT IS THE FUTURE OF POST-BANKRUPTCY?

Using telepathy Malcolm in Cottingley told me that the future of post-bankruptcy is completely irrelevant because he's

The premise for the *Focus North* TV special was that the show was being transmitted back in time from the future. Therefore the *Focus North* cast had to look futuristic [Image removed for legal reasons].

I thought *Focus North* going to be something that the nation would take to its heart and love for years and years. Like Last of the Summer Wine.

BOB PRIESTLEY
(SMILE ORANGE FILMS)

I thought *Focus North* was going to be my first paid job.

JUSTIN ROBERTSON
(SMILE ORANGE FILMS)

I don't want to talk about Smile Orange.

GUS BOUSFIELD
(SMILE ORANGE FILMS)

recently been convening with twelve-dimensional alien beings from the edges of the Multiverse. Malcolm said he would introduce me to these beings because they could grant me anything I desired; from a highly paid job working for a film funding board to meeting TT racer Guy Martin. The mothership is coming again on Wednesday and I have decided to meet with them. The Kingdom of Video awaits me.

Smile Orange Productions, on the other hand, thought that their journey into the world of moving pictures was going to be an action packed thrill ride. Instead they found themselves confused, without hope and staring at *The Abyss* (Dir: James Cameron, 1992).

FILM FACT

Keep going. Unless you are crap, then stop.

StorytellingGBCreative

135C THE STABLES, LEEDS, WEST YORKSHIRE, LS3 5GH

Smile Orange Films
Address unknown
24th May 2014

Dear Jiglet, Augusticine and Bimp,

Hi guys! Roy Devon, author of 'The Wisdom of Stupidity' here! The amazing news is that I have been offered the role of Head of Funding here at *StorytellingGBCreative*. My predecessor Amanda Fees-Rodeane is no longer working here, I have closed Davidwellsley Car Park Safariland and I am happy to announce I am looking forward to funding a new set of fresh projects. All of them starring the master of the TT racing universe, Guy Martin (with maybe a support role for Benedict Cumberbatch here and there if I'm feeling charitable).

The bad news is that, as your projects are of no value to society, I unfortunately cannot accept any further correspondence from Smile Orange Films. I'm sorry to disappoint with my response and I wish you every success in your future endeavours.

My PA, Malcolm in Cottingley, will be happy to clear up any further queries you might have about the death of your dreams.

Ciao guys!

Roy Devon
Head of Funding
StorytellingGBCreative

APPENDIX I
CONTRIBUTORS

TOM ADAMS played the male presenter of *Focus North*. Also famous for DFS sofa adverts and less so for acting in *The Great Escape*.

ANDREA ARNOLD, OBE is an English filmmaker whose career pinnacle was filming Smile Orange for ITV's *Hotel Babylon*.

TOM ASHCROFT is one of the founding members of Smile Orange and starred in the early films.

CLIVE BALDWIN is the world's greatest minstrel and the inspiration for Smile Orange's *Focus North*.

JEREMY BEADLE was an English writer, producer and presenter of *You've Been Framed*.

JOHN BENTHAM is owner of film distribution company Screen Edge and is still a punk.

PAUL BEVERLEY is an adult film star, bodybuilder and Smile Orange actor.

BIG PAT was Bousfield and Butler's housemate in Nottingham and starred in *I'llkillya!*

ALISTAIR BIRDSELL was a Smile Orange actor, crooner and comedy heckler.

THE BLASTER is an evil entity disguised as a film light. Capable of blinding all cast and crew and burning down houses. Whereabouts unknown.

ANDREW BOLDY was the talented cameraboy and not so talented actor on numerous Smile Orange feature films.

GUS BOUSFIELD is one of the founding members of Smile Orange. He has a pretty loud dress sense but pulls it off well.

HOLLY WHITAKER was a runner on *Focus North*.

JULIAN BUTLER is one of the founding members of Smile Orange. Quite big and cuddly and pretty scruffy.

DANIEL KANYON was production assistant on *Focus North*. He also played Mel Gibson's legs in *Fairy Tale: A True Story*.

MISERABLE CGI LAD is an unknown grumpy lad who did CGI on *Fatliners*. Undoubtedly miserably making billions by now.

CHARLES, PRINCE OF WALES funded the post-production on *The Hunt for the Yorkshire Grimace*.

NIGEL CLARK produced Flux, the late night TV show that serialised *I'llkillya!*

NIGEL 'COOKIE' COOK was an actor in *Fatliners*.

STEVE COOTE was *Focus North*'s production coordinator and liar.

SAM DAWSON was *Focus North*'s art director who failed miserably to create some human-sized turkey drumstick legs.

DECKY is a ferreting video producer who can often be seen around Leeds, looking at knives in we-buy-owt shop windows, with ferret pelts and skulls stitched onto the epaulettes of his army surplus jacket.

ROY DEVON is me, the writer of this book.

GRAHAM DUCKWORTH is one of the founding members of Smile Orange and played Ken Fury in *I'llkillya!*

TONY EARNSHAW is a festival organiser, broadcaster, journalist and inexplicable champion of Smile Orange Films.

AMANDA FEES-RODEANE was the Head of Funding of regional funding body StorytellingGBCreative.

GINO FELICIELLO is an allotment gardener and Smile Orange actor.

MICHAEL FOSTER is an actor, muse and inspiration for *The Pike*.

NIGEL GILL is an actor who played Lumpin Trunk in *Fatliners*.

LYNETTE GREENWOOD is an actress who starred in *Focus North*.

STUART HALL is a disgraced broadcaster and sports commentator.

NICKY HINCHCLIFFE is a twelve-year-old film director.

JENKS jumped off a table in a bin and fucked his arm up.

NEL KEENAN is an actor, writer and co-founder of Shirtflifting Films.

SARAH ANN KENNEDY is a writer animator and performer. Played Emma Gelding in *Focus North*.

RICHARD LEACH created some amazingly sculpted pieces of art for *The Hunt for the Yorkshire Grimace*.

JOEL LEVACK was second unit director on *Focus North*. His style can be described as 'North Face practical meets male model'.

EUGENE LEVINE is a Leeds businessman who played Ooge Appy Daddy in *Fatliners*

MARION LIGHTOWLER is a wardrobe mistress and B&Q retailer.

MALCOLM FROM COTTINGLEY is a dark web researcher and cryptozoologist.

ETHAN MCPEDANT is a primary school teacher, independent broadcaster and intuitive etymologist.

MICK was slashed with a blade in Cannes.

STUART MILLS is a seventy-two-year-old Yorkshire retiree and star of *Focus North*.

DAVE 'DUSTY' MUNDY was *Focus North*'s location sound mixer and Pub-a-Van procurer.

BARRY NORMAN, CBE is a British film critic, writer and media personality.

NOTHING-BETTER-TO-DO-NEIL had nothing better to do than help Smile Orange film *The Hunt for the Yorkshire Grimace*.

AUSTIN OATES is the go-to actor for all Smile Orange Productions.

PENELOPE O'ROURKE is the casting agent to go to if you want to cast Tom Baker but don't mind getting Stuart Hall instead.

PAUL was a member of the Smile Orange cult. He was also a Hare Krishna.

TIM PECK was a camera operator on a Bollywood quiz show and *Best of British*. He was often shunted into oncoming traffic in his car.

FELICITY PENDLE was the female anchor on *Focus North*.

JOHNNY PIGRAM is Smile Orange Film's biggest fan. Hi Johnny Pigram!

MICHAEL ARNOLD, of course! That was his name. I knew I'd remember it in the end. He was technical support on Smile Orange's *The Tasche Amsterdam Show* and body double of *Last of the Summer Wine*'s Compo Simmonite.

DANNY PRICE starred in *I'llkillya!* and ran Bingley's taekwondo gym.

BOB PRIESTLEY is one of the founding members of Smile Orange. He wears dark colours and still practices sucking his stomach in.

RHODESY & TOWNHOUSE are astute and drunken bankruptcy lawyers.

MIKE RIPPS is an ex kite-surfer and entrepreneur who founded multimillion dollar corporate video company SeptumFlashMedia.

MISERY GUTS was technical assistant

at Nottingham Trent University and helped the post-production of *I'llkillya!*

RED BEARD is a lighting technician.

RIVERS AND RHODES are Yorkshire's filthiest comedians and foetus flippers.

RHINOMAN is a half-man half-rhino and star of *The Hunt for the Yorkshire Grimace*.

JUSTIN ROBERTSON was second unit camera on *Focus North*. He is now a global news cameraman who was sacked by Japanese broadcasters NHK for moving a satellite in space without permission.

RICHARD SAINT was a Smile Orange actor and Nazi enthusiast who enjoyed shooting audiences.

OLLY SHARPE commissioned *Focus North*. Currently sailing his yacht somewhere in the Atlantic.

MARK SOMETHING is a highly skilled animation camera operator who was totally inappropriate for *Focus North*

DAVE SPANE was a tutor and post-production supervisor on *I'llkillya!*

DAVE STAMFORD was the totally appropriate camera operator for *Focus North*.

KEITH TENNYSON is one of the founding members of Smile Orange who starred in the early films.

TOOLED-UP ORVILLE is a fun fur marionette and star of *The Hunt for the Yorkshire Grimace*.

BRIAN TURNER is a Smile Orange actor, writer and contributor to this book who co-founded film collective Ontolocide Uberbilde.

UNKNOWN TEXTING WOMAN is Amanda Fees-Rodeane's PA and personal shopper.

JULIET UREN was Smile Orange's online marketer and graphic designer.

BOB VON DAMAGE is a stuntman currently residing on Queensland's Gold Coast but originally from Yorkshire's Cold Coast.

COLIN WARE created some amazingly sculpted pieces of art for *The Hunt for the Yorkshire Grimace*.

PETER WARD is managing director of Penash Beef Communications (part of the Keema-Peas Group). Wardy is less of a Yes Man and more of a No Man and proudly produced many British film failures of the 1970s, straight to video disasters of the 1980s, arthouse flops of the 1990s and unwatched uploads of the 2000s.

SUE WRIGHT was a Smile Orange actress.

APPENDIX II
GLOSSARY

BOMB: A jump into water from a great height. The water should be in a public place such as a river full of holidaying families. If the bomber is fully clothed and masked then even better.

BOOBY-JUICE: Ground-up fun fluid, mixed into Blackcurrant juice as a way of sneaking the liquid over a border and into another country.

BRADFORD LEG: A disease caused by living in Bradford which takes the form of a limping, dragging, twisted shuffle. Colloquialisms include: Doley's sprint and Spaz-heel-Jack.

CAUSE: To slap someone in the face without prior warning. Causing is an important part of the filmmaking process. It is rumoured that on an Antiques Roadshow shoot, Fiona Bruce caused so hard to Hugh Scully he went deaf.

CRY WANK: Australian term. When asked 'what is a cry wank?' the reply was 'it's when you wank and cry at the same time'. No further information available.

DEFERRED PAYMENT: No payment.

DOLEY'S QUIFF: A hairstyle where the hair sticks up in an unruly way on the back of the head. Or the front. Either way it hasn't been attended to. It happens when an unemployed person has an afternoon nap and then leaves the house without noticing that their hair is sticking up at the back. Or the front.

END OF LEVEL BADDIE: In any action film, this is the second-in-command who will, without doubt, be killed by the hero. But not before the hero has to overcome a lot of shit.

HANDRUFF: The flaking of skin on the hands due to stress. If you want to know if you are stressed then look at your hands — if you have handruff then you are stressed.

'I'VE NEVER SEEN IT DO THAT': Technical term used by audio/visual professionals when equipment breaks down on a Smile Orange Production.

'IT'S NOT SUPPOSED TO DO THAT': Technical term used by Smile Orange's Augustin Bousfield when operating sound equipment.

MAGNETOGRAPHY: The technique pioneered (and copyrighted, so don't try owt) by Smile Orange Films that involves the use of magnets to animate cut-outs whilst filming them. Recommended as a method of animation that avoids tedious stop-frame techniques.

MASSIVE FIGHT: It has always been the belief of the Smile Orange producers that all good films should end with a massive fight. That's it.

MY PRODUCTION COMPANY HAS A RAFT OF NUMEROUS AND EXCITING PROJECTS IN DEVELOPMENT AT THE MOMENT: My production company has no work at the moment and none on the horizon.

PILE, THE: A large collection of films lovingly made by a filmmaker over their lifetime which was never watched by anyone and is now collecting dust in a cupboard or lock-up.

PRINCE EDWARD: A typical example of the sort of dumpling who works in the television industry.

RENTAGHOST: Technical term for the sudden appearance, or disappearance, in a film or television show of a character out of, or into, thin air.

SHIT YOUR PANTS MAD: A state of perpetual spiritual bliss caused by self-excretion and the knowledge that from this low position there is nowhere further to fall. Welcome to Nappyland.**SPLINTER-SCRIPTS:** A script written when distracted from writing the script you planned to write. DW Griffith's splinter-script, *The Birth of a Nation*, was written whilst he was distracted from writing the script for a corporate video about the construction of electricity pylons.

THESP-TRAWL: Recruiting of local amateur acting talent willing to be abused on film.

TRAGIC HOUR, THE: Many films are shot in the crepuscular period just before sundown known as the Magic Hour. Smile Orange Films use a different lighting period — the eight grey hours of Yorkshire daylight known as the Tragic Hours.

TURNOVER: A wanky word for 'pressing record'. This is the sort of thing that a clueless producer would slavishly fill in on a call-sheet template that they have downloaded when any true professional would be skinning up. Terms like 'turnover' help people to pretend that they are real filmmakers, but basically just create a whole lot of shit. The fuckers who say 'turnover' are the same fuckers who call headphones 'cans' or a tripod 'sticks'.

TV REALITY ECHO: The phenomena whereby something happens on the television you are watching and then immediately happens for real, in your front room.

VERY ENJOYED: Rugby league terminology meaning happy.

VIDEO GRAFFITI: The technique pioneered (and copyrighted, so again, don't try owt) by Smile Orange Films that involves the dubbing of dialogue over videos rented from the video shop, then retuning these videos to the shop to be rented out by an unsuspecting member of the public.

WEBBOX: Anaemically coloured dog food in a sausage shape made in the North of England. Described on the packaging as 'chubb meal' yet no one knows why. One theory is that 'chubb' is chopped up mess (in Jaws the bait used to attract the shark is called chub). Chubb is also a large obese man in the gay community or another name for a tautog or black Porgy.

WE'LL KEEP YOUR CV ON FILE: Written in an email or letter by a company to which you have sent a CV. Meaning: You will never hear from us again.

WINDSOCKED: When a film is so intense that viewers' mouths and anuses gape open allowing air to rush through the body.

WHOOSH SHOT: This is the correct technical term for the shot that amateurs often mislabel the 'whip pan'.

YORKSHIRE GRIMACE: The Northern version of the Chelsea Smile which involves the complete removal of the victim's lips, leaving them with a permanent fucked-up grinning skull-face.

APPENDIX III
STORYTELLINGGBCREATIVE

I just want to sign off this book with some words from the Chief Executive of Britain's esteemed film funding body StorytellingGBCreative. To run such an incredible company it takes a really extraordinary man and Bill Cambridge is that man, so I was privileged recently when Bill kindly shared with me the wisdom he has gained from his many years of filmmaking. Yours truly, Roy Devon.

DEVON: 'Bill, Could you start by telling me about your track record as a film producer?'

CAMBRIDGE: 'I were producer on *Titanic* wan't I? World's biggest grossest film wan't it? They wanted me to do *Avatar* din't they? But I had to do Mix Master Morris's chill out promo din't I? Cos that were keeping it real wan't it? My idea fo' graphics were better than what they went for on *Avatar* weren't it? There weren't none of that blue people were there? There were just hard-core fucking weren't there? Trance fucking! Like the live show at Manumission weren't it? I did it live once din't I? Cos I'm best fuck in Bingley me aren't I?'

DEVON: 'You've also been heavily involved in music production, can you tell me a little bit more about that?'

CAMBRIDGE: 'I were top dog and DJ for numerous film companies wan't I? I had a company dealing in Balearic beats din't I? I owned every Balearic beat ever din't I? I owned the Balearic islands actually din't I? Were it you that were inspiration fo' Manumission live sex shows? Oh, no, it were me won't it? 'Cept I had hair on me, not bald. I were better than you wan't I? I had far bigger knob din't I? Din't have to shave me pubes to mek me knob look bigger or nowt did I?'

DEVON: 'You then worked as a professional scriptwriter? Could you tell us some more about this experience?'

CAMBRIDGE: I'm still owed some money from Terrance Dicks for writing some *Doctor Who* novelizations aren't I? I think I might have worked on a *Judge Dredd* novel an' all. I were writing a lot back then, might have been paid in speed. In fact I definitely were. And not just speed, cocaine actually. They got me a woman too. It was that Jemima Khan wan't it?'

DEVON: 'You also worked as a sound designer, I believe?'

CAMBRIDGE: 'That were me what did all sound effects on *Ghosts of Mars* wan't it? I just had a couple o' decks din't I? I can do full hand-spin on me deck whilst fucking me bird can't I? And when I'd done 'er she'd give me three quid for a bit of bush wouldn't she? I'd go out and get it, din't I? But instead I had her sister din't I? It were that Princess Stephanie of Monaco wan't it? I've actually also done some foleying on Spike Jones films actually. I made all trainer noises for people walking in trainers in that *Her* din't I? Cos I have best collection of trainers int' world don't I? Nike Airs and Air Jordans which are most expensive trainers which I've got. Limited edition, sent off to America for 'em din't I?'

DEVON: 'Could you tell me a little bit about your experiences in post-production?'

CAMBRIDGE: 'I invented Avid dint I? But turned down royalties cos they dint do it my way dint I? I were editor on Newsnight an all wan't I? 'Ad anal wi' Kirsty Wark din' I? So they sent me into field din't they? I won a Pulitzer for me reports din't I? Danger in War Award for Most Dangerous Areas to be Found Editing in wan't it? An' when I were in Cambodia I fucked Susie Wong din't I?'

DEVON: 'Finally, I believe you have some interesting experience of new digital distribution methods?'

CAMBRIDGE: 'My mate had a van din't he? And he used to drive around and deliver all films to multiplexes, din't he? I could take owt out van I wanted couldn't I? Cos I dealt him wiz din't I? I took biscuits and a copy of *The Mummy* from Safeway didn't I? Just ran out wi' them. As I ran out I shouted "NOW THAT'S WHAT I CALL FUCKING FREEVIEW!!!" The Rock brings me all of his videos to me house dun't he? Just for me to watch. When I'm fishing sometimes Rock comes up and gives me the goods then. I know the Rock me.

I saw him down the gym dint I? I was harder than him wont I? It was me who helped make him huge. And I won't on 'roids or owt.'

DEVON: 'Many thanks Bill, a great man and a great boss.'

CAMBRIDGE: 'Suck my dick!'

APPENDIX IV
THE FILM SEQUEL

Written by Brian Turner (Ontolocide Uberbilde Films)

WHAT IS A SEQUEL?

A sequel is a narrative film that continues the story of, or expands upon, some earlier work. Sequels are usually considered inferior to the original but one example of a sequel that is considered superior is of course *Night-Beast II*. Below, the film's co-producer Brian Turner describes the making of *Night-Beast II*, the aborted partial-making of *Night-Beast III*, and how to plan for a prolonged narrative.

SECTION ONE: NIGHTBEAST II: THE LEGEND OF THE RONIN SWORD (1992)

The officially and unofficially entitled 'The *Night-Beast* Sequels' were a project embarked upon and made by the set of neo-philosophical-neo-filmmakers known as Ontolocide Uberbilde who emerged on the scene in the summer of 1991 based in the Yateley/Camberley/Virginia Waters area in the south of Great Britain. Smile Orange Films' Julian Butler lived in London for a number of years with the team's co-founder and co-prime mover, Brian Turner, and it was in the nation's capital where the two worked on a number of ground-breaking dramatical human projects together such as 'The Emotive Invention of Empathetic Masked Based Street and Tube Theatre', 'Paper Samurai Park and Road Processioning', 'Top Window 24-hour Rave-olution Window Shouting',

and perhaps most infamous, 'The Project of Sehmi-Baiting and Christoff-Teasing to Fibbing Landlord-Werk'.

It was during that time that Butler famously showed Turner Smile Orange Films' *Nightbeast*, after which the latter studied the film intently for several video immersed weeks. Turner then returned to his home town of the time and immediately showed it to his childhood friend and neighbour, Stephen Earl Rogers. The result was that in a joint flash of near epiphanic inspiration, Ontolocide Uberbilde burst forth with these mighty two as co-prime movers, and immediately began work on the plot and script that begat *Night-Beast II: Legend of the Ronin Sword*. Therein, the resultant video movie revolutionised the character and arguably the art of film by combining numerous previously disparate genres such as Westerns, martial arts and bushido, monster, sci-fi, art house and more (and beyond in terms of the planned cycle of a total of six sequels culminating in an ouroboros 'ending').

In terms of the *Night-Beast* making its appearance on the screen, the film starts with a naïve and youthful devil worshipping cult performing a neo-semi-satanic ritual and getting dramatically more than they bargained for when, instead of their version of the *Prince of Darkness*, they resurrect something much more terrifying.

Erupting from the body of the intended sacrifice and immediately striking out against the hapless diabolical wannabe intercessors with unbelievable speed and ferocity.

The eponymous zenomorph immediately kills the cultists with the further resulting side effect of wiping the very idea of the cult from the human consciousness. What ensues is a cacophony of wailing as if in some homage to the choruses of ancient Greek theatre and the highest tragedies therein. At its crux, this catharsis of mortal terror and ontological screaming appears hurricane-like as if each instance in history of the persecution and subsequent execution of suspected practitioners of witchcraft as they burn upon their pyres. And at its proverbial calm eye, the then fully reincarnated Night-Beast resides, and then proceeds on further rampages through the Southern States of Berkshire, Surrey and Hampshire, the ground and being shaking at Its manic pounding at reality, and Its quips and one-liners abound at each kill. And indeed it does so without direction and purpose… in the beginning at least.

Thus, the Night-Beast does not discriminate and slaughters, amongst others, lovers, blind-houses, cowboyesque truants, fisher-men, landscape developers, TV crews, and airport chess players. It is at a humble bus stop however that It recognises Its true being in dispatching… a budding philosopher and, after discussing Heidegger's Being and Time with him, smashes his head against a wall proclaiming 'Thinking, it does your head in doesn't it?'

But an overarching factor of the movie and narrative is that this time around the Beast is not merely the killer and culler of a hapless humankind. This time it has a nemesis: The Ronin, played by Brian Turner, is as his name suggests, a masterless samurai who for many years has wandered immortal and so often lost and directionless though ever searching and waiting, until the Spirits re-guide him upon his quest to dispatch This Foul Creature back to the stars of Limbo. More than that however, their fates are bound in history itself, and the two are brothers in more than one way.

The film itself opens with the shadowy origins of the Ronin, explored in flashbacks as the story develops. All the while though there is a sense of two juggernauts, two Forces of Nature careening towards each other, their fates inseparable and entwined, with Ronin himself also cutting a swathe through more undesirable members of the local population though all the while displaying his innate nobility and love and appreciation for nature, tranquillity and the beauty around him. And running. Always running.

The film also stars the great outsider musician, master DJ, erstwhile singer, all time transcendent human genius, risk-taker, Caesar, Emperor and artist Martin Allen (alias The Road Warrior, The Long Rider, The Beard, 12 Bore Beard) who appears as a kendo stick wielding assassin, quickly dispatched by the Beast. In a similar style to Smile Orange's film, the beast itself is a shape-shifter, played in many different ways by many different people with many different body types. The film ends with the bloodiest of battles between the two. With the Ronin only managing to defeat the Beast by grasping the creature and spearing them both on his sword. The mists of time swirl and the corpses vanish, their souls locked in Hell for eternity.

SECTION TWO: NIGHTBEAST III: LE LEGENDE DES L'EPEE DE LE RONIN (1993)

In this second sequel the franchise goes back in time and pits the Three Musketeers against the reincarnated Night-Beast. Filmed by the same team as *Night-Beast II*, this one was never finished as, embittered by cannabis induced ennui of his cast and crew, Brian Turner fled to Japan to become a Lone Wolf. Later with cub.

APPENDIX V
EXAMPLE TREATMENT

Below is an example of a treatment sent to British television channels and film funding bodies in 2001 by Smile Orange Productions. It was never commissioned. The treatment is copyright. So don't try owt.

Smile Orange Treatment

"Fat Knacker"

Concept:

Fat Knacker is a comedy / horror drama revolving around an ageing British New Orleans Trad Jazz Band who are being murdered one by one. Who is responsible? Who hates the jazzers so much and WHY?

Characters:

- Trumpet: Fiddy "Tubs" Chuffer
- Drummer: Fats Mallinson
- Banjo: Peter "Big Boned Butcher" Leach
- Sousaphone: Fatos "Vasectomy" Cuckoldi
- Clarinet: Uncle "Gutty" Butterfield
- Parade Marshall: Dicky "Fat" Knacker

Plot outline:

The band "Knackers, Full Figure Flash Four, Plus One", are marching and playing, Knacker is leading in his high heels; he gets them stuck in the drain, the band have to march past. When he catches up after they have finished playing they have an argument about Knackers high heels and the fact that the clarinettist wants to play some modern jazz. Knacker gives an ultimatum and the band sack him.

Knacker goes away rejected

As the band are packing up the drummer is killed in the street: decapitated by a thrown cymbal. We see his final death beat and collapse.

Is Knacker to blame?

Knacker goes to see a Voodoo priest who sprinkles some powder over Knacker and tells him to watch his friends.

The band go on and attend a practice without Knacker and the dead drummer. The drummer is replaced by a drum machine, programmed by the Clarinettist. During the practice Trumpet player has poison smeared around his mouthpiece and dies.

In the confusion surrounding his demise, the mad banjo butcher, Peter Leach is found garrotted by his banjo string. Who is killing the Full Figure Flash Four, Plus One?

On his way home the sousaphone player dies having his limbs cut off and crammed into his large instruments bell. He is found the next day.

Knacker hearing of the death of his entire band goes to see the clarinettist as he is setting up for his now solo gig. Knacker approaches him and they try to come to an agreement about his heels and the playing of modern jazz. For a split second Knacker turns his back on the Clarinettist and is smashed unconscious.

He wakes up in a wheelchair with his eyes Sellotaped open as the clarinettist is walking round him showing him Charlie Parker album covers and demanding to know who else knows he is there:

"Names Knacker, I want names!!!"

He begins to torture Knacker whilst wearing a Sun Ra pyramid hat and Miles Davis hair and a psychedelic poncho with small blue shades.

Knacker's eyes start to close after too much torture we see an after death experience sequence with Knacker dancing towards the light.

cut

We see a Mardi Gras funeral coming down the street, at the head is the clarinettist playing away with pall bearers (one of whom is the voodoo priest) bearing the coffin with a "FAT KNACKER" Wreath. Suddenly the coffin bursts open and Voodoo Zombie Knacker jumps out. Last shot is him sinking his teeth into the clarinettist.

The end

APPENDIX VI
PRODUCER'S NOTES

This empty page is a place for you to write down all your important production notes. It is definitely not just a way of padding out the book.

⚠ IMPOLITE NOTICE

RULES ON PUBLIC DISPLAYS OF LITERACY IN THIS PUB

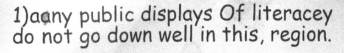

1) aany public displays Of literacey do not go down well in this, region.

2) Writing with a lap-top in this pub will not be tollerate

3) The bar-area is reserved for alcoholic lunatics. If you attempt to write here, they, will approach you and say "I always wondered how writing happened?." an and they will ask you if they can Help. Be aware they nevercan.

4) Even if you are writing in a notebook you will be approched and told "we thought that— you we're a copper"

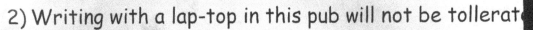

WALLOP

5) If you are found typing stuff up anywhere else in this Pub you will be moved so that the bar staff can set-up for, Breakfast!

6) trhis pub is for drinking !!!

mein hosts __( )__ xx

YOU HAVE BEEN WARNIED!!

ACKNOWLEDGEMENTS

We must give resounding praise and heartfelt thanks for their help
with this book to John Bentham, Andrew Laird-Boldy, Lowry Butler, Tony Earnshaw,
Gino Feliciello, Mike Gillette, Mark Goodall, Lynette Greenwood, Neil Keenan,
David Kerekes, Big Pat, Joel Levack, Douggy Pledger, Stephen Earl Rogers,
Brogan Sohanpaul, Dan Thomas, Brian Turner, Karen Williams, Stuart Wright
and his Mighty Holiness Lord Salamanca the Slow Worm. Hi Johnny Pigram.
Cover illustration: Steven Earl Rogers. Cover design: Dougie Pledger. Illustrations of
Authors: Michael Gillette

PHOTO CREDITS

All photos © Smile Orange Films, except for the following:

CHAPTER ONE: Ramunas Geciauskas 'Idea Bulb', likeaduck 'Squirrel', jimmyweee 'rugby', gnat Gorazd 'JVC Victor GR-C1 camcorder side rear view', Philip Hutchinson 'Jeremy Beadle', KurtClark 'Today in 1970 - Elvis Meets Nixon', theNerdPatrol 'Nightbeast b movie bingo'. CHAPTER TWO: Hazel Nicholson 'Old Radio Rentals sign, Banbury', Eva 'Goopy gak'. CHAPTER THREE: Tim Green 'Bradford's Magistrates' and Coroner's Court, Bradford', Levent Ali 'Cameraman' (**https://creativecommons.org/licenses/by/2.0/**). CHAPTER FOUR: chrisjtse 'Script', Carole Raddato 'Portrait of man, from the great baths, early 3rd c. AD, Archaeological Museum, Dion', Carole Raddato 'Marble portrait that attributes and old but dynamic man with hairdressing and characteristics that refers to the early portraits of the Roman emperor Trajan, 98 - 117 AD, Philippi Museum'. CHAPTER FIVE: ete 'Project 365 #125: 050510 Take Note', Derek Harper 'Cotswold House, Warren Road, Torquay', (**https://creativecommons.org/licenses/by-sa/2.0/**), [[user:]] 'VegasBitch198' (**https://commons.wikimedia.org/wiki/File:VegasBitch198. jpg**). CHAPTER SIX: włodi 'The Big Red Button' (**https://creativecommons.org/ licenses/by-sa/2.0/**), State Library of New South Wales 'William Reed filming "The Romance of Runnibede", Sydney, 1927 / Sam Hood' (**https://www.flickr.com/ commons/usage/**), RRT877 'Panasonic MC-10' (**https://creativecommons.org/ publicdomain/zero/1.0/deed.en**), U.S. Embassy London 'Robert Redford and Sir Ben Kingsley' (**https://creativecommons.org/licenses/by-nd/2.0/**). CHAPTER SEVEN: Evan Wohrman 'Disney's Hollywood Studios - Lights, Motors, Action!' CHAPTER EIGHT: John Athayde 'An old analog edit suite', Mr Thinktank 'DSCF9156', Royal Opera House Covent Garden 'Richard Wagner, photograph by Franz Hanfstaengl (1804–77)', © Natalia Balcerska Photography 'Napalm Death' (**https://creativecommons.org/licenses/ by-sa/2.0/**), Jon Farman ' Bingley Town Centre' (**https://creativecommons.org/ licenses/by-sa/3.0/**). CHAPTER TEN: marc falardeau 'LADDER', www.david baxendale. com - Nadaam Horses - A Mongolian "cowboy" collects his racehorses at the end a rural

Nadaam annual festival 25km race in the Altai Mountains (**https://creativecommons.org/licenses/by-sa/2.0/**). CHAPTER TWELVE: Diana Robinson 'Male Lion at Sunrise, Ol Pejeta Conservancy, Kenya, East Africa', Ashley Van Haeften 'Abbey from the river, Bolton Abbey, England-LCCN2002696397', Prisoninfo 'Old Gate - HM Prison Leeds' (**https://creativecommons.org/licenses/by-nd/2.0/**). CHAPTER THIRTEEN: Didriks 'Alessi at Local Root', Ben Salter 'Celebrity boat trip' (**https://creativecommons.org/licenses/by/2.0/**), Jes 'charge of the lycra brigade' (**https://creativecommons.org/licenses/by-sa/2.0/**). CHAPTER SIXTEEN: Tess Watson 'Sound Waves: Loud Volume', Mvuijlst 'rances Densmore recording Mountain Chief2'. CHAPTER SEVENTEEN: LadyDragonflyCC - >;< 'Hugh Jackman *** Smile ***'. CHAPTER EIGHTEEN: Môsieur J. [version 9.1] 'Light#6', Kenny Louie 'Vectorial Elevation revisited', Goran Zec 'Ozric Tentacles in Zagreb 44' (**https://creativecommons.org/licenses/by/2.0/**). CHAPTER NINETEEN: Ben Cooper - Empire Strikes Back boxed costume C-3PO - 1977.jpg, Harry Wood - Trickling blood and bin liner, Ballerinas from the Boris Volkoff Ballet, Toronto / Ballerines du Ballet de Boris Volkoff, Toronto (**http://creativecommons.org/licenses/by-sa/4.0/**), Ben Sutherland 'Henry VIII'. CHAPTER TWENTY-ONE: Tim Green 'Hebden Bridge', Dan Marsh 'Prince Charles'. CHAPTER TWENTY-SIX: Beau B 'Diet Coke on the Rocks', john bentham 'john bentham & mohammed ali' (**https://creativecommons.org/licenses/by/2.0/**). CHAPTER TWENTY-EIGHT: Paul Boxley 'Fruit Machine :D', 'Done' (**https://creativecommons.org/licenses/by-sa/2.0/**). CHAPTER TWENTY-NINE: j4p4n 'Censorship is like an Old Man', Central Board of film certification, India 'Waarish film censor cerificate' (**https://openclipart.org/share**). CHAPTER THIRTY: Bamboofurniture 'Guy Martin TT 2013 01' (**https://creativecommons.org/licenses/by-sa/3.0/deed.en**). CHAPTER THIRTY-ONE: Bs0u10e0 'Carlton Cannes', manuel | MC 'Andie MacDowell was in Paris'. CHAPTER THIRTY-THREE: Roman Harak 'North Korea - TV' (**https://creativecommons.org/licenses/by-sa/2.0/**), [[axg ⁝ talk]] 'Calendar (News) Studios' (**http://commons.wikimedia.org/wiki/File:Calendar_(News)_Studios.JPG**). CHAPTER THIRTY-FOUR: Tim Green 'Old White Horse, Bingley'. CHAPTER THIRTY-FIVE: Vegan Feast Catering 'Exotic Fruit Gift Basket', Didriks 'Heath Plates', Glen Wallace 'Megabus SP07 CAA' (**https://creativecommons.org/licenses/by/2.0/**). CHAPTER THIRTY-SEVEN: Community Spaces Fund 'Richard and Judy at Saltash', Ben Mills 'GHB-3D-balls' (**https://creativecommons.org/licenses/by-nd/2.0/**). CHAPTER THIRTY-EIGHT: MariaAndronic 'Robbie Williams 2' (**https://creativecommons.org/licenses/by-sa/2.0/**), coniferconifer 'Crayfish' (**https://creativecommons.org/licenses/by/2.0/**). CHAPTER FORTY-ONE: JonONeill 'Countdownset' (**http://commons.wikimedia.org/wiki/File:Countdownset.jpg**), gettheshot75 'Setup' (**https://creativecommons.org/licenses/by/2.0/**). CHAPTER FORTY-THREE: Brendan Wood 'my power bill' (**https://creativecommons.org/licenses/by-sa/2.0/**), Images Money 'Tax Return and Calculator', Mike Mozart 'TGI Fridays Restaurant 6/2014 Waterbury CT. TGI Friday's Logo Sign pic by Mike Mozart of TheToyChannel and JeepersMedia on YouTube'. CHAPTER FORTY-FOUR: GotCredit 'Bankrupt' (**https://creativecommons.org/licenses/by/2.0/**), Ped Saunders 'Cuffed Links', Paul Ferguson 'What's black and white and red all over?', Ian Carroll 'sinister' (**https://creativecommons.org/licenses/by-sa/2.0/**), Ryk Neethling 'Open Bible'. CHAPTER FORTY-FIVE: Vitor Lima 'call center' (**https://creativecommons.org/licenses/by/2.0/**), West Midlands Police 'Day 188 - West Midlands Police - Custody Interview Room' (**https://creativecommons.org/licenses/by-sa/2.0/**), Mike Roberts 'Pub Car Park 1', Magnus D 'Pocket money' (**https://creativecommons.org/licenses/by/2.0/**).

IMAGINE THE FACE OF THE ACTOR YOU LOVE WHEN YOU GIVE THEM THIS...

Male or Female, Young or Elderly, Dead or Alive, Mythical or Archetypal

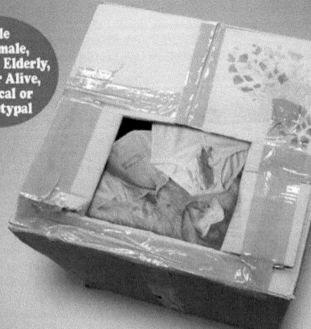

"It's not any but it is many!"
– Bullet McDuke (Actor)

Back in the day a professional film costumier would head down to Spastics on Boar Lane, Leeds to fit out their cast for under a tenner. Not any more! Now all the best stuff is chucked.
Chances of getting a full white top hat and tails set for 20p - 0.0043%

So how would you fit out your whole cast for £10 now? Easy the Universal Thespian Wardrobe
contains enough clothes to create every costume you will ever need.

Deep within the flaps of this prestige box are five items of clothing which, in a variety of combinations, can dress every character in every Multiverse (apart from Sportsworld 89) : Including Lollypop Man/Pervert, Cone Placer, Potential Employee, Actual employee, Twenty Year Old Long Standing Employee, Retired Employee, Coffin Wear for When You're Laid Out, Olympic Swimmer, Hostage, Hostage Negotiator, Terrorist, Feral Man.

Also available: Bullet McDuke's Universal Action Film Wardrobe Kit: Includes two items: 1) Vest 2) Bald head wigs.

Universal Thespian Wardrobe System

Film costume and wardrobe solution centre

Contents: A two piece black suit, Tie, High vis vest, drexs, shoes. Note. This product is suitable from ages 14 to dead.

Lightning Source UK Ltd.
Milton Keynes UK
UKHW031827230219
337848UK00004B/25/P